ROADRUNNER
Rock tours in 60's London

ROAD

RUNNER

Rock tours in 60's London

Lars Madelid

PREMIUM PUBLISHING
Stockholm

Premium Publishing
Box 30184
SE-104 25 Stockholm
Sweden

Phone: +46 8 545 689 20
Fax: +46 8 545 689 19
E-Mail: info@premiumpublishing.com
www.premiumpublishing.com

English translation by Carl Magnus Palm

Graphic design by Pia Nygren Carlsson/Jocke Wester
Project manager: Wille Wendt
Repro: Mats Sellin
Graphics: Myran Grafiska

Printed by Bulls Graphics, Sweden
Paper: Tom & Otto silk 115 gr

ISBN: 978-91-89136-24-3 English version

This book is also available in a Swedish language version, ISBN: 978-91-89136-21-2

© 2007 Premium Publishing – a div. of Internal AB

Contents

Malmö, Sweden, the summer of 1966. The author, in the middle, on his way to Hamburg and eventually London.

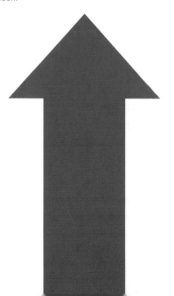

Foreword

The most important background for this book is my love for music, especially the British bands of the Sixties and their music. The British wave that flooded in with great power and energy during the Sixties wasn't only about a new kind of music, but also about a new lifestyle and attitude. London was the city where most of it happened; an exciting world-centre for the youth revolution within music, fashion and other cultural phenomena during a few years in the Sixties. Who wouldn't have wanted to be there?

It was the love for music and London, the metropolis for young people, that made me take to the road at the age of 16. My goal was to hitchhike down to the Star Club in Hamburg, with the view of finally trying to get to England.

I will admit it: I never got to London. Maybe that's why I wrote this book. I never got farther than a water-filled ditch at the Dutch border. Broke and somewhat weary I arrived at the frontier station in Holland one night in July 1966. They looked at me and my pathetic notes and crossed out my passport stamp. This meant not only that London was moved to a faraway planet, but also that Holland was out of reach. A broke and long-haired 16-year-old like me wasn't exactly the kind of person that border guards would welcome with a smile and open arms. But I wasn't going to give up that easily – I quickly hatched a plan. I decided to steal across the border before dawn and fool the grumpy and small-minded guards. I quietly snuck along a path and put my sleeping-bag in a ditch a short distance into the forest, underneath some branches. I was in a deep sleep when I suddenly woke up from having my nose under water. The rain was pouring down and the ditch was completely filled with water. I cursed life and my slyness, emptied the water out of my suede shoes and put on my water-soaked socks. What were meant to be my extra clothes were at the bottom of my water-filled sleeping bag: a pair of white socks, underpants and a black t-shirt.

I spent half the day in a public lavatory, where I let most of the water drain off my clothes while I was sitting in my underwear, locked in a toilet booth. Angry and disappointed I hitch-hiked back home to Sweden. It would be almost 40 years before I finally came to London and was able to visit what remained of the places I had wanted to visit way back when.

I spent a total of four weeks walking around London, to see some of the places I had read about over the years. Many of them, but far from all, I have written about in this book. I know that there were many other places, such as Blaises, the Cromwellian Club, Sibylla's, Revolution, Manor House and many others, but because of a lack of space and to avoid repetition I have made a subjective selection. This selection is also based on the prerequisite that there is still something to see at the location. It's not very much fun travelling across half of London just to see a parking lot.

The biggest difficulty in writing this book has been to determine what most likely happened and when. My experience, after having read innumerable biographies and memoirs, is that most books inherit inaccuracies from each other and that very few of them go back to the original sources. And in many cases the artists themselves are the most unreliable sources. They are often keen to spread myths about themselves, or they don't remember a particular incident, or they confuse one incident with another. Therefore, in many cases I have relied on reports, articles and interviews with the musicians, found in then-current papers and magazines.

Some things I have researched more thoroughly than others, but despite my efforts I am certain that some errors and myths have still made it through.

I have mixed important events in rock history with episodes that many may feel are trivial, but which I still feel say something about the artist or the band in question, or in some way or other reflect the atmosphere of London at the time. It is also worth mentioning that the selection of artists is my own and I mainly write about that which interests me personally in the music business and youth culture in London of the Sixties.

Roadrunner is partly a travel guide for those who are interested in London locations that are strongly connected to the British bands and artists of the Sixties. But since it often gives background information and detailed descriptions of various bands and episodes, it is also a rock-historical depiction, although somewhat rhapsodic.

The purpose of the book is to give a rough answer to the questions "what happened where and when" and "who did what" in London's rock and pop world of the Sixties. But the choices I have made are both selective and subjective. The book does not encompass the first generation of British pop- and rock artists, such as Cliff Richard, Adam Faith, Tommy Steele and many others. Therefore I have not covered places like these artists' first residence, the famous 2 I's Coffee Bar. Instead the story begins in the spring of 1962, when England's first real rhythm & blues club opened in London and became a meeting-place and source of inspiration for many bands and musicians who were to become famous.

Even though many of the music clubs of the Sixties have vanished over the years, I have discovered during my London visits that some of them are still highly active and that many bands and musicians have continued playing out of their love for music. Apart from the places covered in the book, I want to mention that the legendary Eel Pie Club in Twickenham was reformed in 2000. The original club was located on Eel Pie Island, but unfortunately it was destroyed by fire in 1971. At the new club – located just a few hundred yards from the original – you may still see performances by old well-known members from bands such as The Yardbirds, The Pretty Things, Downliners Sect, The Kinks and John Mayall's Bluesbreakers. This I could never have imagined when I missed out on London 40 years ago.

Lars Madelid
London 2007

Introduction

This book is divided into four geographical main areas: Central London, East London, North and Northwest London, and West and Southwest London. Each area has been assigned its own colour at the top of the page to make it easier to use the book. Most of the places covered are noted in the margin, along with the nearest tube or bus.

A four zone travelcard will get you to all the places, but if you're only planning to visit the central parts a one zone card is sufficient. My walks have mainly been divided into the area names, for example Soho and Mayfair, and not according to the geographical interrelation of the places. If you want to visit the places according to geographical proximity you may use the maps and make your plans with the nearest underground station as the starting point. And those who'd rather walk in the footsteps of their favourite band may refer to the index and plan their own route. Most of the places mentioned in the book have been illustrated with a current photograph, so that they will be recognisable.

Many of the places covered in the book are situated in central London, and it might be tempting to just take a walk in Soho or that general area. But for me the most rewarding experience was to visit the suburban areas, such as Muswell Hill and Putney. They feel more genuine and have not changed at the same pace as the tourist areas in the centre of the city, where commercial interests rule.

Finally: use walking-shoes if you are planning a longer walk. Pavements are harder than you might think. Good luck and I hope you will enjoy these trips and walks around London as much as I have.

Explanation of maps:
The locations have been numbered according to the order in which they appear in the book.

Blue numbers mean that the locations are described in the main text.

Green numbers refer to descriptions of the locations in the appendix at the back of the book.

The red box around certain locations indicates that this area can also beviewed on a separate map, placed in conjunction with the description of the location.

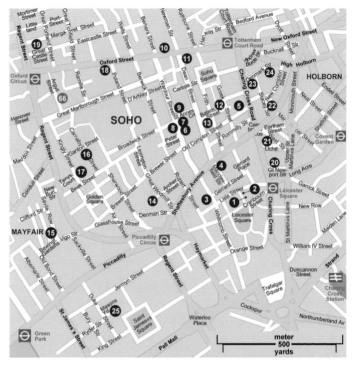

Soho, Piccadilly Circus, Oxford Circus, Covent Garden, St James's

- ❶ Notre Dame Hall
- ❷ Ad Lib
- ❸ Flamingo Club
- ❹ De Hems
- ❺ Pollo
- ❻ Marquee Club II
- ❼ The Ship
- ❽ Bricklayers Arms
- ❾ Trident Sound Studios
- ❿ 100 Club
- ⓫ Beat City Club/Tiles
- ⓬ Les Cousins
- ⓭ Ronnie Scott's Jazz Club
- ⓮ Piccadilly Jazz Club/ The Scene Club
- ⓯ 3 Savile Row
- ⓰ Carnaby Street
- ⓱ Bag O'Nails
- ⓲ Marquee Club I
- ⓳ Speakeasy
- ⓴ Studio 51
- ㉑ Bunjies
- ㉒ Saville Theatre
- ㉓ Giaconda Café
- ㉔ Regent Sound Studio
- ㉕ 6–13 Masons Yard
- 66 Palladium Theatre

Central London

Soho

Soho is surrounded by Oxford Street in the north, Regent Street in the west, Coventry Street in the south and Charing Cross Road in the east. Immigrants of various origins – mostly Italian – began moving to this area of around 1 square mile at the end of the 19th Century. The new population brought their food and drink cultures with them. Soon enough, restaurants and bars began appearing, attracting those who were looking for something a little different.

In the Twenties, Soho became popular among artists and writers, and by the end of the Thirties, there were plenty of artistic and literary bohemians in the area. At the start of the Fifties, after the Second World War, music was the focus for the new generations. This coincided with the entry of the coffe machine and the jukebox into London. Soon there were plenty of coffee bars, many of which stayed open all night long, that served both Espresso and jazz music, and a little later on also skiffle, folk and rock music. In July 1956, the most famous of the coffee bars, 2 I's Coffee Bar, opened at 59 Old Compton Street. Artists such as Tommy Steele, Cliff Richard, Vince Taylor, The Shadows, Adam Faith, Lonnie Donegan, Marty Wilde and Tony Sheridan would perform in the

ROBIN HALL & JIMMIE MacGREGOR
Contact MALCOLM NIXON AGENCY, 46 Maddox Street, W.1
Sole Agency : Storyville Clubs, Frankfurt & Cologne

JOAN REGAN
Direction :
Keith Devon
Bernard Delfont Ltd
Joan Regan Supporters Club,
73, Longlands Road, Sidcup, Kent.

DAVID WHITFIELD
c/o GRADE ORGANISATION
Tel.: REG 5821

ALMA COGAN
c/o SYDNEY GRACE
235, Regent St., W.1.   REG 5821

DOROTHY SQUIRES
Joe   Collins,   Chandos   House,
Chandos   Place,   London,   W.C.2

HELEN SHAPIRO
Sole Booking Agents :
GENERAL ARTISTES LTD.

THE BEATLES
Direction :
NEMS ENTERPRISES LTD., 12-14 WHITECHAPEL, LIVERPOOL 1 ROY 7895

JANIE MARDEN
c/o GRADE ORGANISATION   REG 5821

On February 1, 1963, The Beatles still had to announce their existence in the music press. But only a few weeks later all that had changed. That was when The Beatles first topped the charts with their 'Please Please Me' single. ▶

small room in the basement before they achieved their breakthrough.

During the years 1962–1963 there was a change in Soho, when the blues and the British version of R&B began attracting the young generation. Within just a couple of years, most of the jazz clubs were turned into blues and rock clubs. But today you have to look hard if you are to find any traces of Swinging London in Soho, and because of the exorbitant rents the area is changing constantly.

Notre Dame Hall

Notre Dame Hall
Leicester Square/
Soho
5–6 Leicester Place
Tube:
Leicester Square

I have chosen Leicester Square as the starting point for my walks. Many pubs in Soho are closed on Sundays, so naturally I have chosen a weekday for my wanderings.

I start by walking into Leicester Place, which is a narrow street that will take me to Chinatown. The first address I reach is number 5–6 and Notre Dame Hall. The Who played there a number of times early on in their career, in the summer and autumn of 1963, when they called themselves The Detours. At the time their show consisted of Beatles songs, a few Shadows tunes, blues songs and a couple of Dixieland numbers featuring Roger Daltrey on the trombone (!).

In 1965 the short-lived club *Cavern In The Town* opened on the same premises. In April, The Who were back, but with a much more hard-edged set list; at that time guitarist Pete Townshend had started writing his own songs for the band. Also, Keith Moon was now behind the drums; with his energetic style of playing he attracted everybody's at-

The Detours (The Who) play Dixieland jazz, dressed in suits designed by Pete Townshend. A little over six months later they switched to rhythm & blues, after having seen The Rolling Stones. Left–right: Pete Townshend, guitar; Roger Daltrey, trombone; John Entwistle, trumpet; Dough Sandom, drums. The man at the centre may possibly be singer Colin Dawson.

▼

The Small Faces gave their last performance at the Cavern In The Town on September 11, 1965. This picture is taken a few weeks later in conjunction with their appearance in the film Dateline Diamonds. At the time, Jimmy Winston was still a member of the band, but a couple of weeks later he was replaced by organ player Ian McLagan. Left–right: Jimmie Winston, Kenney Jones, Steve Marriott and Ronnie Lane.   ▲

tention and he was an important ingredient in The Who's new sound and image.

However, the Cavern Club is mainly known for being the venue where The Small Faces achieved their breakthrough. The Small Faces played at the club for the first time on Saturday, May 29, 1965, and although they only had five songs in their repertoire, they were such a big hit that they were booked for five consecutive Saturdays. Those five Saturdays were the starting-point for the band's quick rise to the top. On a slate, Ronnie Lane drew a mod on a scooter, complete with a parka featuring the group's name on the back, and put it on the pavement outside the club. The mods were immediately attracted and after just a few gigs, the venue was packed with people.

The newly formed group was noticed by the famous American duo Sonny and Cher, who generously contributed their advice and plenty of encouragement. The Small Faces also became one of Mick Jagger and Keith Richards' favourite bands and Mick Jagger stated in an interview that "if you don't like The Small Faces, you're getting old". In an interview with BBC London in 2004, Ian McLagan, The Small Faces' organ player, even maintained that Steve Marriott and Ronnie Lane contributed backing vocals to The Rolling Stones' hit single 'Get Off Of My Cloud', in the early autumn of 1965. Word quickly spread about The Small Faces and they were soon discovered by the manager Don Arden, who was able to sign the band by offering them £20 per week and free clothes from Carnaby Street.

Ad Lib

The next door, number 7, was the entrance for the first club for the young Swinging London, the *Ad* Lib. The club

❷

Ad Lib
Leicester Square/
Soho
7 Leicester Place
Tube:
Leicester Square

The door to the Notre Dame Hall is to the right in the picture. The entrance to the elevator, which would transport a visitor directly up to the Ad Lib, is straight ahead behind the glass doors. ◀

was located on the roof, above the Prince Charles Theatre, and it was reached from the street level via a small elevator behind a couple of smoked glass doors. There were no guards or any signs to give any hints about the existence of the club, which held a little over 300 guests. The premises had previously been the location for the WIP'S club, but were taken over by the brothers Al and Bob Burnett, who employed Brian Morris to run the new club. They installed a large and modern sound system, a tiny dance floor, hidden coloured lights in the ceiling, low tables and chairs and lots of big mirrors – highly suitable for narcissists!

A disc jockey dressed in a dinner-jacket provided the music – often Otis Redding, Wilson Pickett, James Brown and Aretha Franklin – with the equipment hidden inside a piano, while piranhas were swimming around in a gigantic aquarium. But the main attraction was the large windows around the premises, which provided a spectacular view of Soho, Piccadilly and Mayfair; the guests could really feel that London was beneath their feet.

The popularity of pop music meant that the bands were important guests as well as attractions at the London clubs. Before there were pure rock clubs, the artists would often visit the exclusive Ad Lib club. The club's profile was so discrete that guests could smoke marijuana freely if they so wished, without anyone interfering. ▶

The club opened on December 13, 1963, but had a slow start until Sandra Cogan – the younger sister of Alma Cogan – attended the place together with her friend George Harrison. He immediately liked the place and brought along Ringo Starr a few nights later. With two members of The Beatles in the same place, the success was immediate: overnight, Ad Lib became the place to be in London.

In 1963–1964 pop music hadn't achieved a breakthrough on a wider scale and there were no clubs exclusively for the new wave of rock- and pop artists. There-

MELODY MAKER, April 4, 1964—Page 13

Jazzshows

Jazz Club
100 OXFORD STREET, W.1
AT 7.30

Friday, April 3rd
MIKE DANIELS BIG BAND
plus THE DELTA JAZZMEN
with DOREEN BEATTY
JOHN CHILTON'S QUARTET
Saturday, April 4th
ALEX WELSH AND HIS BAND
Sunday, April 5th
ALAN ELSDON'S JAZZ BAND
MICK EMERY'S FOLK GROUP
Wednesday, April 8th
MONTY SUNSHINE'S JAZZ BAND
with VAL WISEMAN
DICKIE BISHOP'S FOLK GROUP
Full details of the Club from the Secretary
J.J.C., 22 Newman St., W.1 (LAN 0184)

100 CLUB
100 OXFORD ST., W.1
7.30 to 11 p.m.
RHYTHM AND BLUES
Thursday, April 2nd
GRAHAM BOND'S
Rhythm and Blues Quartet
plus THE FALLING LEAVES
Monday, April 6th
THE MIKE COTTON COMBO
ANDY McKINLEY and the SEE SEE RIDERS
Tuesday, April 7th
THE ANIMALS
THE FALLING LEAVES
and THE PRETTY THINGS
Thursday, April 9th
GRAHAM BOND'S
R & B Quartet
THE MARK LEEMAN 5
and THE BLUEBOTTLES with MIKE PATIO
Full details of the Club from the Secretary
100 Club, 22 Newman St., W.1 (LAN 0184)

KEN COLYER CLUB
At Studio 51, 10/11 Gt. Newport St.
Leicester Square (Tube)
Saturday, 7.30, April 4th
KEN COLYER JAZZMEN
Sunday, 7.15, April 5th
ERIC SILK SOUTHERN J.B.
Wednesday, 7.30, April 8th
KID MARTYN RAGTIME BAND
All-night Session this Saturday
Midnight till Six
DIS DISLEY & IAN WHEELER
with everyone that's in town
Non-members admitted at all Sessions
Next R. & B. All-nighter, April 11th

STUDIO '51
10/11 GT. NEWPORT ST.
LEICESTER SQUARE
RHYTHM & BLUES every
Thursday, 8 to 11, April 2nd
THE SMOKE-STACKS
Friday, 8 to Midnight, April 3rd
THE DOWNLINERS SECT
Sunday Afternoon, 4 until 6.30, April 5th
THE DOWNLINERS SECT
Monday, 8 to 11, April 6th
"THEM"
Non-members admitted at all Sessions
R. & B. All-Nighter, April 11th

THAMES HOTEL
Hampton Court
Friday, April 3rd
ALEX WELSH & HIS BAND
Saturday, April 4th
ALEXANDER'S JAZZBAND
Sunday, April 5th
JOHNNIE TOOGOOD & HIS BAND

JIM GODBOLT presents
SIX BELLS JAZZ CLUB
Six Bells, King's Road, Chelsea
19, 22, 49, 11 Buses
Nearest Station Sloane Square
Friday, April 3
SANDY BROWN
and his band
featuring AL FAIRWEATHER and
Saturday, April 4
BRUCE TURNER
and his Jump Band

JAZZ CLUBS —LONDON

FLAMINGO & ALLNIGHTER CLUBS
33-37 Wardour St., London, W.1
Gerrard 1549. Guests welcome
Dance or listen in comfort
Tony Harris & Rik Gunnell
present:—
THURSDAY (2nd) 8-12 midnight
JOHN MAYALL'S
BLUES BREAKERS
FRIDAY (3rd) 7.30-11.30
CHRIS FARLOW
& THE THUNDERBIRDS
FRIDAY ALL-NIGHT SESSION
12-5 a.m.
ZOOT MONEY'S
BIG ROLL BAND
CHRIS FARLOW
& THUNDERBIRDS
SATURDAY (4th) 7.30-11.30 p.m.
JOHNNY BURCH OCTET
PHIL SEAMAN TRIO
SATURDAY ALL-NIGHT SESSION
12-6 a.m.
DICK MORRISSEY QRT.
SUNDAY AFTERNOON SESSION
GEORGIE FAME
& BLUE FLAMES
3-6 p.m.
TONY SHEVETON
& SHEVELLES
SUNDAY EVENING SESSION
7-11 p.m.
ZOOT MONEY'S
BIG ROLL BAND
MONDAY (6th) 8-12 midnight
MONEY'S MONDAY
ZOOT MONEY'S
BIG ROLL BAND
WEDNESDAY (8th) 7.30-11 p.m.
GEORGIE FAME NIGHT
MEMBERSHIP s.a.e. and P.O. for 10/- to Sec. Flamingo and All-Nighter Clubs, 47 Gerrard Street, W.1.

CRAWDADDY
AT THE STAR, CROYDON
ALSO FRIDAYS, ST. PETERS HALL, KINGSTON, WITH THE AUTHENTICS
Saturday—YARDBIRDS
Wednesday—IMPULSIONS R & B
RICHMOND ATHLETIC GROUNDS
Sunday
MOST R and BLUES WAILING
YARDBIRDS

● THURSDAY ●
TODAY

BRIAN GREEN AND HIS NEW ORLEANS STOMPERS, Tally Ho, Kentish Town.

BROMLEY COURT: Acker Bilk.

FOREST GATE: Tailgate Six at the Rising Sun.

NEW ORLEANS, Rising Sun, St. Leonard's Road, Bromley by Bow.

RHYTHM AND BLUES, George and Dragon, Acton. **ART WOOD COMBO**.

STARTING GATE, Station Road, Wood Green: **LENNIE BEST**, Colin Peters.

THE PLOUGH, Stockwell Road, S.W.9. Pete Winslow and Rex Morris.

● THURSDAY,—contd. ●

THURSDAY NIGHT PRAYER MEETING
PREACHED BY
ALEXIS KORNER'S
BLUES INC.
WITH
HERBIE GOINS
ALSO THE
DON BROWN QRT.
AT THE
MERCURY THEATRE
NOTTING HILL GATE
OPENING TONIGHT!

● FRIDAY ●

BLACK LION, Plaistow, E.13. (Next week April 10). **AGAIN FABULOUS DICK MORRISSEY QUARTET**.

BLUEOPERA CLUB
GRAHAM BOND
QUARTET
RUSKIN ARMS
386 High Street North, E.12
Free Membership Opening Night

BRIXTON, Thames City Jazzmen.

BROMLEY COURT: R & B, Roadrunners.

CROYDON JAZZ CLUB, Star Hotel: Back O'Town Syncopators.

ERIC SILK'S SOUTHERN JAZZBAND. Southern Jazz Club in Ex-Servicemen's Club next door, while Red Lion, 640 High Road, Leytonstone, is being redecorated.

GOLDERS GREEN REFECTORY. **JIMMY POWELL - R&B**

HARRINGAY R&B BLUESVILLE!
SOULSVILLE WITH
JOHN MAYALL
BLUES BREAKERS!
"THE MANOR HOUSE"
(opposite Manor House Tube)

● SATURDAY ●

WOOD GREEN: THE LONDON CITY STOMPERS!!

● SUNDAY ●

AT THE JAZZHOUSE
Green Man, Blackheath Hill,
DON RENDELL QUINTET

BEXLEY, Black Prince: Rhythm and Blues, Jimmy Powell and 5 Dimensions.

BILL BRUNSKILL, Fighting Cocks, Kingston.

BO STREET RUNNERS, Railway Hotel, Wealdstone.

● SUNDAY,—contd. ●

CLUB OCTAVE presents The Dave Morse Quartet with Pete Coe, Hambrough Tavern, Southall.

COOKS, CHINGFORD, Royal Forest Hotel. **FREDDY RANDALL AND HIS BAND**. Just as packed as ever.

ERIC SILKS Jazzband. Ken Colyer Club.

HOT CLUB OF LONDON, 7 to 10.30 p.m. **THE BACK O'TOWN SYNCOPATORS**, Shakespeare Hotel, Powis Street, Woolwich.

METROPOLITAN TAVERN
FARRINGDON ROAD
12-2 p.m.
ROYAL GARDEN JAZZBAND
MUSICIANS WELCOME

THE PLOUGH, Stockwell Road, S.W.9. Lunchtime. Terry Seymour and Jimmy Collins.

WOOD GREEN: ALEX WELSH!!

● MONDAY ●

AT THE HOPBINE
(OPP. NORTH WEMBLEY STN.)
JOHN BURCH PRESENTS HIS
OCTET
AN ALL STAR GROUP
Bob Efford, Hank Shaw, P. J. Perry, Ken Wray, Harry Klein, Danny Thompson, Mike Scott. Admission 3/6.

BEXLEY, Black Prince: Ken Colyer.

BLUEOPERA CLUB
GRAHAM BOND
RHYTHM & BLUES
Cook's Ferry Inn, Edmonton

BROMLEY COURT: R & B, **ZOOT MONEY**.

GOLDERS GREEN REFECTORY
BOB WALLIS

OPENING
MOJO. R.&B. CLUB
White Hart Hotel, Acton. This week: **THE PARTISANS**.

RHYTHM AND BLUES CLUB CONCORDE
37-39 OXFORD STREET, W.1
EVERY MONDAY

THE PLOUGH, Stockwell Road, S.W.9. Duncan Campbell and Rex Morris.

● TUESDAY ●

KLOOKS KLEEK
Railway Hotel, West Hampstead
ALEX HARVEY SOUL BAND plus
ART WOOD COMBO — 3s. 6d.

MORDEN: ALAN ELSDON, Interval: Colin Banagan: The Crown.

WOOD GREEN: THE MIKE COTTON SOUND!!

● WEDNESDAY ●

BLUE ROOM, Islington
LENNIE BEST, Chris Spedding Trio, Angel & Crown, Upper St., (Highbury Corner).

BROMLEY COURT: R & B, **BO STREET RUNNERS**.

GOLDERS GREEN REFECTORY
THE YARDBIRDS - R&B

KLOOKS KLEEK
RONNIE ROSS meets **DANNY MOSS**. 2s 6d.

RHYTHM AND BLUES, George and Dragon, Acton. **ART WOOD COMBO**.

THE PLOUGH, Stockwell Road, S.W.9. Micky Ashman's Jazzband.

JAZZ CLUBS —outside London

1/4d. per word

RICKY-TICK CLUB
Friday, 3rd April
WINDSOR: Star & Garter
ZOOT MONEY
GUILDFORD Plaza
GEORGIE FAME
Saturday, 4th April
MAIDENHEAD, Pearce Hall
GEORGIE FAME
Sunday, 5th
READING Olympia
3-5.30: JOHN MAYALL

● FRIDAY ●

GILES-FOX Hot Four—Sweden

OSTERLEY JAZZ CLUB, Osterley Rugby Club Pavilion, Tentelow Lane, Norwood Green, Southall: **DOUG RICHFORD'S LONDON JAZZBAND**, Colin Kingwell's Jazz Bandits.

● SATURDAY ●

BRENTWOOD JAZZ CLUB
ALAN ELSDONS
JAZZ BAND!!
WITH MICK EMERY TRIO
"THE WHITE HART" HOTEL
Brentwood, Essex. Lic. Bar

HOT FOUR—Stockholm

● SUNDAY ●

HOT FOUR—Stockholm.

● MONDAY ●

HOT FOUR—Stockholm.

● TUESDAY ●

AYLESBURY R&B BLUESVILLE!
MANFRED MANN
MANFRED MANN
READY! STEADY! GO!
BOROUGH ASSEMBLY HALL, AYL
EVERYBODY WELCOME LIC. BAR

BALDRY'S BLUES CLUB
RAILWAY HOTEL, WEALDSTONE
LONG JOHN BALDRY AND
THE HOOCHIE COOCHIE MEN

HOT FOUR—Stockholm

● WEDNESDAY ●

HOT FOUR—Stockholm.

JAZZ CLUBS —Northern

● SUNDAY ●

REDCAR JAZZ CLUB
COATHAM HOTEL
TERRY LIGHTFOOT'S JAZZMEN

HOTELS

1/4d. per word

STONEHALL HOUSE HOTEL.—(20 minutes West End.) Room and breakfast from 18s. 6d. daily. Hot and Cold; fully centrally heated and heaters all rooms. Lounge, TV, and radio. AA and RAC listed —27 Westcombe Park Road, Blackheath, London, S.E.3. Greenwich 1595.

REHEARSAL ROOMS

1/4d. per word

LARGE REHEARSAL ROOM.—George Fierstone Music Centre.—Phone North 4224.

FAN CLUBS

1/4d. per word

BARRY and the Quintones Fan Club: S.a.e. to the Secretary, 66 Spur Road, Orpington, Kent.

GEORGIE FAME FAN CLUB. Sec., 47 Gerrard Street, W.1.

KENNY BALL Appreciation Society. — S.a.e. to Miss Pat Saunders, 18 Carlisle Street, W.1.

TONY SHEVETON & THE SHEVELLES. — S.a.e. to Secretary, 47 Gerrard Street London, W.1.

Alexis Korner's
BLUES INCORPORATED
all enquiries to:
Peter Burman Agency
HAMpstead 6596 or 4994

WALLINGTON PUBLIC HALL
STAFFORD ROAD, WALLINGTON
KIN 1787
THIS SATURDAY (APRIL 4th)
THE
COMMANCHES
and SUPPORTING GROUP
7.45-11.45 p.m. Admission 5/-

PALM COURT HOTEL
RICHMOND
Friday, April 3 DON RENDELL
Saturday, April 4th BOB BURNS
Sunday, April 5th
Lunchtime DICK MORRISSEY & LENNIE BEST
Evening IAN CARR
Resident Rhythm Section
ED FAULTLESS TRIO
Martin Joseph, Dick Brennan
ADMISSION FREE

MANFRED MANN
ODEON LEWISHAM
Friday, April 3rd
also
READY STEADY GO

RONNIE SCOTT'S CLUB
39 GERRARD ST., W.1. Tel.: GER 4752
LONDON'S ONLY
JAZZ NIGHT-CLUB!
Wine and Dine nightly to the Best Jazz in Town!
YOUR LAST CHANCE TO HEAR
THE GREAT
STAN GETZ!
THURS. 2nd, 7.30-3 a.m.
STAN GETZ!
RONNIE SCOTT and the
STAN TRACEY TRIO
JOHNNIE SCOTT QUINTET
FRI. 3rd and SAT. 4th, Two Sessions Nightly, 7 p.m.-11.30 p.m. and Midnight-4.30 a.m.
STAN GETZ!
RONNIE SCOTT and the
STAN TRACEY TRIO
TUBBY HAYES QUINTET
SUN. 5th, Special Sunday afternoon Session, 2.30-6 p.m. Admission 12/6
STAN GETZ!
RONNIE SCOTT and the
STAN TRACEY TRIO
ERNEST RANGLIN TRIO
7 p.m.-Midnight
ERNEST RANGLIN QUARTET
(Stan Getz last appearance at the Marquee)
COMMENCING MON. 6th.
FOR ONE WEEK, 7.30-1 a.m. Nightly
THE WONDERFUL AMERICAN SINGER
MISS
BETTY BENNETT
Plus THE BEST IN BRITISH JAZZ
During Stan Getz's engagement Club Session times are: Mon.-Thurs. 7.30-2 a.m., Fri. and Sat. 7-11.30 and Midnight-4.30 a.m., Sunday afternoon 2.30 p.m.-6 p.m. and 7.30-Midnight.
STAN GETZ will be appearing at all these sessions except MONDAYS
ADVANCE TICKETS (reserved seats) for all appearances can be booked at the Club or by post, please telephone for details.

MARQUEE
90 WARDOUR ST.
LONDON, W.1
Friday, April 3rd
★THE YARDBIRDS
★THE IMPULSIONS R & B
Saturday, April 4th
★JOE HARRIOTT QUINTET
featuring SHAKE KEANE
★RONNIE ROSS QUARTET
featuring BILL LE SAGE
Sunday, April 5th
THE FINAL APPEARANCE OF
STAN GETZ
PLUS! PLUS! PLUS!
MARK MURPHY
TUBBY HAYES QUINTET
RONNIE SCOTT QUARTET
Members: 12/6 Guests: 15/-
Monday, April 6th
MANFRED MANN
★JOHN MAYALL'S BLUES BREAKERS
Tuesday, April 7th
★BLUE BEAT
LESTER DAWSON and the BLUE BEATS with RED PRICE
Wednesday, April 8th
★CHRIS BARBER'S
JAZZ BAND
& OTTILIE PATTERSON
Members 5/- Guests: 7/6
Thursday, April 9th
★LONG JOHN BALDRY
and the HOOCHIE COOCHIE MEN
★ANDY McKINLEY and the SEE SEE RIDERS
Sat: Members 6/-, Guests 7/6
Mon., Tue., Fri., Members 5/-, Guests 6/-
Thur., Members 5/-, Guests 7/6

At the
BULL'S HEAD
BARNES BRIDGE PRO 5241
Thursday, April 2nd
SIX SOUNDS
Ian Hamer - Bob Efford - Tony Archer - Ken Wray - Alan Branscombe - Alan Green
Friday, April 3rd
JOE TEMPERLEY
Saturday, April 4th
BOBBY WELLINS
Sunday, April 5th
Lunchtime—
ART ELLEFSON
Evening—
ALAN BRANSCOMBE
Monday, April 6th
TUBBY HAYES BIG BAND
Tuesday, April 7th
KEITH CHRISTIE
Wednesday, April 8th
BILL LE SAGE
RONNIE ROSS

FOLK FORUM

● THURSDAY ●
TODAY

ADDLESTONE, Dukes Head. **STEVE BENBOW**. N.W. Roy Guest.

STARTING GATE, Station Road, Wood Green, open night 8 p.m. NW Pete Stanley and Wiz Jones.

● FRIDAY ●

CATFORD! COME! The Railway Tavern, Catford Bridge, S.E.6. 7.45 p.m. **ALEX CAMPBELL**, Chris and Jackie, **TAVERNERS**, Colin and Graham. Opening Night. Plus **GUESTS**.

FRIENDS OF OLD TIMEY MUSIC—OSTERLEY.

RORY McEWEN PRESENTS FOLKSONG CONCERT, CECIL SHARP HOUSE, 2 REGENT'S PARK ROAD, LONDON, N.W.1, FRIDAY, APRIL 10, 7.30 p.m., WITH CYRIL TAWNEY, LISA TURNER, MARTIN CARTHY, JULIE FELIX AND SURPRISE GUESTS. TICKETS 5s., 7s. 6d.—GUL 2206. BOOK NOW. LAST CONCERT IN THE SERIES.

● SATURDAY ●

AT THE CELLAR, Cecil Sharp House, Regents Park Rd., N.W.1. Mike Robinson and The Washhouse Three. Commence 7.30 (Folk Time).

AT THE TROUBADOUR, Earls Court 10.30. **NIGEL DENVER, RED SULLIVAN**.

HOOTENANNY, BALLADS AND BLUES, Black Horse, Rathbone Place, W.1. **ALEX CAMPBELL, THE MESSENGERS** (Folk Four), **JOHN BERRY**.

THE SINGERS CLUB, Saturday, April 4, 1964, The Royal Hotel, Woburn Place, W.C.1. Commencing 8 p.m.: Ewan MacColl, Peggy Seeger and guest performer.

● SUNDAY ●

BATTERSEA NAGS HEAD, York Road, Battersea. Residents **PAUL LENIHAN** and **JOHN WARD** with **EVAN JOHNSON** and special guest **LEON ROSSELSON**.

HAMPSTEAD, STEVE BENBOW, CLAIRE and **DAVE**. The Enterprise, opposite Chalk Farm Station. 7.30.

KINGSTON, Union Hotel, Surbiton Road, 8 p.m.: Derek Sarjeant.

POTTERS BAR, "Robin Hood," 7.30 p.m. An American Couple —Sandy and Jeannie.

● MONDAY ●

ALEX CAMPBELL at **ROUNDHOUSE** Corner, Wardour, Brewer St. 7.30. Also return **GERRY LOUGHRAN** plus **PETE DYER**. Many guests.

LEATHER BOTTLE, Edgware. **LINDA DREW, MARTIN WINSOR, HICKORY NUTS**.

SPINNING WHEEL CELLAR Folk Song Club, 8 every Monday. **MICK SOFTLEY**. — The Spinning Wheel, 30 High Street, Hemel Hempstead. Boxmoor 5516.

● TUESDAY ●

CROWN, TWICKENHAM, Johnny Silvo, Farriers, Strawberry Hill Boys.

● WEDNESDAY ●

BROMLEY "STAR AND GARTER" DEREK SARJEANT and **DIZ DISLEY**.

SIDCUP FOLK CLUB
Station Hotel, Sidcup
Res. **BRIAN FRY, MAUREEN FIDDLER, PAUL STARR**. Admission 3/-.

SURBITON, Assembly Rooms, 8 p.m.: Folkvendors (Derek at Bromley).

INSTRUMENTS FOR SALE

1/- per word

ALTO, HAWKES, case, £17 ono. Cornet, £8.—D. Cox, 104 Ainsworth Rd., Bury, Lancs.

BARGAIN. Eb alto sax, Selmer Mark VI, as new. £85 o.n.o.—L/Cpl. Warr, J.S.C., Crickhowell, Brecs.

BARITONE, Pennsylvania, F.A.M. G.L., case/stand. £60. — Box 3353.

FENDER precision bass, pink immaculate, £90 o.n.o.—PIN 3689

GUILD SLIM JIM, immaculate £80 or nearest offer. — Balham 3654 (9 a.m. to 5 p.m.).

HENNESSEY 12-string guitar, as new, £75.—TED 2252, Ext. 230.

IMPERIAL TROMBONE, beautiful condition, £30.—GRA 4228.

LEVIN cutaway electric guitar, professional instrument, c/w case, £57.—BOW 1097.

SOPRANO, £20.—46 North St., Pewsey, Wilts.

TENOR CONN, case, F.A.M., S.P.B.D. £65.—Box 3352.

TENOR SAX, immaculate, £65. —Phone FUL 9839.

INSTRUMENTS WANTED

1/- per word

ARCHITECTURAL student wants very good guitar, pickups optional.—Box 3346.

DRUMS, Guitars, Echoes, Clarinets, Accordions, etc. Bring your instruments for spot cash to Len Stiles Ltd., 233/235 Lewisham High Street, S.E.13. Lee 8018.

GUITARS, AMPLIFIERS, cash waiting, part exchange etc. — Musical Exchange, Wembley 1970.

MUSICAL INSTRUMENTS wanted for cash. — Musical Exchange, Wembley 1970.

SPOT CASH, Gibson Guitars or similar, Amplifiers, Drums etc. Greenwoods, 20 Guildhall Street, Preston 2542.

INSTRUMENT REPAIRS

1/4d. per word

EXPRESS BRASS REPAIR SERVICE by Paxman Musical Instruments Ltd., 36 Gerrard Street, London, W.1. Ger. 4892.

FOOTE FOR BASS REPAIRS. Expert work on the premises. Estimates free.—Chas. E. Foote Ltd., 20 Denman Street, W.1. GER 1811.

JACK DAWKES' saxophone repairs.—6 Chaucer Avenue, Hayes, Middx. (Hayes 4475).

DRUMS

1/- per word

FOR SALE, Premier drum kit, excellent condition. — Cranleigh (Surrey) 680.

LUDWIG KITS. Trade-ins taken. H.P. available. Jon Murray, Gerry Rafferty, 2 Fownes Street, Dublin.

SOUND EQUIPMENT

1/- per word

LEAK TL25 plus amplifier and Goodmans 18in. speaker, in cabinets, £50.—PIN 3689.

RECORDING STUDIOS

1/4d. per word

TOP QUALITY DEMO DISCS at moderate costs. — **TONY PIKE, SOUND STUDIOS**, Putney 4928.

PUBLICATIONS

1/4d. per word

R & B MONTHLY, No. 3 April, 1s. p.o.—M. Vernon, 3b Godstone Road, Kenley, Surrey.

WANTED: Books on music publishing, printing and engraving. —37 Cannon Street, Walsall.

CLUB SECRETARIES AND CLASSIFIED ADVERTISERS PLEASE NOTE
copy should reach this office by 10 a.m. on Fridays if insertion is desired in the following week's issue of
"MELODY MAKER"
161-166 Fleet Street
London, E.C.4

DE MONFORT HALL - LEICESTER
THURSDAY, APRIL 23rd, at 7.45 p.m. ONLY
By arrangement with Harold Davison, Arthur Kimbrell presents
THE MODERN JAZZ QUARTET
JOHN LEWIS, PERCY HEATH, CONNIE KAY, MILT JACKSON
Guest Artist: LAURINDO ALMEIDA (Guitar)
Balcony 12/6, 10/6; Gallery 8/6, 7/6; Stalls 11/6, 9/6, 7/6, 5/6; Stage 5/6
From Arthur Kimbrell, 38 Rugby Road, Hinckley (Tel. 3563), or Municipal Box Office, Charles Street, Leicester (Tel. 27632)
Postal bookings enclose remittance and s.a.e.

PETER, PAUL & MARY
arriving London Airport 1 p.m.
Thursday, 2nd April
Official Fan Club
S.a.e. plus 7/6d. to:
84 Elmshurst Crescent, East Finchley, N.2
TUD 8718

BEDSITTER CLUB
120 HOLLAND PARK AVENUE
LONDON, W.11
Wed., 1st April, 8 p.m.-11 p.m.: BLUEBIRDS
Thurs., 2nd April, 8 p.m.-11 p.m.: CARDINALS
Fri., 3rd April, 9 p.m.-2 a.m.: PHANTOMS
Sat., 4th April, 9 p.m.-3 a.m.: SUGAR BEATS
Sun., 5th April, 8 p.m.-11 p.m.: ROOSTERS

HORNSEY TOWN HALL
Saturday, April 18
DANCE — 7.30 to Midnight
TED HEATH
and his Music
Advance Tickets 6/6 FITzroy 2448
Licensed Bar

From April 14th, resident at
100 Club, Oxford Street
Rhythm and Blues Stylists
THE PRETTY THINGS
All enquiries to Sole Agents
Jazzshows Ltd., 22 Newman St., W.1

BALDING MAN?
Although baldness is incurable, if you have some hair left an entirely new process of toupee construction will give you a natural-looking and vigorous head of hair that defies detection. The U.K. rights in this revolutionary technique are exclusive to
ADRIAN BROOK
Dept. MM., 146A BROMPTON ROAD, LONDON, S.W.3
Write now for details and FREE consultation—your anxieties may well be at an end.

fore, the Ad Lib was attended by actors, fashion designers, models, photographers, gallery-owners and many others from the old and new London jet set. You could meet people like Alma Cogan, Sean Connery, Sammy Davis Jr, Judy Garland, Roger Moore and Diana Dors, mixed with the upcoming, young generation of music acts such as The Beatles, members of The Rolling Stones, Manfred Mann, The Who, The Pretty Things, The Hollies, The Searchers, and many others. Female singers such as Dusty Springfield, Lulu, Cilla Black and Petula Clark also often attended the club regularly.

It was at the Ad Lib that Ringo Starr, at two o'clock in the morning and after a few drinks, proposed to his girl-friend from the Cavern days, hairdresser Maureen Cox, on January 20, 1965. John Lennon used to drink Scotch and Coke and became increasingly condescending in his discussions with people the more he drank. He was often sarcastic about The Hollies, whom he felt were just imitating The Beatles' vocal style. However, there was a lot of mutual respect between The Beatles and The Rolling Stones, and several of the members would hang out together when they had the chance.

The success of the Ad Lib paved the way for other clubs and in 1965 places such as the Cromwellian, Blaises and, in particular, Scotch of St. James, took over as watering-holes for the pop stars. Ad Lib survived until early 1966, when a fire in the kitchen forced the club to close down for good. But through the glass door I can still see the elevator that took the guests up to the Ad Lib, just as discreet as it was back then.

A page of ads from Melody Maker in early May 1964. In just a year the music scene had changed. Many of the jazz clubs are gone, while the choices for those interested in rhythm & blues are almost limitless. ◄

Flamingo Club

Flamingo Club
Soho
33–37 Wardour
Street
Tube:
LeicesterSquare

I walk along Lisle Street to Wardour Street. At number 33–37 there was once a truly legendary club: the Flamingo Club. The Flamingo Club was located in the basement, while its sister club, the Whisky A Go Go, which was fully licensed, was situated on the ground floor. The Flamingo opened in 1957 and quickly became an important show venue for many bands, a position it maintained for many years. The brothers Rik and John Gunnell owned and ran the place; at the same time they were also running a booking agency. Their "All Nighter Club", which started in 1959 and lasted all through the night on Fridays and Saturdays, was very popular.

Whisky A Go Go was located on the ground floor, while the door to the left led down to the Flamingo Club. ▲

Originally, the Flamingo tried to attract an older, more sophisticated jazz audience and was particularly popular with West Indians and black American soldiers stationed outside London. The club was noisy and hot, and fistfights were often part of the entertainment. After a particularly violent brawl the American army stopped the soldiers from visiting the club. In early 1963, Georgie Fame played his first gig at the club with his band, The Blue Flames. The band became the house band at the club and were big favourites during the nightly performances for a long time. Georgie Fame was also a representative for the music that was performed at the club: a cool, jazz-influenced sort of blues. In 1963 he recorded a live album at the club, entitled *Rhythm And Blues At The Flamingo*. Many of the songs in his repertoire were taken from records im-

ported by American soldiers from their home-country, and many musicians from several different groups, such as The Beatles and The Rolling Stones, often came there to listen to new records or to Georgie Fame.

The Rolling Stones got the chance to play at the club on January 14, 1963, which was the first time that Charlie Watts performed with the band. However, the jazz crowd gave the Stones' rocky style a cool reception, but at the same time the group attracted a new, younger audience to the club: the mod movement was on the rise in London. And like so many other London clubs, from mid-1963 the Flamingo was forced to gradually change direction from jazz to soul and British rhythm & blues.

The Animals played their first gig at the Flamingo in december 1963 and quickly became the biggest favourites at the club. The Flamingo increasingly became the mods' favourite hangout, especially during the "All Nighters". Two of the people who attended the club regularly were the founders of The Small Faces: Steve Marriott and Ronnie Lane. At the club they could often see American blues artists, among them Rufus Thomas and T-Bone Walker, who always played at the Flamingo when they visited London. Police raids at the club with its pill-popping audience were recurring events, although the Gunnell brothers often received advance warnings of the raids. A somewhat unusual gig was Paul Simon's performance there in 1964.

According to Georgie Fame, the audience at the All-nighters originally consisted mostly of West Indians, black American soldiers, pimps, prostitutes and gangsters. But when the album was recorded, the mods were already taking over the club. ▲

25

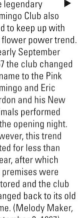

The legendary ▶ Flamingo Club also tried to keep up with the flower power trend. In early September 1967 the club changed its name to the Pink Flamingo and Eric Burdon and his New Animals performed on the opening night. However, this trend lasted for less than a year, after which the premises were restored and the club changed back to its old name. (Melody Maker, September 2, 1967)

Eric unveils the 'new' Flamingo

LONDON'S long-running Flamingo Club has gone hippie under its new name, the Pink Flamingo.

The ceiling is covered in flowers. psychedelic paintings adorn the walls and above the audience, stuffed pigeons, lit by ultra violet lights, sit on pipes.

The stage, extended by some four feet, is decorated with flowers, beads and jewels.

The club was completely packed on Saturday for Eric Burdon and the Animals—but hippies were few. Highspots of a good Burdon show were "San Francisan Nights", which drew the biggest applause, "When I Was Young ", " Are You Experienced?"—which Eric dedicates to Jimi Hendrix—and a great version of "Paint It Black" using an electric violin.

Among the songs he played were 'The Sound Of Silence' and 'I Am A Rock', and although the songs were still unknown his performance received big ovations.

The Gunnell brothers expanded their stable of artists and when they were unable to book them elsewhere, they had them perform at their own club. Besides Georgie Fame, some of the artists in their stable who played at their club were Chris Farlowe, Geno Washington and The Ram Jam Band, and John Mayall's Bluesbreakers. John Mayall's Bluesbreakers became extremely popular and in April 1966 they recorded a handful of songs for a live album at the club. Two of the members of the band that night were Eric Clapton and Jack Bruce, soon would shortly form Cream together with Ginger Baker. The Gunnell brothers also introduced one of the first super groups, Shotgun Express, featuring Peter Green on guitar, Mick Fleetwood on drums and Rod

During the weekends, Flamingo Club offered live music all through the evening and night, where one band would follow another. The downside of these nightly arrangements was that uppers were as frequent as the pigeons in Trafalgar Square. ▶

FLAMINGO & ALLNIGHTER CLUBS
33-37 Wardour St., London, W.1
Gerrard 1549. Guests welcome
Dance or listen in comfort
Tony Harris & Rik Gunnell
present:—
★ Thursday (9th) 8-12 midnight
JOHN MAYALL'S
BLUES BREAKERS
★ Friday (10th) 7.30-11.30
CHRIS FARLOW
AND THE THUNDERBIRDS
★ Friday All-Nite Session
12-5 a.m.
ZOOT MONEY'S
BIG ROLL BAND
JOHN MAYALL'S
BLUES BREAKERS
★ Saturday (11th) 7.30-11.30
RONNIE ROSS QNT.
TOMMY WHITTLE QT.
★ Saturday All-Nite Session
12-5 a.m.
ZOOT MONEY'S
BIG ROLL BAND
DICK MORRISSEY QRT.
★ Sunday Afternoon Session
3-6 pm
TONY SHEVETON
AND SHEVELLES
★ Sunday Evening Session
7-11 pm
ZOOT MONEY
BIG ROLL BAND
★ Monday (13th) 8-12 midnight
MONEY'S MONDAY
ZOOT MONEY'S BIG ROLL BAND
★ Wednesday (15th) 7.30-11 pm
GEORGIE FAME NIGHT
WITH GEORGIE & GUEST STARS
MEMBERSHIP s.a.e. and P.O. for
10/- to Sec. Flamingo and All-
Nighter Clubs, 47 Gerrard Street,
W.1.

Stewart on lead vocals. But the group only survived for a few months and broke up in early 1967.

The club venue, which was a large, dark room, was always packed with people; the only furnishing was five rows of cinema seats in front of the stage. The premises are still there today, although they now function as a pub and everything from the original decoration and atmosphere is long gone.

Zoot Money and his Big Roll Band take a break during a gig at the Flamingo Club. The club's All-Nighters were very popular and lasted until five in the morning. ▼

De Hems
Soho
11 Macclesfield
Street
Tube:
Leicester Square

De Hems

Right opposite the Flamingo is Gerrard Street, the main street of Chinatown, and I make my way through the crowd of tourists to Macclesfield Street, where my next stop is. On this short street, between Gerrard Street and Shaftesbury Avenue, lies the Dutch pub *De Hems*.

While researching this book I got in touch with the Swede Jan "Rock Ola" Olofsson and we have decided to meet up at the pub. Since the early Sixties, Jan has been based in London; he is mostly known for his photographs taken during the filming of the television programme Ready Steady Go!, which was broadcast between 1963 and 1966, and for his book, My 60s. But he was also working as an agent, a record company owner, a club owner and a music publisher. In these various guises Jan got to know most of the big artists and socialised with

them privately in different clubs and pubs. He has promised me to share his personal memories from some of the places I plan to visit.

Jan tells me that he often went to De Hems, since the pub was an important meeting-place for the British music business. Around the corner, on Shaftesbury Avenue, the music paper Record Mirror had their offices, and Jan Olofsson often met Richard Green (later the press officer for The Who) at the paper. It was partly due to the contacts he made at De Hems that he managed to get into the music business. At the pub, jour-

Jan Olofsson together with The Beatles in London, March 9, 1963. The picture was taken at the Granada in East Ham, where the Beatles began their tour together with Tommy Roe and Chris Montez. The 'Please Please Me' single was then at the top of the charts and The Beatles were preparing the release of their first album. ◀

nalists, agents, promoters and managers would get together to make deals, or simply to exchange gossip.

Jan also got to know many of the musicians who visited the pub, among them Keith Moon of The Who, who was often there during 1965–1966, and in 1967 Jimi Hendrix became a regular guest at the pub. Nearby, on Gerrard Street, one of Jimi Hendrix' managers had his offices. Michael Jeffrey handled the negotiations and the business side, while Chas Chandler was responsible for everything concerning the music. In Jeffrey's offices, Jan took one of his most famous photographs of Hendrix, in the spring of 1967.

But there wasn't any wild partying going on at De Hems – not even for Keith Moon! The pub mainly functioned as a warming-up place before going on to the clubs. But Jan tells me that after a particularly alcohol-soaked warm-up, Keith Moon, Richard Green and he were discretely shown the door at the Bag O'Nails, a club that otherwise could withstand most everything. He also says that De Hems still looks like it did in the Sixties, and while we drink our Belgian beer I tell him what little I know about the pub:

Jan Olofsson's picture of Jimi Hendrix, taken at co-manager Michael Jeffrey's offices at Gerrard Street in early March 1967. At the time, Hendrix had just made his breakthrough with 'Hey Joe'. ▶

In the beginning of 1963, the 19-year-old Andrew Loog Oldham was working as a publicist for The Beatles' manager, Brian Epstein. His job was to make the papers write about the new signings Gerry & The Pacemakers and Billy J. Kramer. To this end, he would hang out at the pub all day, usually approaching Peter Jones of the Record Mirror. By mid-April Oldham's work had been done, but at that time he received an all-important tip from Peter Jones. He told him that one of his colleagues, Norman Jopling,

A young and unspoiled Keith Moon. Always ready for new and crazy pranks, which with his growing drug abuse would become increasingly bizarre over the years. ▶

30

had written an enthusiastic article about a group that used to perform at a club in Richmond on Sundays: they were really great. Jones had been to see the band himself and as far as he knew they didn't have a manager. This would be the first time that the paper published an article about a group that had never released a single, so this was something truly unique. Next Sunday an eager Oldham took the train to Richmond, and just about a week later he was the manager for this new group: The Rolling Stones.

Pollo
Soho
20 Old Compton
Street
Tube:
Leicester Square

Pollo

Having finished our beers, Jan and I part ways but decide to meet up later. I walk up to 20 Old Compton Street, where I plan to have lunch at a small Italian restaurant. While I walk along the street I softly sing the old Al Stewart song 'Old Compton Street Blues' to myself:

> "Oh, your pictures they don't really do you justice little girl
> For you're careful not to let the camera touch your private world

Old Compton
Street 1967   ▶

And there's just a hint of sadness in your smile through the dark
As you slip your dress off slowly for the sailor or the clerk"
(Old Compton Street Blues, lyrics: Al Stewart)

Those words will tell you something about the goings-on in this street during the Sixties, while today it is a popular gay street. The Beatles' Magical Mystery Tour film was edited at Norman Film Production, which was located at 76 Old Compton Street, with a dedicated Paul McCartney in attendance for the entire 11 weeks it took to complete work on the film.

I reach my lunch spot, *Pollo* at 20 Old Compton Street, not far from Charing Cross Road, where I order a pasta salad. Syd Barrett, the founder and original front man of Pink Floyd, loved this small and simple but nice Italian pasta restaurant. From the spring of 1966 it was his regular hangout for almost a year, and he would sit there for hours, writing songs, making drawings, having discussions or playing the Oriental board game Go with his

friends and his girlfriend Lindsay Korner. He lived just around the corner on 2 *Earlham Street* — that house has since been torn down — and this was during his most creative time in Pink Floyd, when he wrote most of his songs, among them the band's breakthrough hit 'See Emily Play'. This was also before he started dropping LSD into his morning coffee and tragically withdrew into his own world of madness.

I leave my table to make room for other hungry lunch guests and walk back to Wardour Street, where I stop at the corner to Brewer Street for a while.

Syd Barrett was the natural creative centre at the start of Pink Floyd's career. He was also a leading figure in the psychedelic wave that swept through London during the summer and autumn of 1966. But as early as the summer of 1967 his drug problems and psychological instability were evident to everybody around him. ◄

On 83–85 Wardour Street was the location of the old *Roundhouse* (not to be confused with the Roundhouse located in Camden); the name is still engraved in the wall above the present bar sign. Roundhouse is actually outside the perimeters of my Sixties, but it is so important that I have to mention it. The roots of the British pop music wave can partly be found in skiffle music, and one of the first skiffle clubs, The London Skiffle Club, was opened by Cyril Davies in 1952 on the first floor above the pub.

By the mid-Fifties, Cyril Davies was tired of skiffle and although the club was always full he suggested to his friend and fellow musician Alexis Korner that they should open a blues club instead. A month later the pair opened The London Blues and Barrelhouse Club. Only three people were there on the opening night, and the performing artists usually outnumbered the audience, which mainly consisted of up-and-coming blues musicians such as Long John Baldry, Brian Knight and Geoff Bradford. The latter two would later rehearse with a band formed by Brian Jones, which would eventually become The Rolling Stones.

The club was given a magical aura thanks to the American blues musicians who played at the club many times: Big Bill Bronzy, Sonny Terry, Otis Spann and later on also Muddy Waters. Everybody played acoustically, which was customary at the early blues clubs. The only exception was Muddy Waters, who played at the club in 1960 and sufficiently inspired Cyril Davies and Alexis Korner to invest in a 10 Watt (!) amplifier, which they would own together.

Playing with electric instruments was highly provocative for the really puritanical blues fans and coupled with the fact that the pub owners felt it was too noisy, Davies and Korner were not allowed to continue with their blues nights above the pub. This was the reason they founded the first European blues club, the G Club (better known as the Ealing Club), which played a major role in the emergence of a British rhythm & blues scene.

Marquee Club II
Soho
90 Wardour Street
Tube:
Leicester Square

Marquee Club II

Just a little further up on the other side of Wardour Street, number 90 was once the location of what is perhaps the

MARQUEE
where the
action is

■ Where is the pop corner of the world? For thousands of youngsters it is London's Marquee Club. It is the melting pot of today's hip music, where jazz, folk and pop meet on equal terms, where trends are born and stars emerge. It could be compared with New York's Apollo Theatre, but really there is nothing like it in the world.

■ Look at the record. It was here the incredible Rolling Stones were acclaimed, and Britain's rhythm and blues revolution got under way. It was here that chart-smashing groups like the Moody Blues, Yardbirds, Manfred Mann and the Who built their fan following. Now it is the

turn of the Mark Leeman Five, T-Bones, and Jimmy James and the Vagabonds. All can be heard in the steaming atmosphere in Soho's Wardour Street.

■ Marquee Jazz Club Ltd is run by managing director Harold Pendleton. Co-directors are famous jazz band leaders Chris Barber and Kenny Ball. The club now means many things to many people. At weekends it's the home of exciting jazz from the big bands of Ted Heath and Johnny Dankworth, to the Dick Morrissey Quartet with Phil Seamen.

■ Folk fans flock to hear the Settlers and the new jug bands like the Dedicated Men, Hard Rhythm and Blues

is provided by Long John Baldry, Alex Harvey, T-Bones, Who and the Yardbirds.

■ Pop stars pile in and make use of the recording facilities for Radio Luxembourg and Radio London programmes, and hit records have emerged from the recording studio, hidden behind the main club area.

■ The Marquee has an excellent reputation as a "clean" club. No scandals here or tales of pills and delinquency. Music is the important quantity at the Marquee, and the club goers are London's most aware, adult teenagers. They are broadminded and listen to folk as easily as R&B. All of it is merging to such

an extent it ...
"Marquee Mu...

■ The club use... basement in C... Friday, March ... to Wardour St... the club mainl... pioneered the ... Korner's Blues ... late Cyril Dav... policy diversif... whole gamut o...

■ Atmosphere is ... ent and when ... storming the s... are exploding ... can be few

most famous rock club in London: *the Marquee Club*. If I hadn't already known the address I would never have guessed that this was the location, since all signs of the club are now gone. Today it is hard to imagine that there used to be a long line of people queuing up here almost every night for many years.

After having been forced to shut down the original Marquee Club on Oxford Street in early 1964, the owner, Harold Pendleton, began looking for a new location. He found an old warehouse in Soho, and in order to maintain the atmosphere he brought along the decoration from the old club, but he also put up mirrors on the walls in order to make the premises seem larger. Pendleton referred to the club as Mark 2 and managed to get a

Melody Maker
December 6, 1965 ▲

Manfred Mann, with Paul Jones on vocals, perform at the Marquee Club in 1964. The band's success began when they were asked to write a theme song for the television programme Ready Steady Go! The result was '5-4-3-2-1', which was released in January 1964. In the summer they achieved their international breakthrough with 'Do Wah Diddy Diddy' ▶

Five Live Yardbirds didn't contain anything original, merely the standard repertoire performed by all British R&B bands in 1964. ▼

leasing contract for the premises for twentyfour years. In conjunction with the move, Harold Pendleton broadened the repertoire of the club, since he'd realised that new winds were blowing and that jazz music had lost much of its position. Rock, pop, blues, jazz and folk music would share the same stage, but on different days, and this was where new trends and new stars were born.

Already from the start, the new Marquee Club was an important playing ground for the emerging British rock and blues scene during the Sixties, and for many years it continued to be one of the most important venues to play for new bands. It was part of the club's policy to encourage new bands by giving them regular gigs, but only the best of them would be given that opportunity.

On the opening night of March 13, 1964, The Yardbirds, Sonny Boy Williamson and Long John Baldry played, which defined the level of ambition from the word go. Just a week later, on March 20, The Yardbirds recorded their album *Five Live Yardbirds* at the Marquee. Eric Clapton always used really thin strings that would break after just a few songs, and while he changed strings the audience would slowly clap their hands, giving him the nickname "Slowhand". The Yardbirds played more than forty gigs at the club, the last one occurring in June 1966 with Jeff Beck on guitar and Jimmy Page on bass.

The Who had regular engagements on Tuesdays, starting November 24, 1964, but only a few faithful fans

from the Goldhawk Club turned up in the rotten weather. The fans were immediately given the task to go out in the streets and distribute invitation cards that promised "Maximum R&B" at the Marquee for just half the price of a regular ticket. Still, they only managed to attract around 30 people to The Who's first gig at the club, which was mostly known as a jazz club at the time.

The group that played more gigs than anybody else was Manfred Mann, but

they also played many times at the original Marquee Club. One of their most spectacular gigs happened at the end of 1965, when Eric Burdon of The Animals appeared onstage with them to sing a duet with Manfred Mann singer Paul Jones.

On Sunday, January 30, 1966, New Yorker Steve Stollman began arranging something he called Spontaneous Underground, a forerunner of the mix of music and other art forms that would later be known as "happenings". Stollman was looking for a suitable band that could be a part of these events, and one of his friends, Nigel Gordon, recommended his old friends in The Pink Floyd Sound. It was during one of these Sunday gigs, in May 1966, that Pink Floyd were discovered by their future managers, Peter Jenner and Andrew King.

The Move released a live recording from the Marquee Club, the EP *Something Else*, in January 1968. ▲

The Birmingham band The Move made their debut at the club in April 1966. With a skilful song writer like Roy Wood in the band, a broad musical competence and spectacular live gigs, they soon got a record contract, followed by well-deserved success. During one of their gigs at the Marquee, when they performed 'Fire Brigade', they set fire on the stage and the real fire brigade had to get there quickly to save the club. The band's tarnished reputation meant that they were banned at all English theatres for a while. In the early Seventies, Roy Wood, drummer Bev Bevan and the new member Jeff Lynne dissolved the band, changed musical direction and formed the Electric Light Orchestra.

The Moody Blues and Ten Years After are other examples of groups that played the Marquee Club at the start of their careers. Ten Years After made their debut at the club in June 1967, as an opening act for John Lee Hooker and the Savoy Brown Blues Band. They were such a big hit that they secured regular bookings at the club and then went on to become the main attraction every Friday.

At the back of the club, with an entrance from 10 Richmond Mews, there was a combined recording and rehearsal studio for the artists, where musical history was also written. In this studio The Moody Blues recorded their breakthrough hit, 'Go Now', in the late autumn of 1964, and a year later The Who recorded their first demos of their breakthrough hit, 'My Generation'. Spencer Davis Group had already achieved their big breakthrough, with songs such as 'Keep On Running' and 'Somebody Help Me', when they spent half an hour in this studio writing 'Gimme Some Lovin' in the early autumn of 1966.

But playing the Marquee was no guarantee for success; most of the bands remained unknown and some of them only achieved their breakthrough later on. Mr Jones and the Lower Third made their debut on October 8, 1965, but their lead singer would later become more well-known as David Bowie. He was given the chance to perform at the Marquee for many years without attracting any audience or be discovered. But when he finally achieved his breakthrough he returned the club's generosity by recording several of his videos at the Marquee. The mod band The Action were very popular in London and played several gigs between 1965 and 1967, but without achieving any major breakthrough and certainly not on an international level.

It was quite demanding for a band to play the Marquee, for the audience was knowledgeable, critical and had already seen most everything. One group that really set the sceptical audience on fire was The Small Faces. They played two gigs at the club, in March and June 1966, and created such chaos that they had to escape out the back door onto Richmond Mews after the gigs.

Someone who studied the band, and especially Steve Marriott, was the band's constant companion Robert Plant, but also Jimmy Page, who wanted Marriott to join a super group he was planning together with Jeff Beck. Page's interest subsided fairly quickly, however, after receiving a nightly phone call where the gruff-voiced caller asked him if he would be able to play the guitar with his fingers broken. In all likelihood The Small Faces' manager, Don Arden, had used his contacts in the East End to make sure that he would hold on to his cash cows.

In mid-June 1966, John Mayall's Bluesbreakers played at the venue, and as usual the enthusiastic audience were shouting "we want more God!" and "give God a solo!" whenever Eric Clapton was on stage. What they didn't know – nor did John Mayall for that matter – was that Clapton had decided to leave the band and was secretly rehearsing with a new group. A couple of months later, Eric Clapton returned to the Marquee stage, but now as a member of the legendary band Cream. In the meantime, the expectations on Cream had grown so high that many found their appearance disappointing. One explanation is that the group had too few rehearsals behind them, but also that their repertoire was much too limited. Led Zeppelin were better prepared when they made one of

The north London Mod band The Action in 1966. They are one of the best bands never to achieve a breakthrough in England, despite many well-received gigs at the Marquee. The band was supported by The Beatles' producer, George Martin, but split up as early as 1967 because of a lack success with their records. ◀

their first performances at the Marquee in October 1968, although they still used the name the New Yardbirds.

When The Jimi Hendrix Experience performed at the Marquee on Tuesday, January 24, 1967, the line along Wardour Street was more than 600 yards long; people were very curious about this group, who released their first single, 'Hey Joe', just a few weeks earlier. Jan Olofsson tells me that he attended a concert arranged by German television in March of that year, to take some photographs on behalf of the German television programme Beat Club. Among the performers that night were Jimi Hendrix, The Who, The Smoke and Geno Washington. On that occasion only a fraction of the long queue of people was able to enter the club, which was extremely crowded and sweaty. Jimi Hendrix played once more at the Marquee, together with

Jimi Hendrix at the Marquee Club in March 1967, during a recording for the West German television programme Beat Club. The line stretched around half the block before the concert, which was Hendrix' first at the Marquee ▼

Pete Townshend of The Who. To avoid creating chaos they were advertised as Gypsy when they did this concert in memory of Beatles manager Brian Epstein on January 29, 1969.

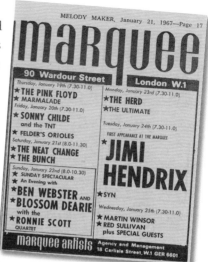

But it is only because of the artists that the Marquee Club has become legendary, for the actual premises were primitive, dark and shabby. On the stage there was only room for the most essential part of the equipment, and the sound would bounce off the walls, across the audience and then back to the band. Behind the stage there was a small and narrow room without a toilet or washing facilities, where the bands would traditionally sign their names on the wall. Even so, the club was popular among musicians, thanks to the positive atmosphere and the enthusiastic audience.

Going through the classic Marquee's database of bands who played at the club, is like going through a large part of the British blues and rock history. But among the missing names are The Beatles and The Rolling Stones, although the Stones played at the old Marquee. They were much too big and established when Mark 2 opened. However, The Rolling Stones made two unofficial gigs at the Marquee. The first time was in December 1968 – when they were rehearsing for their Rock And Roll Circus film – and the second in March 1971, when they recorded a farewell television performance in conjunction with their move to France.

In 1988, Harold Pendleton's lease expired and the club had to move to Charing Cross Road. Today, the entrance to Mark 2 has been altered and is much smaller than before. Although all traces of the legendary club are now gone, there is still a certain atmosphere surrounding the place, but this isn't something those rushing by will notice.

The Ship
Soho
116 Wardour Street
Tube:
Leicester Square

The Ship

I continue my walk just a few yards to the corner of Flaxman Court and The Ship, which is closely connected to the Marquee Club and its artists. Since the Marquee lacked an alcohol licence on their Sixties blues nights (it was felt that the audience was much too young), many artists went here to have a beer every now and then. For example, when The Yardbirds recorded their Five Live Yardbirds album at the Marquee Club in March 1964, the band would rush over here to have a beer during each break. Apparently, the beer did nothing to calm their nerves, however, since they played the songs in a maniacally high tempo.

In the mid-Sixties, The Ship also became a hangout for record company people and managers, who would have a couple of beers before they went on to the Marquee Club in the hope of making a new discovery. Eric Burdon would often come here and one evening in early September 1967 he was sitting together with a friend, planning his last night as a bachelor before his wedding to Angie King two days later. They were planning a psychedelic wedding, where everything would be flower power style with all the guests dressed in hippie clothes. They planned a route for the following day and night, where Burdon would make one last intimate visit to a number of the women he had been involved with in London. While I drink my beer I try to imagine what the groom Eric Burdon must have looked like at the wedding, and I wonder whether the bride, Angie King, knew about his busy schedule.

New Musical Express
September 16, 1967 ▲

During 1968, The Ship became the place where drummer Keith Moon (The Who) and his partying buddies would gather before they went on to some club a little later at night. It was virtually a daily routine that Moon would show up at The Ship after having picked up some money from the band's managers, who were based nearby on Old Compton Street. The Ship was also where George Harrison met up with Peter Frampton, when he wanted Peter to play on his first solo album, All Things Must Pass, which he was recording just around the corner, at Trident Studios.

Although The Ship still looks like it did during the Sixties, I'm surprised that the pub doesn't treasure its connection to rock history. There are no photographs or anything else that tells you about its history in the Sixties, but unfortunately this is quite common in London. However, there's a nice atmosphere at the pub, but after just one beer I have to leave and continue my walk.

Bricklayers Arms

Bricklayers Arms
Soho
7 Broadwick Street
T-bana:
Leicester Square

Almost opposite The Ship, at 7 Broadwick Street, there is a record shop, but in the early Sixties a pub was located here: *Bricklayers Arms*. The storeroom above the pub was the place where Brian Jones formed The Rolling Stones in 1962. For a couple of months, starting in mid-May 1962, Jones would hold auditions for a band he hoped would spread the blues all over the country. The first member to join the band was the pianist Ian Stewart, who showed up on a racing bike, dressed in leather shorts and with a packed lunch in his hand. The pub owner had seen to it that an old piano was available in the store room, and Stewart sat down at the piano and had no problems playing each and every song Brian suggested. At the same time, he was looking out the window, partly because he

On May 25, 1962, Mick Jagger, Keith Richards and Dick Taylor checked out Brian Jones and Ian Stewart's rehearsals, which were held in the store room above the pub. Just a little over a month later, Brian Jones named the newly formed band The Rolling Stones. ▶

New Musical Express September 4, 1964 ◀

12   NEW MUSICA

Meet Stew the sixth Stone....

IF you saw Ian Stewart (above) walking along any street, you probably wouldn't give him a second glance. He's a fair size, sported a beard until a few weeks ago and has normal length hair.

But one thing that makes him different from the rest of the herd is the fact that this week he and the Rolling Stones have taken an EP way up the top ten.

Stew is, in fact, the Stones' road manager, but on the " Five By Five " EP he plays organ. He's in there swingin' on the LP, too. This time on organ and piano.

He isn't one to hog the limelight and when the Stones aren't working, like this week, he's not always easy to locate. I eventually tracked him down to a bungalow on the London-Dorking road.

" I've got this place with two friends," he told me. " It stands in its own grounds so we can make a lot of noise. Which we do. I've just connected my record player to a great big amplifier. You only have to touch the volume control and the thing blasts out."

In a corner of Stew's room stands the organ he used on the Stones' LP. It hasn't been played since.

" I don't get that much time to," he explained. " When we made the EP in America, I used a Hammond that the studio had. When we're here, we're nearly always away from home and I can't take it with me."

By RICHARD GREEN

Stew is probably the sixth Rolling Stone, though he's not as obvious to the public as he used to be. When the Stones were just getting started many moons ago, Stew played with them.

" I joined before Charlie or Bill Stone, and when we wanted a new drummer, I suggested Charlie to Brian," he explained over a coffee. " We used to play a lot of stuff like ' Poison Ivy ' and ' Love Potion No. 9 ' in those days, not like now.

" About a year ago I left because of one or two things and the Stones stayed as just five blokes instead of six."

Stew left just when the mobbing bit was beginning for the Stones. Nowadays, things are much worse and torn clothes and pulled hair is

part of life for them.

" I don't want to be pointed at in the street and get torn to pieces, so I'm better off like this. I don't want to go to places like the Ad Lib Club at night either, so I'm happy collecting the odd three farthings that come in from the record," Stew pointed out.

We were joined by Spikey, Stew's young, long-haired assistant. Spikey loves the mobbing that the Stones get and wants to join a group playing tambourine and maraccas.

" He can have all that," Stew said quietly.

I don't know what the majority of Stones fans feel, but to my mind " Now I've Got A Witness " is one of the best tracks on the LP. And as far as the new EP is concerned, it's a knockout. And the organ definitely helps.

" I don't think I'm a great organist," Stew commented. " I think I'm okay, then I hear someone else and think I'm no good. Long John Baldry's pianist is marvellous and someone who's nearly very, very, very good is the Nashville Teens' pianist."

Ask Stew which organist he likes best and he'll jokingly reply: " Eric

THE ROLLING STONES

ALL NITE RAVE
MIDNIGHT TO 6 a.m.
CLUB NORFIK

wanted to keep an eye on his bike, but also to comment on all the women passing by. Despite his leather shorts, Ian Stewart became the first member to join Brian's band. Through his contacts with Alexis Korner and the Ealing Club, Brian Jones found a number of musicians to audition for his band, among them guitarist Geoff Bradford and harmonica player/guitarist Brian Knight. Bradford was widely acknowledged as a competent and experienced blues guitarist, with very firm opinions on what counted as real blues music. The singer and harmonica

49

player Paul Jones – with whom Brian had played before – was asked to join the band, but turned the offer down since he didn't believe in a future as a professional blues musician. He would later change his mind and become the lead singer in Manfred Mann.

Brian Jones also met Mick Jagger and Keith Richards at the Ealing Club and Brian invited Keith to rehearse at The Brick. Mick Jagger was already the singer of Blues Incorporated, but accompanied Keith to the rehearsals, along with Dick Taylor. Taylor was a guitarist, but since there was no bass player he had to change instruments. On a number of occasions Mick Avory was at the drums, but he didn't want to join the band on a professional basis; he would just play sporadically at their gigs during the autumn of 1962. After having realised his mistake a year or so later, he joined the newly formed Kinks instead. The band also used Tony Chapman and Carlo Little as drummers, but they didn't find a suitable drummer until Brian Jones finally managed to persuade Charlie Watts to join them in January 1963.

The new band would rehearse three times a week at The Brick, but soon there were major confrontations within the band. Geoff Bradford and Brian Knight were blues purists and found Keith Richards' fondness for artists such as Chuck Berry and Bo Diddley annoying. A split was inevitable and Keith Richards was certain that he would be the one asked to leave, since the others were much more experienced as musicians. But Brian Jones liked Keith and fired Bradford and Knight instead.

Even though Mick Jagger was gigging regularly with Blues Inc. he was starting to rehearse regularly with Brian's as yet unnamed band. After the band made their debut at the Marquee Club in July 1962 – with Mick on vocals – the singer decided to join the band permanently. For this gig Brian named the band The Rollin' Stones, although "Rollin'" later was changed to "Rolling", without the apostrophe.

Bricklayers Arms was mostly frequented by street vendors and shop assistants out for a quick lunch, and although there were loud discussions and laughter, no-one was offended. However, Brian, Mick and Keith would attract a certain attention with their ragged clothes and long hair, but other guests often bought them beers and the proprietor would let them buy on credit when they needed to. The band, which now consisted of Brian Jones, Mick Jagger, Keith Richards, Ian Stewart and Dick Taylor, continued rehearsing at The Brick three times a week during the autumn, before Brian found a rehearsal room on Kings Road in Chelsea in November.

Although Bricklayers Arms closed down as a pub as early as 1964, there are still traces of the old pub on the outside, and the store room is still there. After having determined that Ian Stewart's racing bike is no longer there, I cross the street to *St. Anne's Court*. According to Marianne Faithfull this somewhat obscure street was where she spent a year in the early Seventies sitting on a wall, all drugged-out and unrecognisable, far away from her earlier, glamorous life.

St. Anne's Court is an extremely narrow street in the centre of Soho, and just a few yards down the street is a recording studio that appears to be just as unassuming. But looks may deceive, for it has been and partly continues to be an important part of music history.

St Anne's Court, with Trident Studio to the left. ▶

Trident Sound Studios
Soho
17 St Annes Court
Tube:
Tottenham Court Road

When George Harrison became a solo artist he could prove what an amazing treasure of songs he possessed. The album was released in the autumn of 1970, but many of the songs were unused compositions from his years with The Beatles. ▶

Trident Sound Studio

Trident Sound Studios was opened in 1967 and because it was the first recording studio in Great Britain with Dolby and 8-track recording facilities, it immediately became popular among many bands.

The first hit recording to be made here was 'My Name Is Jack' by Manfred Mann in May 1968. On July 31, 1968, The Beatles entered the studio to record 'Hey Jude' and this recording is an example of how random events may influence the creation of a masterpiece. When Paul Mc-Cartney started playing the opening part of the song, he didn't notice that Ringo had just gone to the bathroom – which was located just behind the drum set – and consequently he just continued playing, which meant that Ringo started playing the drums much later than originally intended. Although the song's length exceeded seven minutes, the group immediately realised that this was how it should be performed.

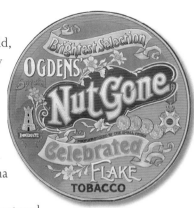

The studio owned a hundred-year-old, handmade Beckstein piano with a very special sound that can be heard on 'Hey Jude'; it was also used by Elton John when he recorded 'Your Song'. 'Hey Jude' was recorded during sessions for The Beatles' so-called *White Album*, and songs like 'Dear Prudence' and 'Martha My Dear' were also recorded here.

On May 6, 1968, The Small Faces entered the studio to start recording what was to become the group's most important album, *Ogdens' Nut Gone Flake*. They spent around three weeks in the studio and then continued the recordings at the Olympic Studios in Barnes.

The Small Faces' LP *Ogdens' Nut Gone Flake* was a little odd in many ways. The record sleeve was round and made as a copy of a tobacco tin, and the songs were linked by a narrator. This approach worked well in England, where the album was number one for six weeks. ▲

The artists who released their records on The Beatles' Apple label often chose Trident as their recording studio, among them Mary Hopkin, James Taylor and George Harrison, who recorded his triple album *All Things Must Pass* at this studio. Among the many other famous recordings made here are David Bowie's *Space Oddity* and *The Rise And Fall Of Ziggy Stardust And The Spiders From Mars* albums, Lou Reed's *Transformer* and Harry Nilsson's version of 'Without You'. In early February 1970, Mick Jagger and Keith Richards used the studio for the final mix of *Get Yer Ya-Ya's Out*, recorded during the Stones' US tour of 1969. Queen, Genesis, Supertramp and Marc Bolan also used Trident Studios for several of their recording sessions.

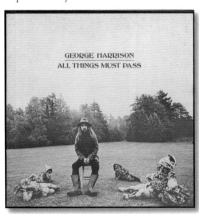

Apart from the advanced technology, the studio was characterised by a relaxed atmosphere. This was an added attraction for the many great artists who chose to make their records here for several years, up until the studio was sold in 1981. The present owners, The Sound Studio, took over in 1993, and even if no major bands are recording here these days, some famous names can often be seen on the premises.

100 Club

100 Club
100 Oxford Street
Tube:
Tottenham Court
Road

I continue my walk up Wardour Street until I get to Oxford Street, where I cross the street to one of the two clubs that have been around since the Sixties: the 100 Club. If you don't feel like walking, you may take the tube directly to Tottenham Court Road. It is only three in the afternoon when I start banging the door at 100 Oxford Street. No-one opens the door, but I'm determined to

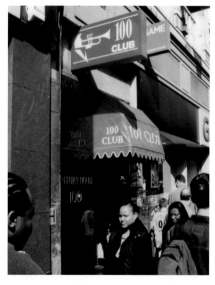

enter the legendary rock club, so I go on banging. Finally the door is opened by the club owner, who is both annoyed and surprised. I beg and plead, explaining that I've travelled far to get here, and after some hesitation I'm allowed to enter the legendary club.

When I reveal that I know a thing or two about the club, particularly its history in relation to The Pretty Things, he brightens up and takes the time to talk with me for a while. The Pretty Things happened to be the house band at the club in 1964

BIG BEAT GALLERY

Five twenty-year-olds who can't understand just why people keep staring at them—that's The Pretty Things.

The Merseybeats—almost as familiar a quartet as The Beatles to the patrons of Liverpool's famous Cavern.

The Pretty Things at the 100 Club. Drummer Viv Prince, behind the bar, serves beer to his mates in the band. The other members, left–right: Brian Pendleton, Dick Taylor, John Stax and Phil May. (Pop Star no 4 1964) ◄

and 1965 and gained a reputation as one of the hottest bands in London. He tells me that his parents owned the 100 Club during that period and that The Pretty Things have returned many times since then, most recently just a few weeks earlier.

When I walk around the premises it becomes clear to me that the club is mainly suitable for an audience without any demands on elegance. The floor in front of the stage is empty, and orange-coloured plastic chairs and small, round white tables are placed along the blood red walls, which in turn are covered with pictures of artists and earlier gigs. A good location for listening as well as partying, jumping around and dancing; in other words, everything you want from a good rock club.

As early as 1942 a jazz club was opened here at 100 Oxford Street, which changed its name a number of times before the club changed both its direction and its name in 1964 and became the 100 Club. The club immediately became an important live venue for the emerging British

100 CLUB

100 OXFORD ST., W.1
7·30 to 11 p.m.

RHYTHM AND BLUES

Thursday, April 9th

GRAHAM BOND'S ORGANISATION
The MARK LEEMAN 5
The BLUEBOTTLES with MIKE PATIO

Monday, April 13th

THE MIKE COTTON SOUND
THE WHO
The EMBERS

Tuesday, April 14th

THE PRETTY THINGS
The MARK LEEMAN 5
The TRIDENTS

Thursday, April 16th

GRAHAM BOND'S ORGANISATION
JOHN LEE and the GROUND HOGS
The OUTRIDERS
Full details of the Club from the Secretary

100 Club, 22 Newman St., W.1 (LAN 0184)

An ad for The Pretty Things' first gig as headliners at the 100 Club on April 14, 1964. Among the opening acts were The Tridents, featuring Jeff Beck on guitar; one year later he would replace Eric Clapton in The Yardbirds. The previous day The Who did their first gig at the 100 club as the opening act for The Mike Cotton Sound. ▲

R&B scene. Apart from The Pretty Things, some of the names who played at the club were The Animals, The Who, The Kinks, The Yardbirds, Spencer Davis Group, The Jeff Beck Group and John Mayall's Bluesbreakers. The club also hosted concerts by major American blues artists such as Muddy Waters, Otis Span, Albert King and Bo Diddley.

The Who made their debut at the club on April 13, 1964, but when they played two weeks later their drummer Dough Sandom was fired from the band. Not because he was bad, but because the record company felt he was too old. Pete Townshend gave himself the painful task of delivering the news to Sandom after the gig. For a couple of weeks the band used various drummers, before a certain Keith Moon appeared for an audition in mid-May and was asked to play 'Roadrunner' together with the band. In the space of just a few minutes he managed to destroy both his drum sticks and the bass drum, but the band realised they had found the drummer they were looking for, and it is no exaggeration to claim that Moon's drumming constituted a turning-point for the band.

In April 1964, a seventeen-year-old Steve Marriott performed at the club with his band The Moments, a year before he formed The Small Faces together with Ronnie Lane. The unusual thing about their repertoire was that it didn't just consist of the usual Chuck Berry and Buddy Holly covers, but that Steve Marriott had already started writing his own songs.

Among the many other interesting concerts at the 100 Club is Sonny & Cher's only official stage performance in England, and over the years the club has been welcoming both the old and the new music movements in London. During the Seventies it was the stronghold for punk music, and in the early Nineties, Suede and Oasis did some of their first concerts at the club.

In 1986, The Rolling Stones held a private memorial concert as a tribute to founder member Ian Stewart, who had recently passed away. The gig also functioned as a sort of reconciliation between Mick Jagger and Keith Richards. Keith had been angry with Mick Jagger, who had run out of ideas for the Stone's *Dirty Work* album after having completed his solo album, *She's The Boss*. During the gig, old friends such as Eric Clapton, Jeff Beck and Pete Townshend also went up on the stage to jam with the band. Unfortunately, I wasn't invited.

Before I leave the club, the owner tells me that out of all the classic live venues in Soho, the 100 Club and Ronnie Scott's are the only ones that are still around, and he is debating whether he should also close down because of high rental costs. For a moment I wonder what will happen if all the classic music venues disappear from London, and it feels like I'm a long, long way from the old Swinging London. Such thoughts make me crave for a beer, or rather a number of beers, but unfortunately there is no pub outside; instead, I continue my walk along Oxford Street in the direction of Tottenham Court Road. After having passed by Dean Street, I reach the next destination.

Beat City Club/Tiles

Beat City Club/Tiles
Soho
79 Oxford Street
Tube:
Tottenham Court
Road

Number 79 Oxford Street was once the location of *Beat City Club*, which opened in April 1964, with Alexis Korner as a part-owner. Shortly after returning from their first US trip, The Rolling Stones played here on July 18, 1964, with an unknown Tom Jones and his backing band The Squires as the opening act. With 600 people in attendance, the club was packed and the heat was unbearable for both the bands

and the audience. The staff had to throw buckets of water at the bands and plenty of people who fainted had to be carried out of the club. The Rolling Stones were now so popular that this became their last club gig in London.

Spencer Davis Group from Manchester did one of their first gigs in London at the club, and Them, featuring Van Morrison on lead vocals, performed here in early 1965. Van Morrison is not an artist who exactly jumps around onstage, nor was he back then, but before this early gig in Them's career Morrison was told by the band's manager that he had to move around a little more. And Van Morrison really tried: he ran back and forth from one side of the stage to the other and even jumped up on the speakers, all the while screaming the lyrics out-of-breath into the microphone. Someone who enjoyed Van Morrison's performance was Rod

Stewart, standing at the very front of the audience and cheering.

The Swedish group The Shanes performing at Beat City, late October 1964. ▲

After a year the club closed down, but it was reopened in April 1966 as *Tiles*, a slightly more posh club. One of the first guest performers was Wilson Pickett, who was followed by groups and artists such as Otis Redding, The Small Faces, Pink Floyd, The Kinks and Manfred Mann. A fairly unknown David Bowie played at the club together with the band The Riot Squad in 1967. But although the pirate radio station Radio Luxenbourg did broadcasts from the club, Tiles never became really popular. Many felt that the atmosphere wasn't quite right and too many unknown and anonymous bands dominated the stage, which led to the club's closing in 1967. Today the premises are empty and it's only because of the blue-painted entrance

that one can surmise that there was once a club on this location.

Les Cousins
Soho
49 Greek Street
Tube:
Tottenham Court
Road

Les Cousins

It's time to turn back and I walk around the corner towards Soho Square, continuing down Greek Street to number 49, which was the location for *Les Cousins*. This was one of the few clubs in Soho that held "All-Nighters": one night each week there were gigs all night long.

These All-Nighters began when the tube stopped running and ended when the tube started again. This made The Cousins – which was the name Londoners preferred to use for the club – a good place to meet up with friends and listen to music.

The premises could hold only fifty people and was very unassuming: there was no furniture, so the audience had to sit on the floor, and the stage was built on loading pallets. Along one of the walls there was a coffee bar, but no alcoholic beverages were allowed. On the other hand, the entrance fee was only a little over £1 in today's money value.

Originally, Les Cousins was a popular place for folk singers of the day: artists such as Bert Jansch, Donovan, Al Stewart, Cat Stevens and Ralph McTell. Someone who rarely missed out on a Bert Jansch gig was Jimmy Page; Jansch was one of his very biggest idols. Paul Simon would often play at Les Cousins when he lived in London in 1964–65. During the summer Art Garfunkel came to visit and they would perform at the club together several times. Paul Simon's then-girlfriend, Kathy Chitty, was often in the audience, and Simon's 'Kathy's Song' was dedicated to her. But the folk singers would only perform on ordinary

Tiles primarily tried to attract a crowd with dance-friendly soul and ska music, except on the nights when a famous band was performing. The club's specialty was to arrange lunch dances for youths, providing the latest music. ◄

Today, the G clef on the wall is the only reminder that there was once a music club here. ▼

Paul Simon remained ▶ in London until December 1965, when his American record company ordered him to come back home after 'The Sound Of Silence' had reached number on the singles chart. But the actual song had been completed in London as early as February 1964.

nights and not during the All-Nighters. Someone who did, however, was Alexis Korner. He played at Les Cousins each week, starting in the autumn of 1966, with a shifting band line-up. There were often jam sessions during the nights and both Eric Burdon and Paul Jones occasionally performed with the house band, while John Mayall would often sit in a corner writing songs.

One late autumn night in October 1966 Jimi Hendrix came there. He paid his entrance, plugged-in his Fender Telecaster, and then quickly proceeded to display every imaginable variation on how to handle a guitar, before he left the stage – leaving the blues purists in the audience in a state of shock. What on earth was that? Who was this strangely attired character who turned the blues into a show and played the guitar in a way that no-one had seen before? There was confusion all around and no-one knew what they were supposed to think about what they had just witnessed.

The small G clef on one of the mosaic stones outside the entrance – which no-one seems to notice – suggests that there was once a music club here, but there are no other signs.

Les Cousins was probably the most popular folk music place in Soho. The guitar playing of Bert Jansch attracted many artists, even those who were rock acts, among them Jimmy Page. During the weekends the club closed at 11.30 pm. They opened again half an hour later to start the popular nightly gigs. ▶

In May 1969 The Who premiered their rock opera *Tommy* at Ronnie Scott's. In August of the same year Humble Pie, featuring Steve Marriott and Peter Frampton, made their debut at the club. ◄

Ronnie Scott's Jazz Club

To cheer myself up I turn around the block and walk to 47 Frith Street, which is the location of the other club that has managed to survive the years: *Ronnie Scott's Jazz Club*. When I read the advertisements outside I learn that Charlie Watts and his hobby band are playing this week, and that they will only be performing for two more nights. Unfortunately, I haven't made plans for attending any concerts and however deeply I dig through my pockets, I finally realise that the band will have to play without me. But I know that one or more members of The Rolling Stones, plus other music celebrities, usually show up on one of the final nights, so I remain outside the club.

The club owner, Ronnie Scott, moved his club from Gerrard Street (in what today is known as Chinatown) to Frith Street the week before Christmas 1965. Scott himself was a saxophonist and played on The Beatles' 'Lady Madonna'. In the spring of 1968 the club was rebuilt and an upper floor was opened to make room for rock and

Ronnie Scott's Jazz Club
Soho
47 Frith Street
Tube:
Tottenham Court Road

.

63

pop bands. In May 1969 The Who performed their rock opera Tommy at Ronnie Scott's in front of the press, shortly before the release of the album. They played song after song from the album – the smashing of instruments and speakers was now a thing of the past.

In September 1970 Eric Burdon and his band War performed here for a week and after a few nights Jimi Hendrix showed up to meet his old friend Burdon. At the time, Jimi Hendrix was in the throes of a deep depression and lately he had hardly shown his face around town. He wanted to get up onstage and play with the band, but since he was clearly under the influence of something, Eric Burdon asked him to return the following night. And the day after, on a Wednesday night, he was back: sober and carrying his Fender guitar, and this time he was invited to play on some songs. Together with Hendrix the band closed the show with Memphis Slim's 'Mother Earth', on which Hendrix played an amazing guitar solo, according to Burdon. This, sadly, was the last time Jimi Hendrix performed onstage. Two days later he was dead.

As I'm walking back and forth outside Scott's, I see someone who looks very much like Marianne Faithfull arriving in a taxi and then entering the club. Illusions are shattered only when they become visible, and I decide that I must be mistaken. I'm in a ponderous mood as I start walking towards Piccadilly Circus, which, among other things, was once the location for one of the most important live venues on the mod scene.

Piccadilly Jazz Club/ The Scene Club
Soho
41 Great Windmill Street
Tube:
Piccadilly Circus

Piccadilly Jazz Club/The Scene Club

In the early Sixties a large basement room at 41 Great Windmill Street, called the Ham Yard, was the location

for Giorgio Gomelsky's *Piccadilly Jazz Club*. The club was mostly frequented by black Americans and Jamaicans and was known for playing blues records and Jamaican ska music, which was hard to find in England. Many people went to the club just to listen to records, among them Brian Jones and Keith Richards, who used to hang out there in the autumn of 1962. On a Saturday night, when the club was open all night, the small dance floor in the middle of the room would be packed with twohundred guests.

The Record Nights at the Scene Club, with the legendary Guy Stevens, were very popular. He owned a gigantic collection of R&B records, and many artists went there to hear the latest American imports ▲

At the end of 1962, Piccadilly Jazz Club began featuring British blues bands one night every week, and The Rolling Stones played their first gig at the club on November 30, 1962, with Ricky Fenson on bass and Tony Chapman on drums. Bill Wyman and Charlie Watts had not yet joined the group. The headliners were Blues Incorporated (featuring Charlie Watts on drums) and Dave Hunt's Rhythm & Blues Band. That night, a young guitarist named Ray Davies tried out with the latter band. Davies was more impressed by The Rolling Stones' rougher version of the blues and realised that this was the type of music he really wanted to play. A few weeks later the Stones performed at the club again, at which time Bill Wyman (still known as Bill Perks) tried out with the band. There were only a handful of people at the venue and the band felt that the gig was more like a rehearsal. In the audience was Ray Davies' younger brother, Dave, and he was also excited by The Rolling Stones' raw sound.

In early 1963, the Piccadilly Club closed and Giorgio

Gomelsky found his way out to Richmond, where he opened the Crawdaddy Club. On the Piccadilly premises the *Scene* Club opened instead, with an audience that mainly consisted of mods who soon took over the club and made it their favourite hangout. The disc jockey Guy Stevens had a huge record collection, partly because he managed the Sue Record Label, which specialised in American rhythm & blues and soul. He would eventually become legendary through his involvement with bands such as Free, Spooky Tooth, Mott The Hoople and later also The Clash. Stevens also knew The Paramounts who renamed their group after his cat, Procol Harum, at the end of 1966.

Among the many people who often went here to listen to the music were names such as The Beatles, Brian Jones, Keith Richards, Mick Jagger and Georgie Fame. Starting on June 20, 1963, The Rolling Stones played at the club four Thursdays in a row, and at one of the shows The Beatles showed up after a recording session at the studio in Abbey Road. At the time it was still possible for them to move about freely among ordinary people.

In December 1963 The Animals from Newcastle played their first gigs in London at the Scene Club, after the venue had received a tip about the band from The Rolling Stones, who had met them at a club in Newcastle. The stage was so small that when The Animals had entered the stage with the drums and their organ, there was no room for Eric Burdon who had to stand on the dance floor singing. The stage was also occupied by a large piano and Eric Burdon has related how he eventually tired of standing on the floor, jumped up on the piano and stamped it to pieces, cheered on by the audience.

The Who – still known as The High Numbers at the time
– played regularly at the Scene Club, starting on August 5,
1964, and this was where they built up their reputation as
a mod band. At the time, Pete Townshend hadn't yet started
smashing his guitar, but was happy enough having a go at
the speakers. The Who's first manager, Pete Meaden, was
aware of the emerging mod scene quite early on, realis-
ing the importance it was going to have; he himself was
New Musical Express   one of the leading mods. Therefore, he re-styled the band
May 15, 1964   ▼   and made sure that they acquired the right haircuts and

NEW MUSICAL EXPRESS ✱   Friday. May 15, 196

Great big swinging Animals !

MY dictionary defines the word
"animal" as " being endowed
with life, sensation, and voluntary
motion." You try multiplying that
by five and see what you get !
  You get one great big swinging
r-and-b group who play what they
want to play simply because they
want to play it. There is no pre-
tence with the Animals.
  They don't even claim that they
are playing r-and-b as such. To
them, and to all true fans, r-and-b
is Negro music. Talk to them and
the names of Jimmy Reed, John Lee
Hooker and Chuck Berry keep
cropping up. That's because they
admire people who stand for r-and-b.
  The Animals come from Newcastle
and it wasn't even their own idea
to have that name. They started
out as the Alan Price Combo, but
gradually it dawned on them that
the people who paid the two bobs
to listen to them called them by a
different name.
  That name was the Animals
and it has stuck with them ever
since.
  It is a good, commercial name,
but it is not just the name that
attracts the crowds like the latest
fashions have people scurrying off
to Paris. On stage, the Animals
live up to their name in no uncertain
manner.
  " When you play in a club, you
have more time to get going," said
singer Eric Burdon. He's the one
who can—and often does—talk at
great length about what is and what
is not blues music. Just 23, he seems
to know an awful lot about r-and-b
and has a scrapbook full of cuttings
on the subject.
  When the Animals played the
Scene in Piccadilly recently, Eric
finished up on top of the piano
yelling things like: " Let's smash
the thing " and " We're gonna tear
the place apart."
  These are the kind of comments
that prompt adults to launch fresh
attacks on young musicians. But it
only reflects the kind of music the

Animals play raw, uninhibited stuff
that appeals to the fans.
  When I went along for a drink
with them this week we found a
little pub tucked away in a side
street in Mayfair. We all trooped
in and decided that the hot weather
demanded nothing less than pints.
  That was fine and we all began
chatting at once . . . until the phone
rang behind us in the booth. Eric
dived for it, snatched it off the
cradle and exclaimed: " Hello, can

known each other for years. Three
of us live on one side of the river
and the others come from the
opposite bank."
  Besides Eric and Chas, there
are Alan Price who plays electric
organ, lead guitarist Hilton Valentine and drummer John Steel.
  " We just met up because we all
like r-and-b, nothing else," commented Eric. " All this business
about getting together and playing
because Newcastle is a hard, rough

place is a load of rubbish. It'd ha
been no different if we'd come fro
London or anywhere."
  At the moment, Chas is getti
quite excited about the curre
visit of Bob Dylan, who he like
You may not like Bob, but y
can't argue with Chas.   Why
Because he's 6 feet 4 inches a
goes 14 stone !
  "I reckon Bob Dylan's goo
anyway," he said between mouthfu
of a sandwich. " I like a lot
blues singers, but the least of all
like Jimmy Reed. He sounds li
an old man crying."
  " That's why he's so good, tha
what blues is," Eric quickly put i
" You can't say a bloke's no goo
because of that."
  Back to Chas. " I don't me
he's no good, it's just that I li
so many, I've got to like one t
least. I know Reed's good, I nev
said he wasn't."
  This is typical of the kind
discussion that can so easily beg
with the Animals. They all kno
their subject and they like to tc
ideas and opinions back and for
like that.
  " When I was at school, th
teachers used to accept the fact th
you were going into ship buildi
or engineering," Eric told me.
  " I wanted to go to art scho
and when I went to the You
Employment Officer he said h
would get me a job signwritin
But he meant writing names c
the sides of ships !"
  It's a good job there are peop
like the Animals around to ke
on the scene, there's no danger
that music dying.   They're to
interested in it to let things get th
far.
                    RICHARD GREE

WHY
BE BALD ?
ANY DEGREE OF HAIR LOSS IS
UNSIGHTLY AND UNNECESSARY

The ANIMALS are HILTON VALENTINE (lead guitar), ALAN
PRICE (organ), ERIC BURDON (vocals), JOHN STEEL (drums),
CHAS. CHANDLER (bass guitar).

clothes. Then, Pete Meaden stole a blues song, changed the lyrics and had the band release their first single, 'I'm The Face'. "Face" was a mod expression that referred to the coolest mods. Meaden was also responsible for the name The High Numbers, where "Numbers" meant "ordinary mods" and "High" signified a high position in the mod hierarchy. Naturally, the expression also had an additional meaning among the pill-popping mods.

A band like The Who, with a talented songwriter such as Pete Townshend, would not have needed to use tricks like these, but it contributed to their rapidly growing popularity among the mods. When Kit Lambert and Chris

The Animals from Newcastle achieved their London breakthrough at the Scene Club, six months before they released their monster hit 'The House Of The Rising Sun' in 1964. Front row, left–right: Chas Chandler and Alan Price. Back row, left–right: Eric Burdon, Hilton Valentine and John Steel. Alan Price left the group in the spring of 1965, forming the Alan Price Set. ▲

Stamp became the band's new managers in November 1964, the name was changed back to The Who.

Among the regular visitors at the Scene Club were Steve Marriott and Ronnie Lane, who used to go there before they continued to the Flamingo, although at this time they still didn't know each other. The police regularly raided the Scene Club and the press wrote about it after the police had stormed in during an Animals concert and ordered the audience to stand completely still. Immediately there was a smattering sound, as if in a hail storm, and the police had to wade through droves of pills.

Savile Row

3 Savile Row
Mayfair
Tube:
Piccadilly Circus

After having spent an hour trying to find the location for the Scene Club, I realise that the premises have been turned into a parking lot. Disappointed, I instead decide to visit nearby Savile Row, which runs parallel to Regent Street. On the roof of 3 *Savile Row*, The Beatles held their famous concert on January 30, 1969. Billy Preston was in the building at the same time and was persuaded by George Harrison to take part in the gig. The concert made up the finale of the Let It Be documentary, and was the group's last performance in front of an audience. On this cold and windy day The Beatles played for forty minutes during the lunch hour and the street below them was quickly jammed with surprised passers-by from the surrounding office buildings, before the police stopped the show. The last song they managed to perform in public was 'Get Back'.

The choice of building was natural since The Beatles' company Apple Corps Ltd. owned the building and had its offices there. The five-storeyed building was bought in June 1968 for the sum of £500,000 and a considerable amount of money was then spent on rebuilding and furnishing. Innumerable fans would literally live outside the building, in the hope of catching a glimpse of their idols.

Carnaby Street

The following day my starting-point is the place where I finished last night: Piccadilly Circus. I follow Regent Street northward until I reach Beak Street, where I walk up to the legendary *Carnaby Street*, which was once a symbol for Swinging London.

Carnaby Street
Soho
Tube:
Oxford Circus

And when he does his little rounds,
'Round the boutiques of London Town,
Eagerly pursuing all the latest fads and trends,
'Cause he's a dedicated follower of fashion
(Dedicated Follower Of Fashion, lyrics: Ray Davies)

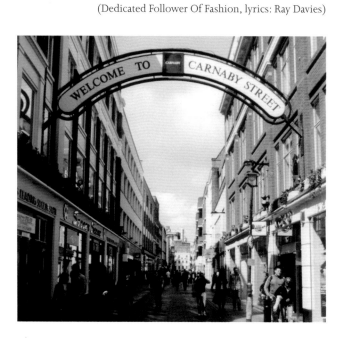

New Musical Express
March 4, 1966   ▲

'Dedicated Follower Of Fashion' is certainly the most well-known song about the fashion hysteria of the Sixties, although The Kinks were actually a part of the very same culture, whether song writer Ray Davies wanted it or not.

Carnaby Street's function as a street associated with fashion began in 1957 when designer John Stephen opened the shop His Clothes. At the time it was a somewhat obscure street, overshadowed by the major shopping streets and the rent was only £7 per week. Stephens made men's clothes that were more colourful than the traditional black and grey, and used other materials than the usual wool, tweed and gabardine. The shop's profile soon attracted rock stars such as Cliff Richard and Adam Faith. They would wear Stephen's clothes during gigs and in films, which soon increased the demand for his clothes among young men. By 1965, John Stephen had eight shops on Carnaby Street, among them The Mod Male and His Clothes. The main competitor was Lord John, which was opened by the brothers Warren, Harold and David Gold in 1963.

The exclusive clothes were expensive, however, and musicians had to achieve a big chart hit before they could afford to shop in any of the stores. The first time

Pete Townshend of The Who visited one of the stores he could only afford to buy a pair of socks, but after the group's breakthrough in 1965, all four members became major clients.

When The Kinks became popular in 1964, Dave Davies became a frequent shopper on Carnaby Street, and he used to visit Stephen's shops several times a week to build up his wardrobe. He was every shop owner's dream client: he would enter the shop, try on a jacket and buy it immediately if he liked it. His brother Ray was a considerably more cautious client, and normally he was the one who chose The Kinks stage shirts. Bob Dylan was also image-conscious and loved to run around shopping on Carnaby Street when he visited London.

Clothes and fashion were intimately connected to pop and rock music, this applied to all artists without exception. Everybody wanted to show of their individuality and John Stephen's rule was that if an item had been ordered by a star, it would not be available to the general public. The frenzied shopping knew no limits: for example, at one point Dave Clark of the Dave Clark Five bought 50 sweaters in one go from one of John Stephen's shops.

The success of John Stephen attracted others and soon the street was full of fashion boutiques and shoe stores, some of them also for girls. But Carnaby Street wasn't where the new ladies fashion with mini-skirts was developed. That was done by the famous fashion designer Mary Quant, whose studio and boutique Bazaar was situated close to Kings Road in Chelsea.

The Small Faces' manager, Don Arden, had his offices at 52-55 Carnaby Street, and instead of paying the band de-

The Small Faces' manager offered them unlimited clothes accounts in Carnaby Street, which they happily used so that they would always be wearing the latest gear. Only afterwards did they realise that the costs were deducted from their income. Left–right: Steve Marriott, Ian McLagan, Ronnie Lane and Kenney Jones. ▲

cently he enticed them with £20 per week plus a clothes account at the shops in the street. And the band made full use of that account: during 1966 they spent £12,000 in Carnaby Street, a small fortune in those days.

In the mid-Sixties, Carnaby Street became a symbol for Swinging London, and innumerable tourists from all over the world were visiting the street. By 1963, the rents were already thirty times higher than what John Stephen had originally paid when he moved in, and they continued to rise rapidly. The original boutiques, featuring their own designs, had to close down or move to another location. After a while all the shops were owned by clothes chains.

And while John Stephen's clothes were always well-made, his imitators didn't feel this aspect was especially important. Carnaby Street became a tourist trap, where mass-produced clothes of very bad quality were sold at very high prices. But the reputation lives on and tourists still visit the street, which today is pretty dull with not very exciting shops such as Puma, Diesel, Boots and Lee.

The only thing of value that remains at Carnaby Street is the pub at its north end: *Shakespeare's Head*. The pub was established as early as 1733 and it would seem not much more than the range of beers has changed since then. Thanks to its relaxed atmosphere and the location on Carnaby Street, it was a popular hangout for trendy fashion-mongers and pop stars during the Sixties.

One frequent guest was Dave Davies, who used to hang out here early in the evenings before he went on to some club. I go up to the bar and order a Directors Bitter, sit down at the old fireplace in the corner, and almost as if to particularly please me, 'Itchycoo Park' by The Small Faces starts playing on the speakers. I watch the sturdy ceiling

Shakespeare's Head, at the north end of Carnaby Street, is still worth a visit. ◄

beams, one of which bears the legend "Friends, Romans, Countrymen, lend me your ears". It could have been the start of a Bob Dylan song, but it is in fact the first lines out of Shakespeare's Julius Caesar. The Small Faces are followed by 'Out Of Time' by The Rolling Stones, then The Kinks ... and I order another Directors Bitter.

Bag O'Nails

Bag O'Nails
Soho
9 Kingly Street
Tube:
Oxford Circus

It is late as I walk along to Kingly Street, which runs parallel to Carnaby Street. Number 9 was the location for the *Bag O'Nails* club in the Sixties. As I arrive, tailor-made suits and handmade shoes are stepping out of cars and into the Miranda, which is the name of the club today. I ask the doorman if I may step in and have a look, but unfortunately that isn't possible; it's a members-only club. I ask him how to become a member, and he tells me that a recommendation

is required, along with an unspecified sum of money. For a moment I wonder whether I should discreetly put a five-pound note in his breast pocket, but I forget all about it when I realise that I would probably have to multiply that sum by a hundred. Nothing appears to have changed: the Bag O'Nails was also a members-only club and it was just as hard to become a member in the Sixties.

The Bag O'Nails was started around 1930 as a music club. Originally, the music played at the club was swing and jazz. It wasn't a place for danc-

ing, but a club where jazz enthusiasts would gather to listen to live music. The brothers Rik and John Gunnell bought the place and reopened the club with a new concept in November 1966, inspired by the success of Scotch Of St. James. The Gunnell brothers, who had previously owned the Flamingo Club, were also the booking agents for Chris Farlowe, Georgie Fame and John Mayall's Blues-breakers, and when they couldn't get their acts any other bookings, they would have them play at their own club. Accordingly, there were always live gigs at the club.

The Bag O'Nails club quickly became one of the most popular places for the fickle rock elite. Everybody began hanging out here: The Beatles, The Rolling Stones, The Kinks, The Who, The Animals and The Small Faces were regular visitors, and many of them would gladly get up on the stage for a jam session. One night the stage was so crowded with jamming rock stars that Eric Clapton had to make do with playing the tambourine!

I have heard that the club has not been rebuilt since those days, and therefore I'm anxious to get in and have a look

New Musical Express
April 1, 1967 ▲

around the premises. I ask the doorman whether it's possible to visit the club during the daytime and he tells me that I have to ask the proprietor first. I have to visit the club a number of times before I manage to meet the proprietor, Robert Price, who is kind enough to let me enter the premises, once I've explained the purpose of my visit.

The club still looks very exclusive as I enter the actual club, which is reached via a long and narrow, red carpet staircase. My eyebrows raised, I look around. My immediate impression is that I've ended up at a sophisticated strip club for well-to-do middle-aged gentlemen. Everything is coloured red: red velvet couches and discreet lighting in the shape of small lamps with red shades on the walls. The tables are made of smoked glass, and their feet, which are as wide as sturdy pine-stumps, are made of beaten copper.

On the walls there are large mirrors with golden frames and topless girls engraved in the glass. The room is smaller than I had thought and holds perhaps 125 seated guests.

At the far end, in front of a large red curtain, there is a small stage that extends into the room a little and is followed by a long and narrow dance floor. This was the stage where The Jimi Hendrix Experience played at lunchtime on November 25, 1966, when they had their first official reception for the press and the promoters. The band played songs like 'Hey Joe' (which hadn't been released yet), 'Stone Free' and 'Wild Thing', but they still didn't manage to get any bookings. The press and the promoters had never seen anything like them and didn't know how to handle "the wild-man of Borneo", as Jimi Hendrix was called in the press.

He left a much bigger impression with the rock musicians: the London clubs were packed with famous stars whenever Jimi Hendrix played, and they were the ones who paved the way for him. Among his enthusiastic admirers were John Lennon, Paul McCartney, Mick Jagger, Keith Richards, Brian Jones, Eric Burdon, The Small Faces, Donovan and Steve Winwood – those were just a few of the names that would flock around Jimi Hendrix at his gigs, many of which were held at the Bag O' Nails. More shocked and shaken were the musicians who had been the guitar heroes up to that point: Eric Clapton, Jeff Beck and Pete Townshend. They could do nothing but simply watch as their world was turned upside down. After having seen Hendrix, a shocked Jeff Beck went home to his wife and explained that he had to find a new job, while Eric Clapton and Pete Townshend met up to discuss how to handle this new situation.

New Musical Express
January 14, 1967   ▶

One of the most popular gigs ever at the club happened in 1967, when Booker T & The MG's and Carla Thomas played a private show. More than threehundred people packed themselves into the club, among them virtually the entire rock elite, The Beatles included. The Beatles had also arranged to have their private limousines pick up the American artists at Heathrow Airport; they would never have imagined that they were so popular in London.

The Bag O'Nails was also Paul McCartney's favourite place to have a meal after late-night recording sessions, and this was where he met his future wife Linda Eastman on May 15, 1967. Paul was at the club to listen to Georgie Fame And The Blue Flames, while photographer Linda was there together with The Animals, whom she knew after having photographed them in New York. Paul watched her from a distance, and when she and The Animals were about to leave he felt that he had to stand up. He introduced himself (as if this were necessary!) and asked Linda if she wanted to come along to another club. She accepted his invitation and together with The Animals they went to the Speakeasy, which was open all night long. More than 30 years later, Paul McCartney wrote the song 'Magic', commemorating their meeting at the Bag O'Nails.

Robert Price tells me that Julian Lennon came here one night to see the club that his father used to go to. He was told that he was welcome back when he was more suitably dressed – which he was when he returned a few days later. After you've failed in your mission to talk yourself into the club, you can drown your sorrows with a beer at some of the nearby pubs. At those places no-one will care who you are, nor how you're dressed.

NEW to the charts

WILD JIMI HENDRIX

THE man for whom the words "Wild One" were invented has hit us! Jimi Hendrix, 22, from Seattle, Washington, U.S.A., courtesy of ex-Animal Chas Chandler—débuts in the NME Chart at No. 24 with his self-arranged "Hey Joe" (Polydor).

Hendrix is a one-man guitar explosion with a stage act which leaves those who think pop has gone pretty with their mouths hanging open. What this man does to a guitar could get him arrested for assault.

This is the story of his life in his own words :—

"Bored to death at 16 I joined the Army—Airborne. A little less than a year of screaming ' AHHHhh ! ' and ' I'm fallllllliing ' all the time, so I squeezed my way out by breaking my ankle and hurting my back—then I tried being serious with my first love —music.

"One of the Isley Brothers heard me playing in a club and said he had a job open. Sleeping between them tall tenements was hell—rats running across your chest, cockroaches stealing your last candybar, so I figured, ' Yeah, I'll gig.'

"But I got tired of playing in the key of ' F ' all the time and turned in my white mohair silk suit and patent leather shoes.

"A tour came through town with BB King, Sam Cooke, Chuck Jackson, Solomon Burke, Jackie Wilson and Hank Ballard. I learned an awful lot when I got a job guitar-picking behind all those names every night.

"In Atlanta I auditioned with Little Richard, copped the gig and worked with him all over the U.S.—finally landing in Los Angeles and playing more gigs with Ike and Tina Turner.

"I quit Little Richard because of a money misunderstanding and to rest.

"But who can rest in New York ? I got a job with another band. I had all these ideas and sounds in my brain, and playing this ' other people's music ' all the time was hurting me. I jumped from the frying pan into the fire when I joined up with Joey Dee and the Starlighters—mind you, this is an out-of-sight group . . . but ?!?!?

"After sucking on a peppermint twist salary I had to quit and began playing with a juke-box band, and finally quit that, too, with nothing but a ' wish ' sandwich (two pieces of bread—wishing I had some meat between).

"Finally I formed up with three other guys under the name of The Blue Flame (no connection).

"I was living off sympathy until my English friend appeared from nowhere and persuaded Chas Chandler of the Animals to come down to where I was gigging and give an ear.

"We came here to England, picked out two of the best musicians—Noel Redding from the Loving Kind for bass and Mitch Mitchell, an ex-Blue Flame, on drums—formed the Jimi Hendrix Experience.

"Now I'm going to make certain I don't fluff it all up ! ".

KEITH ALTHAM.

JIMI HENDRIX plays to himself —on a broomstick !

Marquee Club I
Soho
165 Oxford Street
Tube:
Oxford Circus

Marquee Club I

The last stop on my rock walk around Soho is a club that was one of the first in central London to feature the blues played on electrical instruments: the Marquee Club on Oxford Street. The original Marquee Club was located in the basement of the Academy Cinema, near the corner of Poland Street. Harold Pendleton took over the club in the spring of 1958, presenting both modern and traditional jazz.

Pendleton was also the chairman of the National Jazz Federation and was known as a jazz purist. But business comes before conviction and soon enough skiffle was performed at the club, followed by the blues one day each week. In 1959 Muddy Waters and his pianist Otis Spann played at the club during their tour of Britain, and in the audience was a young man from Cheltenham: Brian Jones. This was the night when Brian Jones decided that he would learn how to play the electric guitar and then form his own blues band.

Harold Pendleton found it difficult attracting an audi-

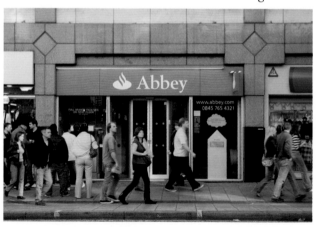

ence on Thursdays and after having witnessed the success enjoyed by Alexis Korner's Blues Incorporated at the Ealing Club, he offered them Thursday night gigs at the Marquee Club. Their first gig in mid-April 1962 was attended only by the onehundred and twenty people who made up their core audience at the Ealing Club. Those who went there were mainly youths who didn't like trad jazz and sickly-sweet pop music. And they were growing in number: soon enough the audience numbered threehundred and fifty, which worried the trad jazz fans.

The blues had arrived in central London: not only was it here to stay, but within a few years it would force most clubs to change their direction from jazz to British rhythm & blues and rock. And all the while Blues Incorporated spawned more blues bands, as Alexis Korner continued the tradition from the Ealing Club to let new, young musicians appear as guest performers with the band.

The Rolling Stones had a very mixed reception when they made their début gig as a group at the Marquee Club on July 12, 1962. While the youths were dancing, the older jazz audience viewed the electrified music with disdain. Brian Jones is in the foreground of the picture and Keith Richards can be seen in the background. ▼

On Thursday, July 12, 1962, The Rolling Stones did their very first public performance. They got the chance because the regular headliners, Blues Incorporated, were scheduled to appear in a radio programme that night. Long John Baldry and his Hoochie Coochie Men replaced them as headliners, but they needed a supporting act. The Marquee Club didn't have an alcohol licence and therefore the headliners used a supporting act so that they could visit a nearby pub during the breaks.

Alexis Korner asked Brian Jones if the band he had formed would possibly be interested. At the time, Mick Jagger was one of the singers in Blues Incorporated, but he also used to rehearse with Brian's band and he offered to be a part of the new band that Thursday night. In conjunction with the gig the group quickly had to find a name, and the first thing Brian Jones could think of was The Rolling Stones, after a Muddy Waters song. The band's line-up this first night was Brian Jones (using the name Elmo Lewis), Mick Jagger, Keith Richards, Ian Stewart at the piano, Dick Taylor on bass (he would become the guitarist in The Pretty Things) and Tony Chapman on drums. The repertoire mainly consisted of songs by Jimmy Reed, Elmore James and Chuck Berry, and the fee was £20 for all six members.

When The Rolling Stones entered the stage the mood in the room immediately became suspicious and almost hostile. Most people viewed rhythm & blues as an offshoot of jazz music and demanded that the bands should have an identical line-up, with lots of horns, a double bass and many instrumental numbers. The Rolling Stones didn't fulfil any of these criteria, but were guitar based. Accordingly, the middle-aged jazz fans in the audience regarded them as a rock and roll band and started booing and jeering the group. However, there was a small group of younger people in the audience who received the band and their repertoire with enthusiasm and with time that group became much bigger.

The Rolling Stones had two more gigs as a supporting act — in September and October, respectively — but each time they were booed by the jazz fans in the audience, encouraged by the owner, Harold Pendleton, who saw the group, their music and their audience as a threat against jazz. Keith Richards finally had enough of the abuse and hit Pendleton in the head with his guitar, which definitely put an end to the Stone's gigging at the Marquee Club for the remainder of 1962.

During the autumn of 1962, the internal conflicts increased within Blues Incorporated, where Alexis Korner represented a jazz-influenced blues. Meanwhile, harmonica player Cyril Davies was an uncompromising devotee of the heavier Chicago style, which led to the formation of the Cyril Davies R&B All Stars. Among the members in the new band were Carlo Little on drums, the phenomenal Nicky Hopkins on piano, Bernie Watson on guitar – he was later in John Mayall's Bluesbreakers – and Long John Baldry and Art Wood alternating as singers. Cyril Davies All Stars began playing regularly at the old Marquee Club and the band also became an important learning ground for young blues musicians. One who was jamming regularly with both Alexis Korner and Cyril Davies was a young guitarist named Jimmy Page, later a legend in The Yardbirds and Led Zeppelin.

In January 1963, The Rolling Stones were again offered gig opportunities at the Marquee, as a supporting act for Cyril Davies All Stars. By this time, the Stones had become a much better group than before, and had been joined by Bill Wyman on bass and Charlie Watts on drums. After a couple of gigs in January, the Stones attracted more people than the headliners, but when they pointed this out to Cyril Davies on January 31 and asked for a higher fee, they were immediately fired. That date became their last gig at the club.

Most of the famous bands of the Sixties that played at the first Marquee, were offshoots of Blues Incorporated and Cyril Davies All Stars: Manfred Mann, Long John Baldry and the Hoochie Coochie Men, The Artwoods, The Graham Bond Organisation and John Mayall's Bluesbreakers. The latter group achieved their breakthrough at the venue, after John Mayall had persuaded Manfred Mann that the Bluesbreakers should be their supporting act. A couple of months later the situation had been turned around: the Bluesbreakers had taken over as headliners.

The Yardbirds did the very last concert at the club before it closed down on March 5, 1964, and then moved to Wardour Street. To be quite honest, there isn't very much left to see on the spot where the club was once located, just a boring bank. There is no atmosphere whatsoever left in the air, unless you count the exhaust fumes of Oxford Street.

Oxford Circus

From Oxford Circus I walk north along Regent Street, until I reach Margaret Street on my right side. The basement on number 48–50 was once the location of one of the most infamous clubs in London during the Sixties and Seventies: *the Speakeasy*.

Today, the steps leading down to the Speakeasy are concealed under the pavement. ▶

Speakeasy
Oxford Circus
48-50 Margaret Street
Tube: Oxford Circus

Speakeasy

When Roy Flynn opened the doors to the Speakeasy on December 15, 1966, the club was crowded with especially invited stars. You had to walk a few steps down to reach the Speakeasy: the entrance was a closet door and the counter was a wreathed coffin. Although this may not sound very encouraging, the Speakeasy became a very popular party club and live venue for rock musicians. The Speakeasy wasn't as elegant as the Bag O'Nails and The Scotch, but had a more relaxed and casual style. The club was one of the few places that were open all night long, and band members would often go here after having visited other clubs.

The Who's drummer Keith Moon was here whenever he could. He would order large quantities of champagne and brandy, and then began subjecting the other guests to practical jokes. This would go on until he was chauffeured home in his purple Rolls Royce in the early hours of the morning. New pals Jimi Hendrix and Brian Jones were often here together, seeing shows by The Turtles on June 4, 1967, and The Moody Blues on December 10.

Jimi Hendrix played some of his first club gigs in London at the Speakeasy and came back to jam here innumerable times, with artists such as Amen Corner, Fairport Convention, Traffic, Eric Burdon, Alan Price and Billy Preston. When John Mayall's Bluesbreakers were about to make a live recording of the song 'The Lesson' in early November 1967, Jimi Hendrix was in the audience. Solo guitarist Mick Taylor handed his guitar over to Jimi Hendrix, and was startled when Hendrix, who was left-handed, proceeded to play the guitar upside down. For contractual

A newly permed Eric Clapton and Jimi Hendrix enjoy a night out at the Speakeasy in the summer of 1967. The profile visible between them belongs to Jan Olofsson. The club was incredibly popular, but not with everybody, since it began salting the major stars' bills. The club knew that it would appear as miserly and embarrassing for world-famous stars to protest or complain about money. ▲

On sale Friday, week ending May 20, 1967   NEW MUSICAL EXPRESS *

Past the Undertaker's 'front'... then through the 'wardrobe'...

Downstairs in the basement entrance, the undertaker's parlour, traditional front for American speakeasy during the days of prohibition. Two members sign in without fear of being pinched!

In the same parlour is a wardrobe—with a difference. It hides the entrance to the club proper. T members are just about to enter. Incidentally, that's an ashtray on the left of the picture!

THIS WAY TO THE SPEAKEASY

NME's Norrie Drummond takes you to London's latest in-place

POP people in their off-duty hours often strike me as being rather similar to migratory birds. For about six months they settle in one club and then suddenly—whoosh, they all flock to another.

At the moment their present nesting ground appears to be the Speakeasy at 48 Margaret Street, just off Oxford Street. I have watched these rare birds fluttering from the Ad Lib to the Scotch, to the Cromwellian, the In Place, Sybilla's, Dolly's and the Bag O'Nails.

Some of these clubs have prospered, some have faded and a few have disappeared—such is the fickleness of the club-going public.

The Speakeasy however has an excellent chance of success. The club is well situated, it's comfortable and the prices are reasonable.

On the occasions I've been to the Speakeasy it has always been fairly busy but never unbearably crowded and the service is quiet and pleasant.

The club is managed by two go-ahead young men Roy Flynn and Mike Carey. Ray told me: " We want the Speakeasy to be a club which people really like to go to rather than one which people go to because it's the done thing. The Speakeasy I think has a very nice relaxed atmosphere and

Frequent visitor to the club, JIMI HENDRIX joins resident group the SOFT MACHINE during a break.

we try to appeal to every musical taste.

" We had the Dudley Moore Trio playing a residency here, and Mary Wells, Ben E. King, the Byrds and Otis Redding have appeared at the Speakeasy."

For those not particularly interested in the music or who prefer to talk, the club has a restaurant at the far end of the dance floor.

Opened last December, the idea was to copy an American speakeasy.

The entrance to the club is through the mirrored door of a wardrobe and the cash desk is a coffin. At the far end of the bar an enormous portrait of Al Capone—painted by Barry Fantoni—gazes down menacingly on sinning drinkers.

The Speakeasy is open seven nights a week, Monday-Saturday it opens at 10 pm. Drinks are sold until 3 am and the club closes about 4 am. Membership is four guineas a year and admission is 10s. most nights.

Co-managers ROY FLYNN and MIKE CAREY relax with guests overlooked by the portrait of Al Capone specially painted for the club by Barry Fantoni.

General view of the bar, where journalists, managers, agents and pop stars can meet and talk in comfort. The dance floor is off to the right.

The stage and dance floor, more spacious than the impression given by this picture. The resident group plays until the small hours.

reasons it wasn't possible to acknowledge on the album sleeve that it was Hendrix playing the guitar. The last time Hendrix jammed at the club was together with Stephen Stills and Billy Cox on August 28, 1970.

New Musical Express
May 20 1967 ◄

The Speakeasy was the venue where Paul McCartney and his future wife, Linda, ended up after their first meeting at the Bag O'Nails, on May 15, 1967. They were having a good time together with Eric Burdon and Keith Moon when they heard 'A Whiter Shade Of Pale' for the first time. Everybody was completely fascinated by the song and tried to guess who performed it. All of them thought it was Steve Winwood, but when Paul went up to ask the DJ, it turned out to be a group that was completely unknown to them: Procol Harum. And they all agreed that it was the best song they had ever heard. Paul and Linda were head over heels about both each other and the song, which they would refer to as "our song". I wonder how many couples who have just fallen in love feel the same way about that song. Afterwards, Linda went back with Paul to his home on Cavendish Avenue, where she was impressed by his famous Magritte paintings...

The underrated Spooky Tooth made their debut at the Speakeasy in early 1968 and Deep Purple made their debut here in 1969. The club was a popular live venue and place of entertainment well into the Seventies.

Covent Garden

From Leicester Square I walk along Charing Cross Road for a short bit, until I reach Gt. Newport Street on my right side.

Studio 51

Studio 51
Leicester Square/
Covent Garden
10-11Gt. Newport
Street
Tube:
Leicester Square

For a long time, the basement of number 10–11 was the location of Studio 51, also known as Ken Coyler's Club since the Ken Coyler Jazzmen were the house band. As the name suggests the club was started in 1951 by two women, Vi Highland and Pat Mayhew, and for ten years it was a popular trad jazz club. But at the end of 1962, the trad jazz era was running to a close and for financial reasons, blues music was now allowed on the premises.

The Rolling Stones played a few tryout gigs at Studio 51, and after March 3, 1963, they had weekly gigs on Sunday afternoons. The band didn't have any proper rehearsal room where they could use amplifiers and drums, so before their Sunday gigs they used Studio 51 for their

rehearsals. There was still a typical jazz atmosphere at the club – "just stand there watching the band, and be cool" – but this was soon changed when the Stones started playing the two hours stipulated by their contract. After just a few months, unconscious people had to be carried out of the packed premises.

On June 7, 1963, the group released their first single, 'Come On', and then they tried to find a suitable follow-up. At the start of the autumn they still didn't have any ideas, but help would arrive from an unexpected place. One Sunday in September 1963, when the group's concerned manager Andrew Loog Oldham was walking towards Studio 51, a taxi cab pulled up. Inside the cab were John Lennon and Paul McCartney, and they started chatting. Oldham told them about his problem, and Lennon & McCartney then offered him a song they were writing at the time, which they thought could be right for the Stones.

They immediately went to Studio 51, where John and Paul borrowed a guitar and a bass and played the first, completed part of the song. The Stones liked what they heard, but wondered when they would finish the entire song. "If you like it, it will be ready in five minutes," the Beatle members said and went out to finish off the song. The result was The Rolling Stones' second single, 'I Wanna Be Your Man', which was not a major hit, but which features an impressive Brian Jones on slide guitar.

At the end of September 1963, the Stones did their

Downliners Sect replaced The Rolling Stones at Studio 51, but were unable to follow their predecessors to the major stages. Van Morrison played at Studio 51 with his newly formed group, Them, in April 1964. As far as I know, this was the Belfast band's first visit to London as well as their premiere gig there. ▶

Downliners Sect got their name from the Jerry Lee Lewis song 'Down The Line'. Their first record, recorded at Studio 51, was released in January 1964, in a limited run of 400 copies. The group achieved no major success with their records in England, but the single 'Little Egypt' was a hit in, above all, Sweden. It reached number two on the Swedish chart in the spring of 1965. ▼

last performance at Studio 51 in front of a packed house, and with hundreds of fans dancing on the pavement outside.

The Stones' successors at the club were the Downliners Sect, who recorded a live EP, *Nite In Gt. Newport Street*, at the club in late 1963. Downliners Sect had an admirer in Van Morrison, who decided to start his own band, Them, after he'd seen the band play at Studio 51. Many other musicians also showed up to watch the band. Phil May and Dick Taylor of The Pretty Things were often guests before they started playing in public themselves, and Long John Baldry would sometimes get up onstage to sing with the band, as did Rod Stewart. Stewart would sometimes perform at the club together with Jimmy Powell and the Five Dimensions, but he would rather have been a member of the Downliners Sect. When he was turned down he was so upset that he got drunk, started a fight and was thrown out of the club. The reason he was turned down was that the band regarded him as too unreliable, since he'd rather go to a football match than do a gig.

One evening in May 1964, Chuck Berry sat listening at the back of the room, wearing a black cap to avoid recognition. But a girl recognised him and was so excited that she ran up to him and pulled off the cap.

STUDIO '51
10/11 GT. NEWPORT S
LEICESTER SQUARE
RHYTHM & BLUES every
Thursday, April 9th, 8-11
THE SMOKE-STACKS
Friday, April 10th, 8 till Midnight
THE DOWNLINERS SECT
Sunday Afternoon, 4 to 6.30
THE DOWNLINERS SECT
Monday, April 13th, 8-11
"THEM"
★★★★★★★★★★★★★★★
All-Night Session this Saturday
LONG JOHN BALDRY
AND HIS HOOCHIE-COOCHIE MEN
NEW ORLEANS STOMPERS
★★★★★★★★★★★★★★★
R & B All-Nighter Next Saturday

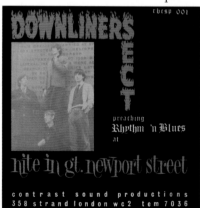

However, underneath the cap was a black stocking, so that his hair would be kept in place for his concert later that night. There he was, everybody's rock and roll hero, with a stocking on his head. Exposed like this he was furious and ran out of the club. As far as I know, however, the incident had no effect on his concert that night.

Ken Colyer and Studio 51 have been honoured with a blue English Heritage memorial plaque, which has been placed on the wall outside. But the plaque only identifies

Them with singer Van Morrison 1965 ▼

Studio 51 as a jazz club and there is not a single word about its role as a home for British rhythm & blues bands, where The Kinks and Manfred Mann also played at the start of their careers.

After a short walk along the book shop street, Charing Cross Road, where it's easy getting stuck at one of the shop windows, I reach the next side road: Litchfield Street. At the start of the street is number 27, which used to be the location for a well-known folk music club: *Bunjies*.

Bunjies

Bunjies
Leicester Square/
Covent Garden
27 Litchfield Street
Tube:
Leicester Square

When the coffee machine became popular in the Fifties, a number of coffee bars quickly opened in Soho. Going out for a cappuccino at nights became a sophisticated yet cheap diversion. In 1954 Bunjies, named after the owner's hamster, opened, and at the same time another new phenomenon was welcomed in the bar: skiffle music.

Melody Maker

1965   9d. weekly

Melody Maker, 1965, 9d. weekly

BEATLES NEW SINGLE

BEATLES day approaches. On April 9, the Beatles' new single, "Ticket To Ride", goes on sale.

Will it go straight to the top of the Pop 50? John Lennon spoke on the subject this week. "It's not at all certain that it'll be another immediate number one," he told the MM. "We're not taking it for granted, by any means. Ask me the day before it goes into the shops when I know the final advance order figure."

The Beatles star with "Ticket To Ride" on TV's "Lucky Stars" on Saturday (April 3); "Eamonn Andrews' Show" (11) and "Top Of The Pops" (15).

Adds Lennon: "It's the slowest A side we've done, I think. It's not that unusual though — I mean, it's still US. It's no more unusual than we are — does that make it unusual? We're quite pleased with the record. But let's emphasise this business of the number one thing. It's not BOUND to make it first go." The Beatles' new single is reviewed on page 12.

● JOHN

DONOVAN AT 5!

BOB DYLAN LEAPS TO No 13 AS CHART HOTS UP

DONOVAN at five, Dylan at 13. That was the hit parade score this week as the two new stars from the folk world became the hottest chart movers. Donovan's chart rise with "Catch The Wind" is a leap of ten places, and Bob Dylan, the 24-year-old American is up 19 places in the Pop 50 with "The Times They Are A-Changin'."

The British boy hits out on page three today at critics who accuse him of being on a Dylan kick.

And Donovan has put back an American trip for five days — until April 21 — because he is too busy in Britain. His first major concert will be at the British Song Festival, the Dome, Brighton, on May 24.

Concert sell out

TV dates for him include Southern's "Day By Day" (today, Thursday), the first "Ready, Steady Goes Live" tomorrow, TWW's "Discs A Gogo" (7) and "Thank Your Lucky Stars" (10).

Dylan jumps from success to success in Britain. His second London concert—on May 9—was a sell-out this week within hours of the Albert Hall box office opening.

He will appear in his own TV spectacular while in Britain. And with his first single in this country riding high, Dylan has another due out on April 23. It is "Subterranean Homesick Blues", another song he wrote, and currently climbing the US chart. The single is reviewed on page 12.

While Donovan and Dylan battle it out for the folk-style honours in the chart, there were other records soaring to the top.

Cliff Richard jumped seven spots to three with "The Minute You're Gone".

Stones

The Yardbirds streaked from sixteen to four with "For Your Love".

But the biggest threat of all was by Unit Four + 2, with "Concrete And Clay". Up three places to number two, they are now only one position behind the Rolling Stones, who cling to the top for the fourth successive week with "The Last Time".

DYLAN Second London concert sold out within hours this week.

DONOVAN He has put back his American trip for five days.

PROBY
HAS HE SUFFERED ENOUGH?

CENTRE PAGES

The shape and size of the premises decided what music could be played in there: the bare and narrow room would guarantee a stone-deaf audience if amplifiers were used, and the low ceiling would cause severe brain damage if anyone felt like jumping around to the music. The room was so small that it looked as if a group of friends had gathered in someone's kitchen, but this also provided a very intimate atmosphere. And the acoustic instruments worked really well in this small room.

In the early Sixties, folk music took over at Bunjies and there would usually be two main attractions each night, after which the stage was open for spontaneous performances. Innumerable world-famous stars took their first, in some cases faltering, steps here: Donovan, Rod Stewart, Sandie Shaw, Cat Stevens, Jeff Buckley, Tom Paxton, David Bowie, Paul Simon, Tom Robinson, Bert Jansch, Al Stewart and Phil Collins all performed here, many of them regularly.

In 1964, Paul Simon rented a room in an apartment in the East End, where he wrote many of his classic songs. At Bunjies he met Martin Carthy, who taught him his arrangement of Scarborough Fair. The song was later recorded by Simon & Garfunkel, with the duo claiming full credit for the arrangement.

Bunjies was one of Bob Dylan's favourite hangouts when he lived in London during the winter of 1962/1963, but he would often prefer to just sit and listen, learning new melodies he could use. Unfortunately, the high rents forced Bunjies to close down in 1998, and today there is a North African shop with a little café on the premises.

Saville Theatre

The next stop is Shaftesbury Avenue, where I walk eastward and soon reach a large building on the left side, the Odeon cinema. The building was once known as *the Saville Theatre* and for a couple of years in the Sixties it was one of the most popular concert venues in London, with performances by many world-famous artists. The Saville Theatre opened in 1931, but in 1965 The Beatles' manager, Brian Epstein, acquired the license for the theatre, with the purpose of arranging regular rock concerts at the venue. Seating 1,200 people, it was large enough for major arrangements, yet it was small enough to retain a club feeling.

During the autumn of 1966, Brian Epstein began arranging concerts on Sunday nights, which became very popular and which were often attended by The Beatles. The first concert featured the American group the Four Tops, who played two shows at a sold-out Saville Theatre, and new gigs were quickly arranged with the group in the following weeks. The Four Tops were enormously popular and all the famous musicians were there to pay tribute to the group.

Saville Theatre
Covent Garden
135 Shaftesbury
Avenue
Tube: Tottenham
Court Road

With The Who as the headliners, The Jimi Hendrix Experience made their concert debut here – excepting performances at small clubs – on January 29, 1967. Among the audience were a large part of the English music elite, headed by John Lennon, Paul McCartney, Eric Clapton, Steve Winwood and Jack Bruce. The Who, regarded as the heaviest and most exciting live act, had to watch as their reputation was demolished this night by a Jimi Hendrix at the height of his powers. The concert was so inspiring that Cream bassist Jack Bruce went home and started writing 'Sunshine Of Your Love'.

The Who's guitarist Pete Townshend went up on the stage after the Hendrix showcase and explained that his band could not top a show like that and added that the audience might as well go home. After the concert, Townshend was really angry with manager Kit Lambert who'd agreed to have both bands play on the same night, and with Jimi Hendrix opening the show.

The night of June 4 must have been memorable for those who were lucky enough to get tickets. The first act was Procol Harum, who made their concert debut this night. A couple of weeks previously they had released their debut single, 'A Whiter Shade Of Pale', and during the night they were told that they were number one on the charts. The attentive audience sank deeply into their seats as they let themselves be highly impressed by each little note from the band.

The next group onstage were The Jimi Hendrix Experience, who were giving a thank-you-and-farewell performance before their upcoming tour of the United States. They opened with the title track from *Sgt. Pepper's Lonely Hearts Club Band*, to the astonishment of members

New Musical Express
July 1, 1967 ▲

of The Beatles, who had released the album only three days earlier. None of them could understand how Hendrix could include it in his repertoire already, and in his own personal interpretation to boot. Hendrix had let his band members listen to the song on a record player a couple of times in the dressing room, only minutes before they were about to enter the stage. Jan Olofsson was in the box next to The Beatles and he recalls how Jimi Hendrix blew his nose in the American flag at the start of the concert and then threw it on the floor, much to the delight of the audience. This was at the height of the Vietnam war, after all!

Just minutes before Jimi Hendrix was about to conduct two concerts on August 27, 1967, the announcement came that Brian Epstein had died. The last show was cancelled and as a tribute to Epstein, Hendrix added 'Summertime Blues' and 'I Don't Live Today' to the set list of the one and only concert performed that night.

A few weeks later a blues concert was arranged: two shows, featuring acts such as Peter Green's Fleetwood Mac, John Mayall's Bluesbreakers and Long John Baldry. One of the members of the Bluesbreakers was future Stones guitarist Mick Taylor, who'd replaced Peter Green as the solo guitarist that spring. The gravity of the situation made nineteen-year-old Mick Taylor feel that he should have his eyes fixed on his guitar throughout the entire concert. But during the psychedelic year of 1967, the blues wasn't as popular as it had once been, and only a few people attended the concert.

During the short period when the Saville Theatre was used as a concert hall, a string of famous artists performed there: Cream, Chuck Berry, Little Richard, Fats Domino, Bo Diddley, Donovan, The Yardbirds, Manfred Mann, The Jeff Beck Group, Tom Jones, Tim Buckley, Bee Gees and Traffic, to name just a few. A year or so after Epstein's death, the concert venue was turned back into a theatre again, the Shaftesbury Theatre, and this was where the musical Hair was staged in 1968.

New Musical Express
September 30, 1967 ▼

SUNDAYS at the SAVILLE

A NEMS PRESENTATION

OCTOBER 1st*

PINK FLOYD
TOMORROW
Featuring KEITH WEST
GUEST STAR TIM ROSE
*Presented in association with Brian Morrison Agency

OCTOBER 8th

JIMI HENDRIX EXPERIENCE

OCTOBER 15th*

JR. WALKER ALL STARS
*Presented in association with Rik and John Gunnell

OCTOBER 22nd

THE WHO

OCTOBER 29th

THE CREAM

BOOK: TEM 4011

Denmark Street

After a short walk north along Charing Cross Road, I end up at a short street on the right side, where I meet up with Jan Olofsson again. We take a walk together on a street that he and many others in the music business have visited many times over the years: Denmark Street.

> Down the way from the Tottenham Court Road
> Just round the corner from old Soho
> There's a place where the publishers go
> If you don't know which way to go
> Just open your ears and follow your nose

('Denmark Street', lyrics:Ray Davies)

For many years, the short and narrow street was a centre for the English music business and was referred to as Tin Pan Alley, after its American role model. From the Twenties up until the mid-Sixties, the street was lined with music publishers, record companies and booking agents. This was where many of the important decisions were made regarding which songs and which artists would get the chance to reach the public.

The publishers would buy songs – some of them even had their own songwriters employed – and then find artists that were suitable for performing those songs. On the street, songwriters were visiting publishers and trying to sell their compositions. If they succeeded, they would be paid less than £45 per song in today's money value; the publishers could then make a fortune on those songs. This was also where the independent recording studios were located. They were mainly used by unknown artists and bands for the purpose of making demo recordings that could be presented to the publishers. Recording at the studios owned by the major labels was unthinkable due to the high studio fees.

Jan and I stop at a shop window to admire some beautiful electric guitars from the Fifties and Sixties that are seeking new owners. It's easy to understand why guitar heroes such as Eric Clapton, Jeff Beck, Jimi Hendrix, Jimmy Page and Pete Townshend spent a lot of time here. Many have both started and ended their careers with a visit to one of the shops in the street, and reportedly, Bob Marley bought his first guitar here. The Beatles also came here quite often, but mostly just to have a look, and the young Keith Moon used to come here on the chance that

The Rolling Stones outside the Tin Pan Alley Club in Denmark Street. The picture was taken in early in 1964, in conjunction with a recording session at Regent Sound Studio. At the time, Denmark Street was a meeting-place for musicians, song writers and publishers. ▼

he would spot a celebrity. In the 1965 documentary Don't Look Back, Bob Dylan is seen walking around looking in shop windows, while his manager Albert Grossman is negotiating with manager/promoter Tito Burns in his offices upstairs.

Giaconda Café

Giaconda Café
Covent Garden
9 Denmark Street
Tube:
Tottenham Court
Road

Jan Olofsson is eager to point out number 9, which was the location of the *Giaconda Café*, a natural gathering place for song writers, artists and musicians, who used to meet up to share their experiences, their hopes and their despair. Today there is an Indian restaurant on the premises, and we walk in to have a glass of wine and discuss the history of the café. Jan Olofsson tells me that it was the legendary record producer Joe Meek who first brought him to the Giaconda in the autumn of 1963. From that moment on Jan was a frequent guest at the café, where he got to know Pretty Things drummer Viv Prince, who in turn introduced him to Brian Jones in 1964.

Bands like The Rolling Stones, The Small Faces, The Kinks, The Pretty Things and The Moody Blues often visited the Giaconda before their careers got off the ground. Jan would also frequently meet the famous song writers Barry Mason and Mitch Murray, who used to hang out at the café. Barry Mason is the man behind songs such as 'Here It Comes Again' by The Fortunes and Tom Jones' 'Delilah', while Mitch Murray wrote most of the hits for Gerry & The Pacemakers.

If an artist or song writer needed help with a demo recording, he would often ask the musicians that were hanging out at the café. Among them were Jimmy Page and drummer Viv Prince, who used to come here al-

Scotsman Donovan Leitch achieved a breakthrough with his first single, 'Catch The Wind'. It reached number four on the UK chart in March 1965. He used the same studio when recorded the singles 'Colours' and 'Universal Soldier', as well as his first album in 1965. ▶

most daily as early as 1963. This was the place where Phil May and Dick Taylor of The Pretty Things met song writer Johnny Dee in the autumn of 1964. Dee offered them the song 'Don't Bring Me Down', which became the group's first UK hit. Steve Marriott, later the guitarist and singer of The Small Faces, would often hang out at the Giaconda in 1964 and 1965, and would be available for whatever was needed: drums, guitar, bass, vocals or harmonica. The café also became a natural meeting-point for The Small Faces at the start of their career, in the spring of 1965.

Paul Simon learned a lot at the Giaconda in 1964 through listening to other musicians and song writers, who told him about their bitter experiences from the pitfalls of the business. Instead of selling his songs, he founded his own publishing company, Charing Cross Music, hired himself as a song writer and managed to keep all his rights and incomes.

At the Giaconda, David Bowie got the idea for his Ziggy Stardust character in the mid-Sixties, after having met the old rock star Vince Taylor a number of times. At the time, Taylor was pretty confused and in very bad shape, and constituted a living example of the rise and fall of a star.

Today there is nothing left of the classic café, not even a photograph on the wall, and we decide to move on.

Next-door to the Giaconda, at number 8, *Southern Music* had a basement studio, which originally was used for the publisher's demo recordings, but which eventually developed into a real recording studio. This was the place where Donovan recorded 'Catch The Wind' in February 1965, and the following month the single 'Colours', as well as his first album, *What's Bin Did And What's Bin Hid*. 22 Denmark Street is still the location for Tin Pan Alley Studio, where Elton John made his first demo recordings. Number 4, across the street, was the location for the most famous studio, *Regent Sound Studio*.

**Regent Sound
Studio**
Covent Garden
4 Denmark Street
Tube:
Tottenham Court
Road

Regent Sound Studio

Today they mostly sell Fender guitars at the premises, but to Jan's and my unbridled joy the owners have made an exact replica of the old studio sign and placed it above the shop-window. At Regent Sound, Jimmy Page and drummer Viv Prince would often participate in various demo and studio recordings during 1963 and 1964.

However, the band that really made Regent Sound Studio famous is The Rolling Stones. The group had a unique contract that let them make their recordings wherever they wanted to and they weren't forced to use the Decca label's own studio, which they thought was too impersonal and expensive. The Rolling Stones had used different studios before, but immediately liked Regent Sound Studio when they came here the first time to do some demo recordings, on November 20, 1963. At the time, it was only used as a demo studio, but The Rolling Stones liked the small, primitive studio, which was equipped with egg cartons in the ceiling and drapings on the walls

The Rolling Stones impressive debut album featured neither the title nor the band's name on the front of the sleeve. With dead serious faces and nonchalant postures the group looks more like a gang of hoodlums under a street lamp. A pretty cocky attitude from a fairly unknown debut band. The album went straight to number one on the UK chart and remained there for 12 weeks. ◄

to make the sound more muted. They were the first band to use it for real master recordings.

On January 3, 1964, the Stones began recording their first album here, on a two-track Revox tape recorder. The small studio was so crowded that it was impossible to separate the instruments, but sound engineer Bill Farley did the very best he could since this was the first time he had the chance to do a real recording, meant for release on record.

The Rolling Stones were constantly on tour and had to work quickly in the studio during the daytime. Sometimes they recorded as many as five songs in one single afternoon, and there were no retakes. Despite the primitive and tough conditions, the band's burning energy and uncompromis-

THE ROLLING STONES CONFESS TO A 'NOISY' HEADACHE—
Getting stage sound on their discs!

WHILE many artists strive to capture on stage the same sound as they get on record, the biggest headache for the Rolling Stones is getting their stage noise on wax. Judging by their chart successes, they manage pretty well.

Their co-manager, Andrew Loog Oldham, who produces some of their discs, told me : "When the Stones go into a recording studio, they enjoy themselves. They don't look upon it as an ordeal. They can go right on and play a number perfectly first time, but we want to get the same sound as they produce on stage, so we often have to double-track."

But whatever tricks the back-room boys get up to in the studios, the end product is always welcomed by the fans. Seven weeks ago, their EP entered the charts. It is still there.

For a record that costs almost twice as much as a single to sell that well, there has to be something different about it. And that is the Stones all over—they are different.

"We are surprised that the EP has sold so well," Mike Jagger confessed.

R-and-b

"We do 'Poison Ivy' and 'Money' on the record, but they have already been hits. 'Money' is on a Beatles EP and it has sold fantastically by other people. So we couldn't have been more surprised when the disc made the charts."

The EP, produced by the group's other manager—Eric Easton—was cut in just seven hours while they were touring with Bo Diddley and the Everly Brothers at the end of last year.

It had been planned for release at Christmas, but it got delayed. It came along just at the right

by
Richard Green

time to plug the gap between "I Wanna Be Your Man" and "Not Fade Away," which jumps into the Chart this week at No. 10.

Perhaps the most requested number on the EP is the slowest—"You Better Move On." But a lot of people have been decrying it as not r-and-b.

Mike answered the critics : "It is himself.

Keith Richard explained the situation : "We had been working on the number for about five minutes when two of the Hollies turned up, then Gene Pitney arrived. Phil Spector was already there, so everything came to a halt while everyone started talking.

"When we got around to recording again, Phil had grabbed hold of Mike's maracas and was shaking the daylights out of them. He really had a ball, and it's him you hear on the disc."

Tapes

If that sounds a remarkable way of conducting a recording session, listen to what Andrew says about the "B" side, "Little By Little."

"After we had done 'Not Fade Away,' Phil and Mike disappeared,"

who plays maracas—Phil Spector an Arthur Alexander number, and as much r-and-b as 'Memphis' or 'Road Runner.' We have been using it in our act for ages and it has always gone down well ; that's why we decided to record it."

Earlier, I mentioned the Rolling Stones' latest single "Not Fade Away," which was originally recorded by the Crickets. But there is the world of difference between the two versions.

In fact, the Stones' version has the Spector sound !

Don't worry, though, you won't hear the group augmented by violins, pianos and all sorts of gimmicks. The only addition is a sixth member

the number they had just written in the outside corridor.

"It was very good, so we decided to use it as the 'B' side. Mike took hold of his harmonica, Phil found the maracas again, and Gene Pitney and the Stones' road manager, Ian Stewart, sat down at the piano. It was a fantastic scene ! "

The session ended up with everyone cutting private tapes and tunes with Spector-type titles, such as "And The Rolling Stones Met Phil And Gene " and " Mr. Spector and Mr. Pitney Came Too," being written and recorded on the spot.

If those tapes are ever issued as discs, they will be a knockout. One thing to listen for is Phil Spector singing. I am told he has a great blues voice.

Now that Gene Pitney is back in the country, he is spending as much time as possible discussing their LP with the Rolling Stones. He wants

trying to finish it in the next cou of months. But what with tou and everything else, we can when it will be done. 'Ca 'Mona ' and ' Route 66 ' are on and we plan to include some num that people wouldn't associate w us."

It will probably prove anot winner for the Rolling Stones.

TWO GREAT SIDES

Two girl fans reach up to hold hands with the ROLLING STONES, who are only too happy to oblige The Stones are (l to r) BRIAN JONES, BILL WYMAN, MICK JAGGER, KEITH RICHARD an CHARLIE WATTS.

The Rolling Stones liked the primitive conditions at Regent Sound. They used the cramped studio to try to reproduce their live concert sound. This approach differed from other bands, who tried to reproduce their recorded sound on stage. (New Musical Express February 28, 1964) ▲

ing approach gave results: when the album was released in April, it entered the UK album chart at number one.

The singles 'Not Fade Away' and 'Little Red Rooster', and a large part of the group's second album, were also recorded at Regent Sound. The most famous session was the recording of 'Not Fade Away' in early February 1964. The group was tired and in a bad mood after a gruelling tour, and couldn't find any inspiration during the recording. There was no way they could knock the song into shape, and their mood grew increasingly worse. Then, out of pure desperation, manager and producer Oldham phoned Gene Pitney, who was on a quick visit to London together with Phil Spector. The pair went down to the studio with a few bottles of brandy and the mood quickly improved. The deadlock broke and after a while they had recorded 'Not Fade Away', with Phil Spector on maracas.

Now the only problem was that they didn't have anything for the B-side. But nothing was impossible anymore. Mick Jagger and Phil Spector left the studio and soon returned with the lyrics for 'Little By Little'. Then, everybody collaborated on the melody and when the recording started it almost resembled a party, to which Graham Nash and Allan Clarke of The Hollies had also been invited. Gene Pitney and Ian Stewart were both at the piano and Phil Spector was hammering an empty bottle of brandy with a coin, which was referred to as "maracas" when the song was released. 'Not Fade Away' was issued at the end of the month and entered the UK chart at number three. The last Stones recording at Regent Sound occurred in October 1965, when Mick Jagger recorded an Italian version of 'As Tears Go By'.

But the Stones weren't the only well-known band to use the studio early on in their career. Downliners Sect made their first recordings, 'Cadillac' and 'Roll Over Beethoven', in this studio as early as 1963, but the recordings were never released. The Kinks also used the studio, when they were still known as The Ravens. This was where they recorded their first singles, as well as a demo version of 'You Really Got Me', in March 1964.

In conjunction with the recording The Kinks met Viv Prince and tried to get him to join the band, but he turned them down since he preferred working as a session musician. However, a short while later he joined The Pretty Things, who used the studio in 1964 for their first recording sessions, among them the group's first single, 'Rosalyn'. In 1965, Them – featuring Van Morrison – recorded the classic 'Mystic Eyes' as well as 'The Story Of Them'. The studio was made into a four-track studio in 1966.

A few years later, the group Silence and their manager, Guy Stevens, were looking for a new vocalist for the band. The studio sound engineer, Bill Farley, recommended a guy he knew who used to hang around Denmark Street and participate in demo recordings. Guy Stevens' vision was to put together the ultimate rock group: a band that could combine the singing style of Bob Dylan with Procol Harum's keyboard playing and the rhythmic sound of The Rolling Stones.

Bill Farley managed to convince this acquaintance of his to come down to the studio for an audition. The sceptical singer came down, wearing shades – in order to conceal his somewhat rotund face – and performed 'Like A Rolling Stone'. Guy Stevens was really happy with what he heard and saw, and from that moment on the shades were an important part of singer Ian Hunter's image as part of the group he formed together with the Silence members: Mott The Hoople.

Regent Sound gradually improved their technical equipment and Jan tells me that when he used the studio in the Seventies, they recorded on 16 tracks. Along with old pictures of the studio, the guitar shop displays the old master tape recorder that was used during recording sessions in the early Sixties. Today, music is still heard all over the street, emanating from shops and basements. At the far end of the street is the 12 Bar Club, which admittedly doesn't have a very long history, but which features live music seven days a week. Jan and I enter the club to have a sandwich and a beer before I move on towards Piccadilly Circus.

St. James's

Masons Yard

After just a few minutes' walk along Piccadilly I reach Duke Street St. James's, which I follow until I reach a pub on the left side where there is a passage to Masons Yard. On this well-hidden and quiet yard there are no less than three interesting places related to rock history.

6-13 Masons Yard
St James's
Duke Street
Tube: Piccadilly
Circus

Indica Gallery

Number 6, which today is the location of James Hyman Fine Art, was the address of the *Indica Gallery* in the Sixties. The gallery was opened in January 1966 by Barry Miles, John Dunbar (the husband of Marianne Faithfull) and Peter Asher (brother of Paul McCartney's girlfriend Jane Asher). Peter Asher was a member of the duo Peter And

Gordon, who had a hit with 'A World Without Love', and he invested some money in the Indica Gallery, together with Paul McCartney. The gallery was mainly occupied with avant garde art, but also sold Eastern and "psychedelic" literature and attracted many of the pop stars of the day.

The Indica Gallery was the place where John Lennon and Yoko Ono met for the first time, in November 1966. Lennon had been invited by John Dunbar to view Yoko's exhibition Unfinished Paintings and Objects the day before the opening. His first impression was that the entire thing was a joke or plain fraud: £200 for a fresh apple and £100 for a bag of nails was not what he had expected! But an item entitled "Painting to Hammer a Nail In" aroused his interest. The hammer was hanging in a chain above a table with nails on it, and he asked if he could hammer a nail in. At first Yoko said no, but after Dunbar had whispered in her ear that Lennon was a millionaire – she

didn't know who he was – she said that he could hammer a nail in if he paid five shillings. Lennon replied that he would give her an imaginary five shillings and hammer an imaginary nail in. That comment was the start of a relationship that led to the pair becoming a couple less than two years later.

Gered Mankowitz' Studio

Number 9 was the location of photographer Gered Mankowitz' studio, which he opened in December 1963 at the tender age of seventeen. After a number of pictures that attracted a great deal of attention he was given

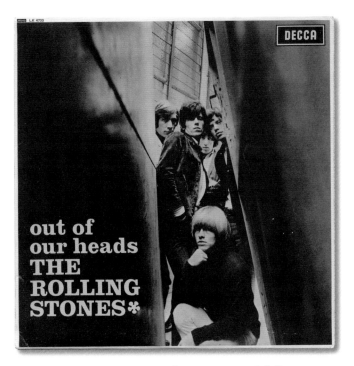

the assignment to photograph Marianne Faithfull in 1964, after her breakthrough with 'As Tears Go By'. Through her, Mankowitz got in touch with the man who discovered her: Rolling Stones manager Andrew Loog Oldham.

Oldham asked Gered Mankowitz to photograph The Rolling Stones and one of the pictures ended up on the cover of *Out Of Our Heads* (the *December's Children* album in the US). In my opinion, this is one of the best rock photos ever; it was taken at Ormond Yard, behind the studio. Mankowitz then became the band's official photographer between 1965 and 1967. He joined the group on their tour of the United States in 1965, and also took the pictures for a number of record covers, among them *Got Live If You Want It* and *Between The Buttons*.

Then Mankowitz went on to work with many of the big names of the time, such as Jimi Hendrix, The Yardbirds, The Small Faces, Free, Eric Clapton and Traffic; he also worked for Oldham's new record label, Immediate. In the Sixties, Gered Mankowitz' studio was a meeting-place for many artists and Jimi Hendrix would often come over to have a talk and to gossip a little before he went on to Scotch of St. James, which is situated next-doors, at number 13.

Scotch of St. James

Scotch of St. James, often called *The Scotch*, was opened by Louis Brown and John Bloom in March 1965. It replaced the Ad Lib as the musicians' favourite hangout in London. Rod Harrod was given the task of managing the club, and since he was also a music journalist he already had good, solid contacts with the musicians. He invited The Animals, headed by Eric Burdon, to the opening night. They became the first guests and remained as loyal visitors to the club. They would recommend the club to their

musician colleagues, which meant that The Scotch soon became the club to go to.

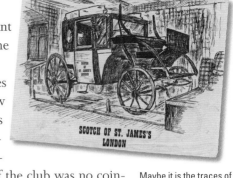

SCOTCH OF ST. JAMES'S
LONDON

Although the Scotch of St. James was located just a stone's throw from Piccadilly Circus, the guests could arrive completely undetected, thanks to the club's hidden location in a backyard. The name of the club was no coincidence. The premises were decorated in a Scottish style: bagpipes on the walls, tartan patterns on lampshades, curtains and carpets, and the waiters were dressed in tartan waistcoats. The bar was constructed from hundreds of empty whisky bottles – Scotch, naturally – and the liquor was served in unopened miniature bottles, an idea that was imported from the Ad Lib. On the ground floor there was a bar and a restaurant, and in the basement there was a dance floor and another bar. Next to the minimal dance floor the disc jockey would be standing in a 17th Century wagon, playing the very latest records at a deafening volume.

Maybe it is the traces of Eric Burdon's beer glass that can be seen on this coaster from 1967? ▲

At the Scotch, you would meet the very elite among musicians: The Beatles, The Rolling Stones, The Who, The Animals, The Small Faces, The Hollies, Eric Clapton, Jeff Beck, Jimmy Page, Rod Stewart, Spencer Davis Group, Donovan, Dave Davies and eventually Jimi Hendrix. Eric Burdon lived close the club, on Duke Street, and spent every free minute at the club, forever celebrating something. The Moody Blues spent so much time there that they had a corner named after them: "The Moody Blues Corner".

The Scotch was where Keith Moon went up to The Beatles and asked them if he could join their band. Ringo caustically replied that they already had a drummer. A few minutes later, Moon approached The Animals and asked if he could join their band. Poor Moon never really felt comfortable in The Who.

The Scotch was more than a club for the top groups; it was their "home" where they would be left alone and no-one would bother them. One night a guest asked George Harrison for an autograph and was immediately thrown out by the club manager, Rod Harrod. To be seen but not disturbed was apparently the motto. The two biggest bands, The Beatles and The Rolling Stones, had their own tables with their names engraved on brass plates. So did The Animals, thanks to their loyalty towards the club, and those three bands were the only ones who never had to pay their bills at the club. Rod Harrod wouldn't allow any other guests, no matter how rich they were, to sit down at any of their tables if one band member was there.

Friday nights were the most popular, since that was the time when the producer of the Ready Steady Go! television show would bring along the night's performers to the club, where they would often do guest appearances. Four Tops, Sonny & Cher, The Supremes, Stevie Wonder, Otis Redding and Wilson Pickett are just some of the American artists who visited the club. Eric Clapton was eager to help out as a backing musician when Wilson Pickett performed, and Paul McCartney and Stevie Wonder began a friendship that would last for many years. Sometimes Tom Jones would be onstage to celebrate and perform his latest hit, but his performances were usually ignored by most of the rock audience.

Thanks to its exclusive guests, the Scotch of St. James was an important club to play when a new band was to be launched. On September 24, 1966, Jimi Hendrix and his

New Musical Express
January 28, 1967 ▲

manager Chas Chandler – formerly the bass player in The Animals – landed at London's Heathrow Airport. It was Hendrix' first visit to England, who was unknown at the time, and already on that first night he visited The Scotch and jammed with the house band. When he began playing, the whole club went quiet, as if struck by lightning, but after a few songs Chas Chandler took Jimi Hendrix off the stage, since he didn't yet have a work permit. During that night, Jimi Hendrix also met his future girlfriend, Kathy Etchingham.

Less than a month later, on October 19, Jimi Hendrix and his newly formed band, the Experience, made their club debut in London at the Scotch of St. James. They performed songs such as 'Have Mercy', 'Killing Floors' and 'Hey Joe' in front of a growing number of star musicians, who had heard the rumour about Hendrix' spectacular

Eric Burdon of The Animals lived next door to the Scotch and would hang out there as often as he could. Considering The Animals' enormous success during the years 1964–66, he had every reason to celebrate. ▶

performances at the London clubs. Hendrix returned to the Scotch a few weeks later and went up to jam with the VIPs, who were friends of Chas Chandler. Chandler had yet to acquire a record contract for Hendrix, but The Who's managers, Kit Lambert and Chris Stamp, attended this performance. Lambert and Stamp had just started a record company, Track Records, and when they heard Jimi play, Lambert almost knocked tables flying in his eagerness to reach Chandler. A record contract was immediately drawn up on a beer coaster and Lambert also promised to arrange two performances on the Ready Steady Go! television show. Lambert and Stamp succeeded, and the rest of the story is well-known.

At the passage into Masons Yard, there is a pub that was often visited by Eric Burdon. I go in and sit down at the window facing the backyard, watching these three memorable places, while having a drink. There are some cars parked on the inner yard, but otherwise there is no sign of life. No-one seems to be aware that this place was once crammed with limousines and sports cars. If you plan to visit Masons Yard at night, you should be aware that The Scotch today is a strip club called Director's Lodge Club.

Before I leave this neighbourhood I have a look at the building where Eric Burdon used to live, 6 *Duke Street*. He was overjoyed when a friend let him take over the apartment on the third floor, which was located close to his favourite hangout. He would buy his favourite Beaujolais wine from a large importer who had their offices further down the street. On the ground floor there was an Italian restaurant that was nice enough to serve him food in bed when he had a bad hangover. It's not hard to understand why Eric Burdon loved this neighbourhood.

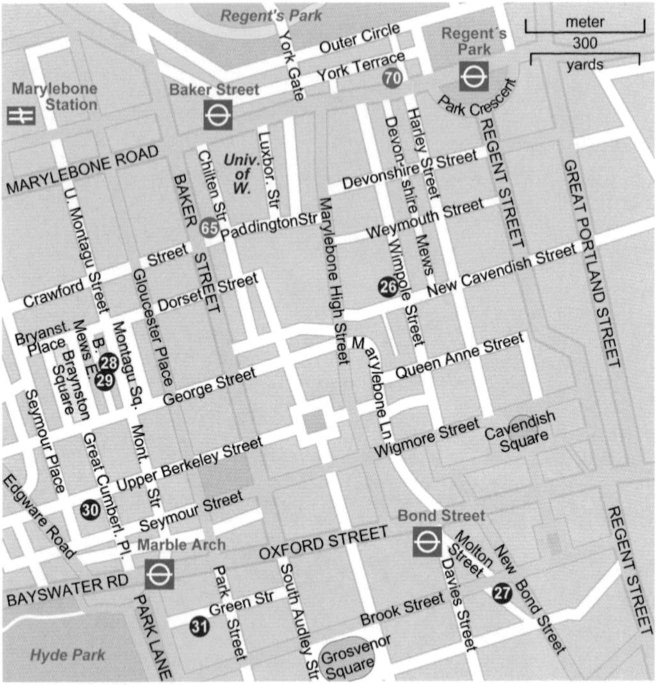

Marylebone, Mayfair

26 **57 Wimpole Street**
27 **23 Brook Street**
28 **34 Montagu Square**
29 **13a Bryanston Mews East**
30 **43 Upper Berkeley Street**
31 **57 Green Street**

65 **Apple Boutique**
70 **52 Marylebone Road**

Marylebone

Between Portland Place and Baker Street there are a couple of districts that by tradition are populated by doctors and other highly educated people.

Wimpole Street

Jane Asher's father was one of those doctors and the family lived at 57 *Wimpole Street*, in a somewhat narrow house that was sandwiched between two larger buildings. Paul McCartney moved in with his girlfriend Jane Asher and her family in November 1963 and stayed here for two and a half years. While the other members of The Beatles moved out in the country, Paul preferred staying in London. The entire six-storey 18th Century building belonged to the family, and Paul moved into a small attic room at the back of the house, with a window that overlooked Browning Mews.

57 Wimpole Street
Marylebone
Tube:
Bond Street/Oxford
Circus

It was in this small attic room that Paul woke up one morning in May 1965 with a melody ringing in his head, got up and went to the piano and started playing the song that was to become 'Yesterday'. The larger room next to his, overlooking Wimpole Street, belonged to Jane's brother, Peter, who was one half of Peter and Gordon. For them Paul wrote the song 'A World Without Love', which was a hit in the spring of 1964. Jane's mother was a music teacher and had a music room in the basement, where she

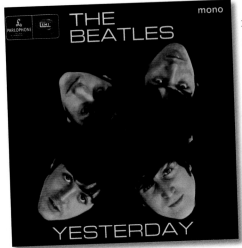

received her students. In this room, which had small windows at the front of the house, John and Paul would meet up to write songs. This was where they wrote songs like 'I Want To Hold Your Hand', the group's first US number one.

When it became known where Paul lived, fans would gather along Wimpole Street, blocking the traffic. The fans even started stealing the cast-iron knobs on the railings in front of the house. I walk to the other side of the house and then into the Browning Mews inner yard. There is an exit between two blue garage doors and this was where Paul McCartney used to get out of the building – via his window, the roof ridges and then through the neighbours' apartments – to escape the attention of the fans.

Browning Mews, where Paul McCartney would sneak out to escape the fans who were besieging Wimpole Street. ▶

This went on for a couple of years, until he and Jane moved to Cavendish Avenue.

I turn south to walk towards the first rock-related apartment building to be adorned with the prestigious blue English Heritage memorial plaque. One major advantage of walking is that you might discover some nice little neighbourhood pub on the way, and I slip into Kings Head, which looks very inviting. After a beer and a quick ethnological study of the local guests, most of whom seem to be well-to-do pensioners out on a long lunch, I head towards the fashionable shopping street New Bond Street. As the observant reader will notice this means that I make a temporary visit to Mayfair.

23 Brook Street
Mayfair
Tube:
Bond Street

Brook Street

After having passed shops such as Cesari, Pellini and Bernini, I reach Brook Street, where the blue memorial plaque has been placed at number 23. It was Jimi Hendrix' former girlfriend, Kathy Etchingham, who managed to persuade English Heritage that the apartment on the second floor was worthy of the prestigious blue plaque. The memorial plaque was unveiled by Jimi Hendrix' friend and Who guitarist Pete Townshend in the presence of more than 2,000 fans. Jeff Beck, Eric Clapton and Jimmy Page were also invited to perform the unveiling, but said no for various reasons.

Managing to make this honour a real-

ity was a major achievement by Kathy Etchingham, especially since Hendrix didn't live in the apartment during the years stated on the memorial plaque: 1968–1969. Although Jimi Hendrix was the one who paid for the apartment, he only lived in the white house on Brook Street for a number of weeks in total. In reality it was Kathy Etchingham who lived here, together with her friend Angie Burdon, the ex-wife of Eric Burdon. Except for a few days in early January 1969, Hendrix only stayed here on and off between early February and March 13. Then he returned to America, where he'd acquired an apartment in Manhattan the previous April. Although 23 Brook Street is the London apartment that Jimi Hendrix spent the least amount of time in, many fans still come to visit this place. It is possible to have a look at the actual apartment since it's now a part of a museum dedicated to Friedrich Händel, who used to live in the building next to this one.

A decidedly more interesting apartment is located not so far away, and I reach it by taking bus number 13 westward from the corner of New Bond Street and Oxford Street. This means that I'm back in Marylebone. After just a couple of minutes the bus turns up on Gloucester Street and I get off after a few hundred yards, at George Street.

Montagu Square

34 Montagu Square
Marylebone
Tube: Marble Arch
Bus: 13

Close to the street is a long and narrow park, *Montagu Square*, and at number 34 there is an apartment which has been occupied by a number of world-famous artists. In early 1965, Ringo Starr bought the apartment, which consists of a ground floor and a basement. When his son Zak was born, on September 13, 1965, Ringo and his family moved out in the country, at which time he began letting his friends rent the apartment.

The first tenant was Paul McCartney, who didn't move in to live there but turned the basement into a demo studio. Poet and author William Burroughs was one of the people who stayed in the ground floor. The idea was that musicians and poets who couldn't afford to rent an ordinary studio would be given the opportunity to experiment with sounds and music. However, the person who used the studio the most was Paul himself. He made sound experiments on the tape recorders as well as various demo recordings, among them 'Eleanor Rigby'. William Burroughs also often used the studio for his sound experiments.

On December 6, 1966, Jimi Hendrix moved into the apartment together with his manager, Chas Chandler; this was Jimi's first London home. Jimi moved into the basement together with his girlfriend Kathy Etchingham, while Chas and his Swedish girlfriend, Lotta, stayed on the ground floor. During the few months that Hendrix lived here, he achieved his international breakthrough with songs such as 'Hey Joe', 'Purple Haze' and 'The Wind Cries Mary'. The last one was written for his girlfriend (her middle name was Mary) in Montagu Square, after one of the couple's many arguments.

In July 1968, Ringo sublet the

apartment to John Lennon and Yoko Ono; it was the first place where they lived together. During the time they were staying here, John made a demo of 'Cold Turkey' and in the basement they took the controversial nude picture for the *Two Virgins* album sleeve. Late in the evening of October 18, a huge police squad with dogs raided the apartment, and the couple was arrested for possession of cannabis. The police force was led by the notorious Sergeant Norman Pilcher, who made a name for himself by arresting famous musicians and making sure that the press was present at the arrest. It was also known among musicians that Pilcher himself often planted the drugs and then demanded a pay-off in return for not filing drugs possession charges. John Lennon had received a tip about the raid and was certain that his apartment was clean, but at the same time he knew that his word carried little weight against that of the police. Had he denied the charges, both he and Yoko would have been convicted. Therefore, he alone pled guilty of possession to protect Yoko, who was under the threat of deportation since she wasn't a British citizen. But afterwards he firmly maintained that he was innocent and that he had been framed by Pilcher. However, the raid provided the building owner with an opportunity to take action, and in February 1969 Ringo chose to sell his apartment lease. A few years later, in 1972, the corrupt Pilcher was sentenced to four years imprisonment for perjury and for planting drugs in other cases. If you feel like buying the apartment, you might be interested to know that it was sold for the sum of £575,000 in the year 2000, but it's probably even more expensive today.

Jimi Hendrix was so cool that he wore his stage costume at the kitchen sink in his Montagu Square apartment. In all likelihood, he neither owned nor needed any other clothes. ◄

29

13 a Bryanston
Mews East
Marylebone
Tube: Marble Arch
Bus: 13

Bryanston Mews East

Ringo and Mick Jagger were able to socialise a great deal in 1965, since Jagger lived just around the corner, at 13*a* *Bryanston Mews East*, in a basement apartment at the far end of long and narrow lane. Mick Jagger moved in there in June 1965, after a short period at a hotel and then with his friend, the photographer David Bailey, who took the sleeve photo for *the Rolling Stones No. 2* album.

From the outside the apartment gives a fairly unassuming and dull impression, with large windows beneath ground level, which are fully exposed to people's view from the lane. However, the 110 square feet apartment stretches throughout the entire building – there is also an entrance from Montagu Square – and consists

of two bedrooms, a living room and a kitchen. It may not sound very impressive, but The Rolling Stones were no world-famous stars when Mick Jagger moved in there. All that would change within a few weeks, when '(I Can't Get No) Satisfaction' was released and hit number one all over the world.

Mick's girlfriend, Chrissie Shrimpton – younger sister of star model Jean Shrimpton – also often lived in the apartment. By the summer of 1965, Mick and Chrissie had been together for a little over two years – years that were marked by constant arguments,

MICK JAGGER'S IDEAL PAD

MICK JAGGER was seated in a very business-like black leather chair in his manager's office, yelling "Help" at the top of his Stone-type voice—not once, not twice, but repeatedly! The singing Stone wasn't throwing a fit, or even being attacked by an army of screaming teenaged girls. Nor was he exercising his voice. He was quite simply repeating the words of the Beatles yet-to-be-released disc, which someone had just played him over the phone.

By SUE MAUTNER

After Mick had calmed down, we started talking about the many problems of a " pad "—like " why did you and Keith leave Hampstead ? "

" It was getting beyond a joke. We had the ground floor flat, which presented problems because we found that as well as sneaking in through the front door, the fans used to climb in through the windows. At weekends there would be about 50 of them.

"We didn't mind signing autographs, but when it came to having the place ransacked and having our clothes taken, it got a bit much. The funny thing was that most things were nearly always returned."

Just then, the elusive fashion photographer, Mr. David Bailey (affectionately known as Bailey to his friends), popped his head round the door to enquire if anyone cared for a 'cuppa.'

"Don't mind, Bailey," Mick replied. "He's got a habit of dropping in unexpectedly — and staying," Mick explained.

"Actually, when I got back from the States, if it hadn't been for Bailey I would have been homeless. Keith and I quit the flat before we left and found staying at the Hilton rather expensive on returning.

" So I stayed with Bailey in his big house in Regents Park and Keith stayed with other friends. Staying with Bailey was like living in a hotel. His pad was quite big, with three bathrooms, and as we were never in at the same time we rarely crossed paths."

quarrels and break-ups, but which also gave Mick Jagger the inspiration for songs like 'Heart Of Stone', 'Play With Fire' and 'The Last Time'. Mick would always retaliate in his lyrics and during his time at Bryanston Mews East he certainly wrote his meanest lyrics about her, in songs such as 'Out Of Time', 'Stupid Girl' and 'Under My Thumb'.

It couldn't have been much fun for Chrissie in April 1966, when the *Aftermath* album was released and the voice of Mick Jagger was heard everywhere: "You're out of touch, my baby, my poor unfaithful baby… / …You're out of time". The situation hardly improved when Chris Farlowe hit number one on the UK chart with 'Out Of Time' that summer. The fact that Chrissie Shrimpton had fooled around with P. J. Proby when the Stones were on tour in America may have contributed to the sarcasm. The couple's stormy relationship would last until December 1966, at which time Mick Jagger had already started dating Marianne Faithfull, and a while later Chrissie Shrimpton began an affair with Steve Marriott of The Small Faces.

New Musical Express
July 23, 1965 ▲

Mick Jagger thought he had moved to a dream flat when he took up residence behind the bars, below the courtyard. The joy probably stemmed from the fact that it was his first own apartment. But Mick Jagger would soon attain considerably more exclusive living habits. ◄

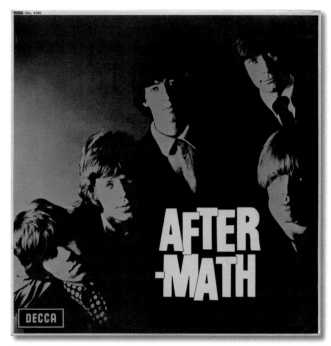

Aftermath was the first Stones album to only contain songs written by Jagger/Richard. But what mainly distinguished the album was Brian Jones' musical contribution on a range of different instruments, which gave many songs their character. *Aftermath* topped the UK album chart for eight weeks.

▶

But the apartment wasn't just a place for arguments. On January 8, 1966, Mick Jagger had a big party, which John Lennon, George Harrison and Ringo Starr attended; the trio could celebrate that 'We Can Work It Out' had hit number one in the US on the same day. They also played their latest album, Rubber Soul, for Mick Jagger, who was mightily impressed; he hadn't yet had the opportunity to hear the record.

The apartment was furnished when Mick Jagger rented it, but he was always looking for a place to live permanently, which he could furnish according to his own tastes. At the end of May 1966, he moved to Harley House on 52 Marylebone Road. During the 11 months he stayed in Bryanston Mews East, he and Keith Richards wrote a number of songs that definitely placed The Rolling Stones at the top, alongside The Beatles. The apartment at Bryanston Mews East is still available to rent furnished; for £600 per week you can take a closer look at it.

Upper Berkeley Street

If you walk south for just a few minutes, towards Edgware Road, you will reach 43 *Upper Berkeley Street*, which was where Jimi Hendrix stayed in London for the longest period of time. In March 1967, Jimi Hendrix and his manager, Chas Chandler, moved into the fourth floor, together with their respective girlfriends, Kathy Etchingham and Lotta. In this apartment, Jimi Hendrix wrote a number of songs that Chas Chandler would help him edit; Hendrix' songs were often six to seven minutes long, and were edited down to three to four minutes. Chas Chandler brought with him plenty of science fiction books that Hendrix began reading, and they provided him with ideas for several of his lyrics, such as 'Third Stone From The Sun' and 'Up From The Skies'.

When Hendrix and Chandler weren't writing songs or planning Hendrix' continued career, they often used to play their favourite game, Risk, together with their girlfriends, and in the evenings Jimi Hendrix would often visit various clubs for jam sessions.

The release of the 'Purple Haze' single in March and the first al-

43 Upper Berkeley Street
Marylebone
Tube:
Marble Arch

Jimi Hendrix lived in apartment number 9 on the fourth floor. ▼

bum, *Are You Experienced?*, in May 1967, quickly turned Jimi Hendrix into an international star. After his breakthrough in the United States, at the Monterey Pop Festival in June 1967, the relatively small-time gigs in England were increasingly replaced by concerts at the big arenas in USA and Europe. But Hendrix was still based in London, and the second Jimi Hendrix Experience album, *Axis: Bold As Love*, was recorded during his time at Upper Berkeley Street.

Despite his popularity and success, Jimi Hendrix only had a few really close friends in London, and during this period one of them was Brian Jones of The Rolling Stones. They would often visit clubs like the Speakeasy together, watching various bands, and after the club visits they would spend the rest of the night in the apartment, jamming on acoustic guitars. Jimi Hendrix also invited Brian Jones, together with Dave Mason of Traffic, to attend his recording sessions in January 1968, when songs like 'All Along The Watchtower' were recorded. Brian immediately showed up in a taxi, dragging his sitar along with him.

But thanks to his great international success, Jimi Hendrix began spending more and more of his time in the USA. In April 1968 he acquired an apartment in Manhattan, where he felt most at home, even if London always had a special place in his heart.

Jimi Hendrix mostly used his Epiphone acoustic guitar when he wrote the songs for *Axis: Bold As Love*. Then he tried them out in the bathroom of the apartment, where he thought the acoustics were good. The A-side was rush-remixed shortly before the release in December 1967, after Hendrix had forgotten the master tape in a taxi after a party. ◄

Mayfair

The Brook Street passage should really have been placed here, in the Mayfair section. But for practical reasons I visited the street during my walk in Marylebone. From a certain spot it is more natural to walk to the place that's closest, although it may be located in another area. I hope that those with a keen sense of order will accept this minor transgression.

57 Green Street
Mayfair
Tube:
Marble Arch

Green Street

My next goal is to visit the only apartment in London where the four members of The Beatles stayed together. I walk south from Marble Arch, until I reach 57 Green Street, where manager Brian Epstein found an apartment on the fourth floor for The Beatles in the beginning of Septem-

ber 1963. Because they spent so much time in London, the idea was that they should use the apartment to save on hotel costs. It may sound like a dream: four incredibly successful boys, sharing an apartment in central London. But this was never how it was, quite the opposite in fact.

Paul was the last one to arrive in the apartment and had to choose the only room that was left: a tiny and stuffy room at the back of the apartment. They had beds, but the rest of the apartment was just empty rooms and bare walls, and no furniture whatsoever. They had money, of course, but there was no time to furnish the apartment and they didn't even have a

teapot. They hated the apartment and John and Paul got out of there as quickly as they could.

When the press found out that John was married and had a son, there was no reason to try to keep this fact a secret anymore. The Lennon family moved to 13 Emperor's Gate in Kensington; the building has since been demolished. Paul moved into John's room, but still hated the apartment and soon moved in with his girlfriend, Jane Asher, at her parents' house in Wimpole Street. George and Ringo remained in the apartment until the beginning of 1964, when they moved to a nicer flat in Whaddon House in William Mews. The house is beautiful and has an attractive location close to Hyde Park, and the façade shines with success and money. But a beautiful façade isn't everything, apparently.

The Beatles in July 1963, shortly after moving to London. After staying at various hotels for a couple of months, they moved to a shared flat in early September. But they never had the time to set up anything that resembled a home. Tours, radio and television appearances, and recording sessions for their *With The Beatles* album, kept them busy round the clock. ▲

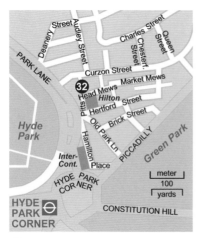

1 Curzon Square
Mayfair
Tube:
Hyde Park Corner

Curzon Square

I will now step sideways into the Seventies, but I justify my decision by the fact that the artists are very closely connected to the Sixties. They are Mama Cass of The Mamas And The Papas and Keith Moon of The Who.

I take the bus down to Hyde Park Corner and then walk a short bit northward along Park Lane to 12 Curzon Place, where the building is supposed to be. The area is being rebuilt and after an hour's search, I find out that the name of the street has been changed; the address is now 1 Curzon Square. On the fourth floor of the brown house is apartment number 9, where the both legends died in the same bed, but four years apart from each other. The apartment belonged to the American singer and song writer Harry Nilsson, but since he spent most of his time in the United States he used to sublet the flat to his friends.

Mama Cass died in bed at the age of thirtythree on July 29, 1974. At first it was thought that she had choked to death, either on a sandwich or her own vomit. But upon closer examination it was revealed that she had died of a heart attack, caused by long-term obesity combined with unsupervised crash dieting and drug abuse.

The wild drummer and party animal Keith Moon of The Who died in bed on the afternoon of September 7, 1978. After an especially rough time in California over the past three years, he had returned to London at the end of 1977, a shadow of his former self. When he died he was only thirtytwo years old, but it's still a miracle that he lived for so long. Ironically, he died of an overdose of Heminevrin, a medicine he had been prescribed to cure his alcohol abuse. The alcohol level in his blood at the time of his death corresponded to no more than a glass of wine, which he had had the night before at a party in memory of Buddy Holly, arranged by Paul McCartney. It's a double irony, since Moon had spent several years washing down handfuls of pills of assorted colours with alcoholic beverages, preferably brandy.

Keith Moon was certainly the most colourful, and perhaps even the best, drummer in rock. The epitaph on his gravestone reads "There is no substitute", which is an accurate observation; The Who were never the same again after his death. In front of the house there is a black sculpture that looks like a coffin to me, but that may just be because of my own feelings about the place.

Keith Moon with his Swedish girlfriend, Anette Walter Lax, at the première party for The Buddy Holly Story. It was Keith Moon's last evening alive. ▼

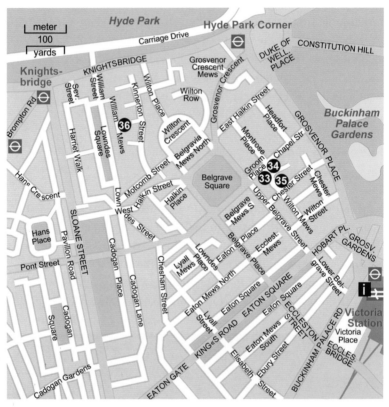

Belgravia, Knightsbridge

③③ Horse & Groom Groom Place **Tube:** Hyde Park Corner **Bus:** 8,16 to Green Park

③④ 24 Chapel Street Next to Groom Place.

③⑤ 13 Chester Street Next to Groom Place.

③⑥ Whaddon House, William Mews **Tube:** Knightsbridge Station

Belgravia

Jan Olofsson and I have decided to meet at Hyde Park Corner and from there we walk to Chapel Street, which we follow to Groom Place, a small, peaceful and beautiful inner yard. This is the location of the pub the Horse & Groom, which is shut off from people's view. If you're at Victoria Station, you may also take the buses 8 or 16 and get off at Green Park.

Horse & Groom

Jan tells me that the Horse & Groom was The Beatles' favourite pub for a couple of years and that he went there with them several times. The most memorable occasion occurred on May 19, 1967. The Sgt. Pepper album was about to be launched and Brian Epstein hosted a private party in his apartment around the corner, on 24 Chapel Street. The Beatles were invited, naturally, but so were Jan Olofsson as well as Lulu and Linda Eastman, whom Paul

Jan Olofsson's photograph of The Beatles as they're sitting on the stairs leading to Brian Epstein's flat at 24 Chapel Street. The Beatles were often there, since Epstein liked to arrange various receptions and parties in the building. ▲

McCartney had met a few days earlier. In the afternoon they first went to the Horse & Groom and had beers and whisky before they headed for the apartment. That was when Jan took a photo of the group, sitting on the stairs to the building, dressed in clothes typical of the year 1967. It's a classic picture, which has been published in several books and magazines the world over.

Brian Epstein was serving gourmet food and exclusive wines, but Jan tells me that Epstein soon disappeared from the party, annoyed by John Lennon's habit of dropping the ash from his cigarette on the floor in his elegant apartment. There was a lot of drinking at the cheerful party and in order to make it last longer Jan offered to go down to the pub and buy more whisky, which had the consequence that he passed out on Brian Epstein's bed towards the small hours.

Epstein bought the apartment in December 1964 and often arranged parties since he wanted to surround himself with people. When the American group the Four Tops visited London in November 1966, Epstein hosted a big party. Among those invited were John Lennon, George Harrison, Mick Jagger, Keith Richards, Charlie Watts,

Melody Maker
September 2, 1967 ▼

Epstein (sixth from right) with his first signings — the Beatles (left) Gerry and the Pacemakers, Billy J. Kramer and the Dakotas.

EPSTEIN

millionaire who feared loneliness

BRIAN EPSTEIN is dead and world show business has lost its most spectacularly successful manager.

In his short but fantastic career he guided the Beatles, Cilla Black, Gerry and the Pacemakers, Billy J. Kramer and others to the pinnacles of pop success. He had his failures too along the way, but they were overshadowed by the stupendous conquests of John, Paul, George and Ringo.

Epstein's career as a manager, paralleled theirs as entertainers. Before that he'd become bored with acting, window dressing, selling furniture, records and books. People often asked—did he make the Beatles or did they make him? And Epstein himself was always the first to say the Beatles would have been as big without him. But his strongpoint was his deep belief in their fabulous future when they were still unknown.

He told the world they would outstrip the great Elvis Presley and was laughed at. He was right. But, characteristically, he didn't have the last laugh. He was too polite for that.

CALCULATED

Last month, the Melody Maker ran a remarkable series of interviews with Brian Epstein. They were arranged and written by Kookie, Belgium, where Epstein's team of singers from his NEMS Enterprises had just won the European Song Contest. With candour and complete honesty he talked to the MM on three lengthy sessions.

On his possible addiction to LSD and marijuana, both of which he'd admitted sampling, he commented: "I took that risk. It was a calculated risk."

On his own failings he said: "I reproach myself most often for being bad tempered and for being mean from time to time." On failings in others he said: "I think I have overcome a very large ego so I'm very forgiving and tolerant of egomaniacs." When asked if the Beatles would have been so successful if managed by someone else he replied: "They may have been as successful, but I don't think they would have been as happy."

Asked to comment on suggestions that he'd used the Beatles to promote other artists he replied: "This is absolutely untrue. I have always been perfectly single-minded about this and I must say in fairness that the Beatles have been easy to manage." On the possibility of him marrying being remote he said: "It is one of the biggest disappointments to me because I must be missing out somewhere not having a wife and children."

Asked if he'd ever contemplated suicide he replied: "Yes. But I think I've got over that period now."

All You Need Is Love sang the Beatles to a world TV audience and, as usual, Epstein was there to listen.

Billy J. Kramer was an early NEMS success thanks in part to Epstein's personal management.

'I hope I'll never be lonely.'

Georgie Fame and Donovan, as well as Eric Burdon and Hilton Valentine of The Animals. They all admired the American group greatly and were keen to express their appreciation of their latest hit, 'Reach Out I'll Be There'.

Despite all the parties, Brian Epstein was unable to get to grips with his loneliness. He was found dead in the apartment on August 27, 1967, after overdosing on pills.

The weather is nice, so Jan and I prefer to eat and have a beer at one of the tables outside the pub. In this same place, Brian Jones used to sit in 1964, since this was his favourite pub as well, when he lived around the corner in the other direction, on 13 Chester Street.

Brian Jones lived in the basement flat behind the bars, while The Pretty Things had their dwellings on the floors above. ▼

13 Chester Street

When Mick Jagger and Keith Richards moved in together with manager Andrew Loog Oldham in the autumn of 1963, Brian Jones first chose to move in with his girlfriend, Linda Lawrence. But shortly afterwards, in April 1964, he moved into the basement flat in Chester Street.

He got the apartment thanks to The Pretty Things, who lived on the floors above his and whose record company rented the building. The Pretty Things still hadn't enjoyed a really big hit, but the Fontana record label put a lot of faith in them in their hunt for suitable rivals to The Rolling Stones. Therefore, it was almost like sleeping with the enemy when Brian Jones moved into the building, but the bands got along well: The Pretty Things' guitarist, Dick Taylor, even started his career as the bass player in an early version of The Rolling Stones.

The white Victorian buildings after Chester Street, close to Buckingham Palace, used to be inhabited mostly by people of the aristocracy, who kept their servants in the attic flats and the basements. But by the early 1960s, times had changed. Thanks to The Pretty Things, and especially their drummer, Viv Prince, 13 Chester Street was soon known as a party hangout, where wild parties were always going on. Viv Prince felt that you could never overdo the drinking or the partying.

★ NEWCOMERS TO THE CHARTS ★

'Pretty Things' hit will mean another party!

THE Pretty Things (below) used to hold great, raving parties almost every night in a house in Belgravia. Then they got thrown out and all went to live in different places.

Now they hold parties no less raving at other people's houses. They view their entry into the NME Chart at No. 17 with some pleasure in this respect.

"This means we'll be able to invite more people and more refreshment," exclaimed drummer Viv St. John Prince guardedly. Viv often refers to himself as the "Lord Mayor Of Belgravia."

Viv was in the charts once before as part of Carter-Lewis and the Southerners, when he had short hair. Now he has very long hair and is a Pretty Thing as much as Phil May, Dick Taylor, John Stax and Brian Pendleton.

I was invited to lunch with them on Monday. But when I arrived at the appointed time they were half-way to Sheffield. Instead, I ate with their managers, who are equally r-and-b minded and young.

The Pretty Things who, except for Nottingham-born Viv, come from around Dartford, make more noise on stage than most other groups. So do their fans, who fight tooth and nail to protect their idols against the kind of criticisms that comes from having long hair, being rather casual about dress and slouching about.

They don't like being compared to the Rolling Stones, although lead guitarist Dick used to play with them. They object to being called unclean and point out that their bills for hair shampoos are tremendous.

"Loon" is a word you will hear used often if in the company of the Pretty Things. I'm not quite sure what it means, but it has something to do with going places.

So I suppose we could say that on the showing of "Don't Bring Me Down," the Pretty Things are looning.   **RICHARD GREEN.**

PRETTY THINGS (l. to r.): DICK TAYLOR (lead guitar), PHIL MAY (vocals), VIV PRINCE (drums), JOHN STAX (bass guitar) and BRIAN PENDLETON (rhythm guitar).

New Musical Express
October 30, 1964   ▲

Party prone guests visiting London and the in-club the Ad Lib, were invited to come along to parties that lasted all night: Judy Garland, Rudolf Nureyev and Diana Dors are just some of the somewhat unusual guests invited by Viv Prince. Bob Dylan visited Chester Street in May 1964, invited by rhythm guitarist Brian Pendleton of The Pretty Things. Dylan liked the anarchic style of the band so much that he offered them 'Mr. Tambourine Man'…but they turned his offer down!

On the same occasion Bob Dylan also met Brian Jones and they immediately became close friends. Brian Jones and Dylan would spend hours on the phone to each other across the Atlantic, and Dylan was highly sympathetic to Brian Jones' situation in the Stones. The following year, Bob Dylan and Robbie Robertson of The Band even discussed a possible collaboration with Brian Jones, after they jammed together in a New York studio for an entire night. But Brian Jones always remained loyal to The Rolling Stones, even if he was badly treated by the band. Bob Dylan's friend, Richard Farina, also gave Brian the appalachian string instrument dulcimer, which he then used on several recordings, among them 'Lady Jane' and 'I Am Waiting'.

During the time at Chester Street, Brian Jones made desperate attempts at writing his own songs for The Rolling Stones, but his insecurity and self-criticism meant that he never dared present anything to the band. And he definitely didn't receive any encouragement from the Jagger/Richards team to make contributions. Brian Jones began feeling more and more like an outsider in the band he had once formed, and therefore he sought the company of friends outside the band, among them Viv Prince and The Pretty Things' lead singer, Phil May.

Another of his pals was Jet Harris, the celebrated bass player of The Shadows who nevertheless was fired from the band because of his wild partying. According to Harris himself, the partying was because he found it too hard to stand behind Cliff Richard onstage, knowing that Richard was having an affair with his wife. Jet Harris then began a solo career and managed to score a UK number one hit in 1963 with 'Diamonds', featuring a certain Jimmy Page on guitar. Brian Jones and Jet Harris met each other when the Stones and Harris performed at the same show in 1963. Perhaps it was both the partying and the feelings of being outsiders that brought them together.

The fallen star Vince Taylor was another of the artists that befriended Brian Jones during this time. Gordon Waller, of Peter And Gordon, also often visited Brian Jones, and in the afternoons they would have a beer in the sun at one of the wooden tables outside the Horse & Groom. In the late autumn of 1964, Brian Jones moved out and soon afterwards The Pretty Things were forced to

Brian Jones during his time at Chester Street in 1964. Here we see him with his famous eyedrop guitar, the Vox Phantom Mark III. But piano and clarinet were the first instruments he learned to play. In The Rolling Stones he was to play more than 15 different instruments. ▼

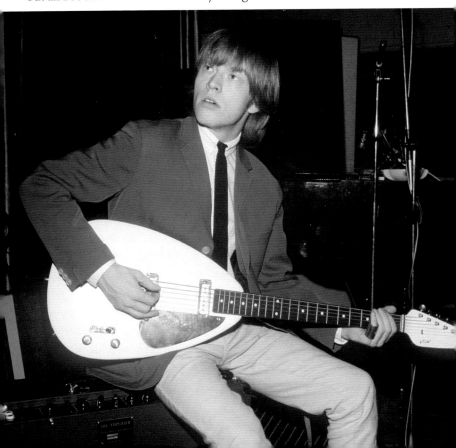

leave the house, after many complaints about late parties and police raids in the house.

Today it is peaceful and quiet in Chester Street and the buildings look like they're inhabited by the tenants they were once built for: the British aristocracy. The Horse & Groom pub is small and simple, but friendly, and with its peaceful location it's easy to understand that both The Beatles and Brian Jones liked it here. It looks like it's going to rain and so we finish our second beer before we move along. Jan heads for home, while I open my umbrella and start walking towards Knightsbridge.

Knightsbridge

Whaddon House

With Sheraton Park Tower as a landmark I head towards

Brian Epstein's flat with a balcony was on the top floor of this five-storey building, in the foreground of the picture. George Harrison and Ringo Starr had their balcony at the other end of the building, at the far left. ▼

yet another quiet inner yard. This one has a boom gate in front of the entrance, but that's no problem for a pedestrian.

William Mews mainly consists of low single-family houses, but at the far end there is a brown five-storey brick building: *Whaddon House*. As I approach the building an old man says, "That's where they sat" and points towards the balcony at the top floor of the building. He says it before I have the chance to ask, since the residents are used to visitors from all over the world and know what people are curious about. At the end of December 1963, The Beatles' manager Brian Epstein

Ringo Starr 1964 ◄

moved in on the top floor of the building, with a balcony at the far corner. A week later, Ringo Starr and George Harrison moved into a luxuriously furnished flat next to Epstein, in the opposite corner, and in front of the house, George Harrison's Jaguar E-type used to be parked.

There were always a steady stream of guests here, invited by Epstein. After The Beatles' first tour of the US, Epstein held a big party on August 12, 1964. Apart from The Beatles, the guests included Keith Richards, Mick Jagger, The Searchers, Alma Cogan, Cilla Black, Peter And Gordon, Tommy Steele, George Martin and Judy Garland; a mix of the old and the new times, in other words.

It was at Whaddon House that a nervous Ringo prepared himself for his wedding to Liverpool girl Maureen Cox on February 11, 1965. He chose a light grey suit with four buttons, a white shirt, a blue tie and ankle-high boots. Epstein helped out by putting a white carnation in the button hole and then Ringo was ready. After the wedding Maureen also moved into the flat, but the couple immediately began looking for their own apartment and shortly afterwards they moved to Montagu Square.

However, no visitors seem to be aware that another rock legend lived in the house a couple of years later: Steve Marriott of The Small Faces. But he just lived here for a few months, before the neighbours as usual had enough of the loud music and the late night parties. Steve Marriott had constant problems with his neighbours – or rather, they with him – and was forced to move from place to place. His next dwelling was in Chiswick, where he wrote a song about his complaining neighbours, 'Lazy Sunday', which was a huge hit in 1968.

Steve Marriott was a person who could never keep a low profile. Much later, in 1974, when Mick Taylor was to be replaced in The Rolling Stones, Keith Richards wanted Steve Marriott to join the band. Before the audition, Keith called Steve and gave him some good advice: he was told to stay in the background, not to move and to keep quiet. It worked for a few songs, but finally Steve was so caught up in the music that he found it impossible to hold back and burst out in a scream of joy. And so, that chance was killed!

He quickly learned that the spotlight belonged to Mick Jagger and that no-one is allowed to occupy too much space when Jagger is onstage, which Brian Jones also had experienced. On the other hand, it's hard to see how it could have worked having Steve Marriott in the band. Firstly, he was by nature too much of a front man himself, and he would have been unable to subordinate himself to Mick Jagger in the long run. Also, there was too much rock'n'roll in Marriott for him to fit in the disciplined and well-oiled Rolling Stones machinery.

As I'm standing there, looking at the not very attractive building, I think about what a strange coincidence it is that Steve Marriott ended up in the same house that George and Ringo once lived in, considering the size of London.

Pimlico

I walk back onto Sloane Street and take the C1 bus to Victoria Coach Station, where I get off, cross the street and walk to the district of Pimlico, not far from the Thames. The nearest underground station is Victoria Station, if you're arriving from another direction than I am. The Small Faces are without a doubt one of the most influential groups of the Sixties and for me it's a must to visit the place where they lived together.

Westmoreland Terrace

22 Westmoreland
Terrace
Pimlico
Tube:
Victoria Station
Bus: 24

As I arrive at 22 *Westmoreland Terrace* in Pimlico, I'm surprised by the still and quiet streets. The area has an atmosphere of middle class residential district, which doesn't
quite match up with young guys from the lower class East
End. Although the street is fairly close to Victoria Station,
there is hardly any urban feeling to the area; low, white
houses, very few shops and no noise from traffic or people. It's an environment that you associate with families
with children, but hardly with one of the hottest bands
in Europe during the Sixties.

It was on Boxing Day 1965 that Steve Marriott, Ronnie
Lane and Ian "Mac" McLagan moved together in the small
four-storey house in Westmoreland Terrace. The band's
drummer, Kenney Jones, was forced to stay with his par-

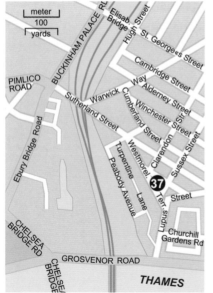

ents; he had only recently turned
seventeen and they felt he was too
young to leave home. In the Small
Faces household there was also a
German housekeeper named Liesel,
who was later the housekeeper for
Ron Wood. They didn't have to worry about cleaning or cooking, which
was like heaven for a few young kids
from London's East End. Don Arden,
the band's manager, had got them
the house, since it was more practical to have everybody living in one
place.

On the ground floor there were
two small rooms, where Ronnie and

Ian moved in, and above them there was a big living room. On the top floor of the house there was a bathroom and a bedroom that Steve secured for himself. In the basement there was a kitchen, which was also used as a mini-studio and contained several tape recorders, guitars, speakers, Mac's Hammond organ and an old piano. In there, Steve Marriott and Ronnie Lane wrote many of the group's songs. The team of Marriott/Lane was one of the very best song writing teams, with songs such as 'Tin Soldier', 'All Or Nothing', 'Itchycoo Park' and 'Lazy Sunday'.

Although the band had enjoyed a reasonably-sized hit during the autumn with their first single, 'Whatcha Gonna Do About It', this was still very early in their successful career. But they were already so popular that they couldn't go out partying in public, and therefore wild parties in Westmoreland Terrace became a habit between all the gigs. Among the many regular guests were names such as Steve Winwood, Marianne Faithfull, Georgie Fame and naturally Eric Burdon – he never missed a party. There would often be so many people in the house that Steve Marriott had to write new songs in the toilet.

The band's nightly partying was certainly fun for them, but not so much fun for the neighbours. The neighbours also had problems with the group's fans, who would gather outside the house all day long and scream every time they caught a glimpse of a group member in the window. The fans used to disappear around 9 pm, and at

The Small Faces had a truly appropriate name: none of them was taller than 5 ft 6 in. The picture was taken in 1966, when they made their major breakthrough. Left–right: Organist Ian McLagan, drummer Kenney Jones, singer and guitarist Steve Marriott and bass player Ronnie Lane. After Steve Marriott's defection in 1969, the other members formed The Faces together with Rod Stewart and Ron Wood.   ▶

New Musical Express July 29, 1966   ▼

11 the band headed for the studio to start new recordings.

With hits such as 'Sha La La La Lee' and the self-written 'All Or Nothing', they became a group that everybody talked about in 1966. They hated 'Sha La La La Lee'; it was recorded to please the group's manager and their record company, who were eager to get a hit quickly. When Steve Marriott wrote 'All Or Nothing', he was thinking of Rod Stewart's girlfriend, Sue Oliver, who later also became Steve's first wife. The song topped the charts in a number of countries.

During the time in the house in Westmoreland Terrace, they wrote a number of further songs, among them 'My Mind's Eye'. It also became a big hit, although the song was really a demo version. However, without consulting the band, manager Don Arden and the record company decided that it should be released as a single immedi-

ately. That was one of the reasons they decided to leave their manager in early 1967, which also meant the end of the shared house in Pimlico. When they moved out, they left behind almost everything; there were droves of shoes and clothes from their shopping rounds in Carnaby Street. The Small Faces literally left their fashionable clothes behind and entered a new phase of their development, which would result in the brilliant album *Ogden's Nut Gone Flake*.

As I'm standing there contemplating the house, the present owner comes out and asks if he can be of any assistance. I explain that I'm looking at the house because of The Small Faces. He proceeds to tell me that he's been trying to get English Heritage to put up a blue memorial plaque on the house for a long while, but they have said no. Fortunately, it's not up to English Heritage to decide which groups are important in rock history!

Before I leave Westmoreland Terrace I take the opportunity to visit the simple local pub at the corner, The White Ferry House. Fortunately, wherever you are in London, you never have to walk hungry or thirsty.

The Small Faces' first album contained seven self-written songs and was a great success. It reached number three on the UK chart in May 1966. However, the nice and "pop-friendly" sleeve was completely inappropriate. The music was far from ingratiating and polite, but was mainly tough R&B, soul and pop with a personal touch. ◄

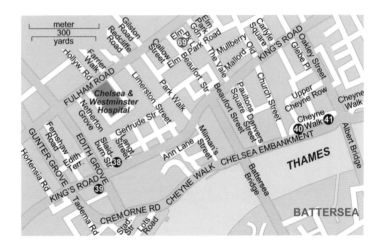

㊳ Wetherby Arms

㊴ 102 Edith Grove

㊵ 48 Cheyne Walk

㊶ 3 Cheyne Walk

㊱ 7 Elm Park Lane

Chelsea

After a while I take the short walk back to Buckingham Palace Road, enter bus number 11 and then travel along King's Road in Chelsea. If you're in Trafalgar Square you may walk to the Strand or Whitehall and take the number 11 bus from there.

King's Road

Together with Carnaby Street, King's Road was the leading fashion street in London in the Sixties. As early as 1955, the fashion designer Mary Quant opened Bazaar, the first boutique in the area, and this was where Quant would achieve her fame by creating the first mini-skirt. At World's End, at the end of King's Road, the Granny Takes A Trip shop opened in the mid-Sixties. It was one of the many imaginative and exclusive boutiques that opened in the area after the tourists had invaded Carnaby Street and mod fashion had become mainstream.

Sargasso Sea, I Was Lord Kitchener's Valet and Hung On You were other boutiques, all of them mainly featuring exclusive clothes of their own design for those who really wanted to make an impression and could afford to pay for it. The Beatles, The Rolling Stones, The Who, Donovan, The Move, Syd Barrett of Pink Floyd and Jimi Hendrix were frequent clients in the boutiques, where the price of one single shirt could be a normal monthly wage.

On 152 King's Road, there are shops and a pizzeria today, but in the Sixties the building was known as an artists' colony. In the basement there was a night club called The Pheasantry, which presented live music.

Cream's second album, *Disraeli Gears*, was released in November 1967. The sleeve was a truly psychedelic creation, made by Eric Clapton's flat mate, Martin Sharp. ▲

In the spring of 1967, Eric Clapton – at the time a member of the super group Cream – moved into the upper floor apartment. The underground artist Martin Sharp was one of the people with whom he shared the big apartment. Clapton and Martin Sharp had met one night at the Speakeasy when Sharp wrote down the lyrics for 'Tales Of Brave Ulysses' on a napkin, in the hope that it would lead somewhere. The lyrics turned into a song that ended up on the Cream album *Disraeli Gears*, and Martin Sharp was also entrusted with the task of designing the album sleeve. Later he also did the sleeve for the group's *Wheels Of Fire* album, as well as well-known psychedelic posters of Jimi Hendrix, Bob Dylan and Donovan.

Cream was mostly on tour in 1967–1968, but Eric Clapton still found time to strengthen his friendship with George Harrison. Together with George he wrote the song 'Badge' for Cream while he was living here. The two of them worked together regularly, for example on George Harrison's solo album *All Things Must Pass*.

Although King's Road is not at all what it used to be, recently it has become a little more lively again. When I sit at the front of the double-decker bus, I have a good view of the street. As I get off the bus at World's End, near the Edith Grove crossing, I take the opportunity to walk across the street to 500 King's Road.

Wetherby Arms

This used to be the location of the pub *Wetherby Arms*, which was The Rolling Stones' rehearsal room during the late autumn and winter of 1962–1963. There are no traces left of the pub and on the premises there is now a betting agency. Wetherby Arms was where Bill Wyman auditioned for the group round December 9, 1962, in front of a fairly uninterested Brian Jones, Mick Jagger and Keith Richards. At the time, The Rolling Stones consisted of Jones, Jagger, Richards, Ian Stewart on piano and Tony Chapman on drums. Chapman was the one who had told the band about his friend Bill Wyman.

Wetherby Arms
Chelsea/
World's End
500 Kings Road
Tube: Earls Court,
Bus: 328
Bus: Nr. 11 from
Trafalgar Square

Ian Stewart greeted Wyman kindly and Mick Jagger made an effort to come up with a few polite phrases, while the other two, Brian Jones and Keith Richards, thought Wyman looked like a real geek and continued drinking beer at the bar. But when they saw Wyman's speakers and amplifier they immediately became more interested. It was the type of equipment they could only dream of; they could never have afforded to buy anything like that. Still, they remained sceptical. Bill Wyman was much older, wore trousers with high turn-ups and blue pointed suede shoes and they also

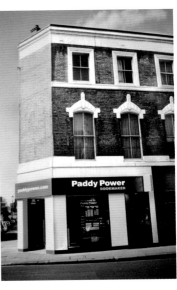

NEW MUSICAL EXPRESS *   Friday, May 1, 1964

1964 STONE AGE

A NEW SERIES FEATURING ROLLING STONES INDIVIDUALLY STARTING WITH . . .

Bill Wyman

WHILE Mick shuffle-shakes about on stage. And Brian thumps a tambourine for all he's worth. And Keith runs backwards with his guitar . . . Bill just stands there and grins through it all !

Holding his guitar so erect that it is almost always parallel to his body, Bill seems oblivious to the pandemonium that is breaking out all around him.

Even when a gift, hurled by an ecstatic fan, hits him on the head, he shows no sign of noticing it.

But that's just the way Bill is. He takes his work as seriously as being a Rolling Stone allows. Yet he has a sense of humour that at times breaks out and sends people into fits of laughter.

That is a typical Stone—always doing the unexpected.

Perhaps the most unexpected thing Bill ever did was to join the Rolling Stones in the first place. It wasn't a thing that he set out to do deliberately from the moment he first heard of them. And if you had told his employers that he would one day be a member of the group whose album was going to shift the Beatles from the No. 1 spot, they would have laughed at you.

"When I left Beckenham Grammar School, I hadn't the faintest idea what I wanted to do," he admitted, as we sat listening to a recording of the Stones playing "Carol."

"I didn't excel at anything, except

By Richard Green

maths. Funny that, being good at maths.

"I went to a firm in Lewisham and started as nothing in a little office job. I really was nothing. I got all the odds and ends that other people didn't want to do."

Then things began to happen. Bill got promoted to a storekeeping job with the same business. Everyone was happy, and things were going well. Then Bill left.

"I'd been there two years when I decided to pack it in," he went on. "I left and went to work for a big department store in Penge."

That was okay, and for a time both he and the bosses got on fine. Then one day—Bill left.

"The first place asked me to go back for about £3 a week more, so I agreed. I was soon in line for a good job. There was one above me, then the manager. I had a good future, and they all asked me not to leave when I began to get on the Rolling Stones kick."

For some time, Bill had been

interested in the Stones and the kind of music they were producing. That was his sort of music, and he was glad to find a bunch of youngsters who played it the right way, his way.

His hair got longer and longer. Visitors to the firm where he was working often threw curious glances at "the boy with the hair," as they called him.

"Eventually, it got so bad with my hair that the management said I would have to make up my mind between the firm and the Stones. I chose the Stones. That surprised the boss !" he exclaimed.

"I was playing with a rock 'n' roll group in Penge before I saw an advert. for a bass guitarist with the Stones. I just went along, practised with them and sat in for a few numbers. We went through loads of tunes and messed about a lot. It wasn't a real audition," he recalled.

"They didn't like me, but I had a good amplifier, and they were badly in need of amplifiers at that time !

"So they kept me on. Later, when they were going to get rid of me, I think I clicked or something, and I stayed. I must have just fitted in. You'd better ask them about that."

"Charlie Watts, who until this time had been silently listening to Bill talk, came in with : "You're no good now !"

Bill smiled, then spoke about his

"double life," which he led until just a few months ago.

"Even though I was playing with the Stones, I hadn't left my other job by then," he began. "I was nearly dead, though. I'd be working with the Stones until 2 am, then I'd go home and have to be up again at 6 am to go to the other place. Half the time, didn't know where I was. So in the end I left my firm and concentrated on the Stones."

But even after he joined the group full-time, he didn't find it all easy going.

"R-and-b clubs were dead in those days and sometimes we'd get hardly any people coming along to listen. I has been a gradual building up of interest. Now, it's better known at over, and clubs get packed ages before we appear.

"But we still get those people who don't want to know us. They pretend we don't exist and just ignore us. They don't like it because we don't conform. But why should we ?"

TRENDSETTERS LTD. PARLOPHONE 'In A Big Way'
AVON ENTERTAINMENTS, Durham House, Bournemouth. Tel. 21370

THE CONTINENTAL *DANCING CLUB*
HERTFORD ROAD, EDMONTON, N.9   FULLY LICENSED

| 5/- FRIDAY, 8th MAY | 7/6 SAT., 9th MAY | 5/- SUN., 10th MAY |
| VINCE EAGER and the SILHOUETTES | BERN ELLIOTT and the FENMEN | THE MARAUDERS |

EVERY MONDAY THE FABULOUS FLEEREKKERS 3/-

Singers!
LESSONS BY POST

Let me help YOU to sing like our MODERN SINGING STARS. TEN carefully prepared postal lessons based on 15 years experience, by Bob Anthony, Top London West End Teacher of Modern Singing, trains you in the phrasing of your own home ! Learn all about Recording, Mike Technique, Cabaret, Rhythm, Voice Control and Breathing, etc. Send 10/- Now for the first lesson, or £4.10.0 for complete course, or write for details sent without obligation :
BOB ANTHONY,
14, Hanover Street, London, W.1

New Musical Express May 1, 1964 ▲

thought his tastes in music were lousy. But after Wyman had bought them fish and chips they became less resistant. Good equipment and money for food finally convinced them that Bill Wyman was the right man for the band. But soon they realised that Wyman also was an excellent bass player. At Wetherby Arms, the classic line-up of The Rolling Stones was formed, when Charlie Watts joined the group in January 1963.

These days, this part of Chelsea is in good shape, but forty years ago it was badly worn and rough.

Edith Grove

It is with a certain sense of solemnity that I approach the building at 102 Edith Grove; I have read so many stories about it. The house has two pillars on each side of the steps that lead up to the red-painted door, and an iron fence in front of the steps down to the basement. Today there are door bells for the apartments, but if you were to visit the Stones during their time here, you had to knock twice on the front door, which meant that you wanted to see the people on the second floor.

39
102 Edith Grove
Chelsea/
World´s End
Tube: Earls Court,
Bus: 328
Bus: Nr. 11 from
Trafalgar Square

It was in September 1962 that Mick Jagger and Keith Richards, both of whom were nineteen years old, and Brian Jones, twenty, moved in together. Mick and Keith came directly from their parents' home, but Brian had a lot more experience. He had moved around a great deal and already had three children with three different women. The first girl was only fourteen years old when she became pregnant and the scandal forced Brian to move to Germany and Scandinavia for a while. When he returned, at the age of eighteen, he immediately made a married woman pregnant, and when the third child was born he was nineteen. And all this happened before The Rolling Stones had even been formed!

The apartment lacked central heating. A simple tub was the only kind of bathroom they had, while the toilet was communal and located on the staircase. The brown wall paper was peeling and all mouldy, and the paint was hanging in chunks from the sooty ceiling, where a naked light bulb was dangling. In the room there was a worn-down double bed in one corner (usually covered by dirty clothes), a chair with only three functioning legs and at the window there was a small table with cigarette burns. On the floor lay a frayed carpet ingrained with dirt, a pile of records and assorted garbage. The idyll was completed by an old radio gramophone, cluttered up with records and cigarette stubs. In the bedroom there were two beds, a bedside table and a wardrobe where the clothes were all piled up on the floor.

The winter of 1962–1963 was the coldest within living memory and since they lacked the money to heat up the apartment, the floors and the damp walls were ice cold. Brian Jones and Keith Richards were unemployed, while Mick Jagger still went to the London School Of Economics. To keep warm, Brian and Keith played their guitars all day long, sometimes without even getting out of bed. They listened to songs by Robert Johnson, Elmore James, Jimmy Reed, Muddy Waters and Chuck Berry, which they then tried to copy.

This was when the Stones created the special sound they became known for, partly through the conditions they were living under during the winter. They developed a loose style that was very tight at the same time, where the guitar playing was interwoven to form a complete unit, and both of them switched between solo and rhythm guitar. Sometimes they would only leave the apartment to beg for food from the neighbours or to steal their empty bottles to get money for cigarettes and coins for the electricity meter.

XPRESS   Friday, August 23, 1963

ROLLING STONES R and B CHAMPS

HE Rolling Stones is a London group with the Liverpool sound, according to some. Rhythm-and-blues fans say they are the only British combo which bears comparison h American r-and-b units.

heir own opinion is simply that they are unique! Spokesman n Jones, who sings and plays harmonica, says: " We believe we sound like ourselves and no one else."

ney are, they claim, first and fore- a rhythm-and-blues group. If refer to them as a beat outfit, frown. If you venture to est that they play rock 'n' roll, positively glower.

appearances on stage they seem resemble long-haired dervishes. the haircuts? Again Brian s explains: " We've had it like for ages," he says patting his luxurious bob cut. Though we didn't grow it this as a gimmick, we see no reason we should cut it off to con- ."

rhaps this is the key to the es. They believe in complete viduality and free expression.

Not that they are beatniks. They aren't!

Their music reflects this freedom. All keen r-and-b fans, they started off playing solid, earthy Muddy Waters stuff. Lately, though, their repertoire has included more generally popular material, by people like Chuck Berry and the Drifters.

Again, this is not because they have been pressured into " going commercial," but, they insist, it is a natural progression.

" I suppose you could say we've made some concessions," says Mick Jagger, lead vocalist and harmonica, " but we still play what we like.

" We consider ourselves profes- sional-amateurs. We still have the enthusiasm to treat the business as an enjoyable pastime, but also the pro- fessionalism to realise that you can't turn up late for dates and that sort of thing.

" We are bound to change. In a way it is already happening, but the changes will be natural. We consider ourselves a flexible group, and as we change, so will our music. In this

respect we resemble a jazz group." Until a couple of weeks ago, they were purely a club group. They had no experience of playing in theatres or dance halls. Since " Come On " entered the chart, though, they have been engaged on a continuous series of ballroom dates.

" We were rather worried about playing these halls," confides Brian. " We had suspicions that some of the hard cases would start taking the . . . er, rise, out of our haircuts. They do a little for the first number, sometimes.

" You know the sort of thing. The boys yell ' Get a haircut ! ', and the girls go ' Ooh ! Who do they think they are ? '

" After the first number, though, they are raving with us. So far, we've raved only in clubs and dance halls, but now we're looking forward to raving on our first theatre tour, with the Everly Brothers, in a few weeks.

" For us, the big thrill is that Bo Diddley will be on the bill ! He's been one of our great influences.

" It won't be a case of the pupils competing with the master, though. We're dropping from our act on the tour all the Bo Diddley numbers we sing." **CHRIS WILLIAMS.**

To amuse each other in the boredom and the cold, Brian and Keith used to pull faces at each other. The worst one was made by Brian, who called it "nanker". I'm only men- tioning it here because "nanker" later became a part of the pseudonym Nanker/Phelge, which the Stones listed as the composers of their first self-written songs, among them 'Play With Fire' and 'Little By Little'. Phelge was the surname of their new lodger, James – usually called

New Musical Express
August 23, 1963 ▲

Jimmy – who moved into the apartment in January 1963 and contributed to the rent through his salary as a printer. By then they had bullied their previous lodger, Richard Hattrell (Brian Jones' old friend from Cheltenham), back to his home town.

During this period Brian Jones was the band's undisputed leader. He guided them musically and was the driving force behind forming a band; he was constantly looking for gigs, writing letters to record companies and newspapers, and handled all negotiations with the promoters. But the Stones hardly had any gigs during their first period together. However, after Bill Wyman and then Charlie Watts joined the band, the number of engagements increased to several per week, beginning in January 1963. At this time, Charlie Watts would sometimes stay in the apartment as well, when he couldn't face the journey home late at night.

When The Beatles heard about them and went to see one of their gigs at the Crawdaddy Club, on April 14, 1963, they went back with the band to Edith Grove. It was the first time the two groups met and although The Beatles already were established, they were all curious about each other. They mostly talked about what kind of music they played and what they liked. John Lennon and Brian Jones were discussing harmonicas; Brian wanted to know what type of harmonica John used on 'Love Me Do' and John wanted a few pointers on how to actually use a harmonica. "You really play it, I just blow in and out," he maintained. Although there was no furniture to sit on, The Beatles stayed until four or five in the morning. This was when the friendship between the two groups was established.

The Rolling Stones' popularity grew quickly during the spring and summer, and Brian, Keith and Mick were finally able to leave the rat-hole in Edith Grove in September 1963. They left the apartment as it was; they took their records with them, but left the old worn-out clothes behind in the apartment. The move also meant the end of the era when Brian Jones was the leader and driving force in the band.

I walk back for a few yards until I reach King's Road, to see if the worker's café that the Stones called "Earnie's" is still there. This is where they usually went when they had scraped together enough money to buy food. The café is still there, surprisingly enough, although it is called John-

The Rolling Stones dressed up in new outfits at the Crawdaddy Club in early May 1963. If the future was looking bright for most of the Stones, prospects were far bleaker for Ian Stewart (back row, far right). He had just been told that his style was wrong for the Stones, according to the group's new manager, Andrew Loog Oldham. Instead, he was offered work as the group's road manager and to play the piano on their records. ▲

The Rolling Stones in early May 1963, when they had just acquired a manager as well as a recording contract. Their manager, Andrew Loog Oldham, quickly provided them with black turtle-neck sweaters, which they got rid of equally quickly. The picture was taken at Embankment, just a few hundred yards from their dwellings on Edith Grove ▲

ny's Fish Bar today. It looks like no-one has touched the building since the days of the Stones' visits here. The worn façade gives you a hint of what this area must have looked like in the early Sixties. However, the Chelsea Drugstore is gone; this was where Mick Jagger and James Phelge bought medicine for Mick's sore throat before a gig in the spring of 1963. That incident may have formed the basis for the lines "I went down to the Chelsea Drugstore ... standing in line with Mr. Jimmy" which turned up in 'You Can't Always Get What You Want' many years later.

I turn back and walk down Edith Grove towards the Thames, following the river along Embankment. This was where the first promotional pictures of the Stones were taken, after they'd signed their record deal with Decca in

May 1963. Along the river there are houseboats, adorned with rows of flower-boxes, and I'm wondering whether they are the same boats that were here in those days.

After a short walk I reach the part of Cheyne Walk where Mick Jagger and Keith Richards later bought houses, when they had become established international stars. It's not too far from Edith Grove, but there are millions of pounds between the two worlds. The location of the two houses in Chelsea, with a clear view of the Thames, is among the most attractive in London.

Cheyne Walk

Cheyne Walk
Chelsea
Tube: Sloane Square
Bus: 319, 19

Mick Jagger, Marianne Faithfull and her son Nicholas moved into the beautiful 16th Century house on 48 *Cheyne Walk* after Mick had bought the house for £40,000 in the spring of 1968. An astronomical sum in those days, but

the two of them wanted to live according to their social and financial status. Their friend and antique dealer Christopher Gibbs helped out with the interior decoration, furnishing the house with exclusive antique furniture from his own store and genuine Persian carpets on the floors.

When you look at the white, fashionable house, it's kind of funny to think that it was here and not in Edith Grove that Mick Jagger wrote most of the lyrics for 'Street Fighting Man'. At the back of the garden Mick Jagger had a recording studio built, which he also used when he learned to play the guitar. During the three years

169

that Mick Jagger lived in the house permanently, The Rolling Stones released the
successful albums *Beggars Banquet*, *Let It Bleed*,
Get Yer Ya-Ya's Out (a live album) and *Sticky
Fingers*. In 1971 The Rolling Stones moved
to France for one year for tax reasons, but
Mick Jagger kept the house in Cheyne Walk
until the late Seventies.

Just a few hundred yards away, on 3 *Cheyne
Walk*, Keith Richards bought a house for
£50,000 in May 1969. That summer he
moved in together with his girlfriend,
Anita Pallenberg. The early 18th Century
house, which was previously owned by
the conservative politician Anthony Nut-
ting, now had to adjust itself to the fact that the rebel and
rock icon Keith Richards installed himself in the rooms.
On the first floor there was a beautiful 18th Century parlour with wood-panelled walls, which Anita Pallenberg
turned into something that looked like a Moroccan opi-
um den. In the living room on the ground floor there was
a large piano painted in a flower pattern.

In the summer of 1968, when The Byrds played in London, Keith Richards and Gram Parsons were very close
friends; a truly deep friendship that lasted until Parson's
death in 1973. After the England visit, The Byrds' tour
was headed for South Africa, but Keith Richards and Mick
Jagger convinced Gram Parsons that this was unwise because of the apartheid system. It all ended with Parsons
leaving both the tour and The Byrds. The country rocker
Gram Parsons instead moved to Keith Richards' coun-

try estate, Redlands, for the summer, where the two of them played and discussed music round the clock, mostly country and blues. When Keith Richards moved to the house in Cheyne Walk, Gram started hanging out there, always with a guitar in hand or sitting at the piano in the living room. He taught Keith Richards most everything about country music and its different styles, but also to play the piano and to use it for song writing.

Although Keith Richards was increasingly caught up in drug abuse, he was now in his most creative period in The Rolling Stones. Shortly before he moved in, between May and July, the group had recorded the Let It Bleed album, with Keith Richards as the musical driving force, and at the same time he was largely responsible for writing the hit single 'Honky Tonk Women'. Inspired by Gram Parsons, Keith began writing more country-influ-

After a pretentious psychedelic excursion in 1967, The Rolling Stones went back to their roots in 1968 with the single 'Jumping Jack Flash' and the Beggars Banquet *album. Many of the songs on that LP and the following album,* Let It Bleed, *were worked out by Mick Jagger and Keith Richards in the studio behind the house. (New Musical Express Annual 1969)* ▼

Jumping Jack
was what they
do best

"I've deliberately refrained from impressing any of my own musical ideas on the Stones and it's worked," said Jimmy. "They've really got it all back together — 'Jumping Jack Flash'—is what they really are. It's what they do best—first class rock and roll!"

Having proved what a little bit of group therapy can do the Stones were now into their album material and if "Sympathy for the Devil"—is not one of the most brilliant things Jagger and Richard have written I am sadly mistaken.

Mick perched attentively on a stool in the control room and watched for my reactions as I heard some of the playback. We got well into our reporters' and pop stars' game.

"The flip-side of 'Jack Flash' is probably the most original thing we've done," said Mick. "That's 'Good Of The Moon'—I expect that to do well in America."

Why?

"Because it is a toe tapping, knee twitching, jog-along, country and western influenced mid-tempo shuffler," said Mick with touching sincerity.

Would there be any love songs on the new album?

"Oh yus—lots of that—plenty of that!" said Mick reassuringly.

Plenty of good solid beat?

Mick nods his head violently and indicates much beat with a stamping of his foot.

All smiles from BRIAN, MICK, CHARLIE, KEITH and BILL, backstage at the NME Pollwinner's concert in May.

During the shooting of the film at the studio there seemed to be dozens of extras and hangers-on among the film crew—half the Chelsea set appeared to wander in with them. Mick apparently did not know who half the assembled people were but made a special point of saying "Goodnight" to everyone. Even those who were not leaving.

A song would suddenly come together in apparently the most haphazard fashion in the studio and the Stones would all stroll back to the studio to hear the playback. The thundering of drums through one speaker, piano crashing chords through another and Keith's traumatic electric guitar on another. The sounds die away.

Jagger looks critically at Keith: "It's much too polite!" he says.

"We could distort the piano," suggests Keith.

"Where's Nicky?" asks Jagger referring to their augmented pianist. He finds him sitting some few feet away. "It's not YAHHHHHH! enough," he informs Nicky distorting his face into a grimace of distaste. Nicky nods understandingly.

In a rare moment of quiet which usually precedes the lull before the electrical storm, Charlie waxes philosophical.

"Pop music runs in cycles," he says. "You can't bring back an era that is dead. If the Beatles went to Liverpool now there would be no need of police cordons and roads blocked off to prevent fans getting at them. The times have changed. There are two kids waiting for us outside the studios at this minute.

"A year ago there were ten and year before that twenty. You've got to change with the times. We stand or fall by our product now."

And that folks is what the Stones are doing now—rolling with the times but still with their heads down charging the Establishment and the big fat man with the cigar who is the epitome of their protest. The Rolling Stones do not protest to be right—they merely defend their right to be wrong!

enced songs for The Rolling Stones, among them classics such as 'Wild Horses', 'Dead Flowers' and 'Sweet Virginia'. As a favour to his friend, Keith allowed Gram Parsons to record 'Wild Horses' before the Stones, who didn't release their version until 1971. According to Keith Richards, he wrote 'Wild Horses' to express his feelings when he had to leave his new-born son Marlon behind and go on an extensive tour of the USA with the band in the autumn of 1969.

While the band was on tour, Marianne Faithfull and Anita Pallenberg sat behind the heavy curtains in the house, injecting heroin. When Keith Richards returned after the tour was completed in December 1969, he also became heavily addicted to heroin, an addiction that almost put both him and The Rolling Stones in the grave many times. The house gradually turned into a dope den, where shady characters wandered about while Keith and Anita often lay collapsed on the floor. It would take ten years before Keith Richards managed to rid himself of his heroin addiction, and during those years it was mainly Mick Jagger who was responsible for the group and its survival. It was the kind of loyalty neither of them afforded Brian Jones in the spring of 1969, when they fired him because his drug abuse had made him unreliable.

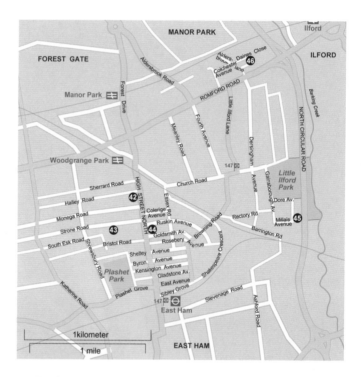

East Ham, Manor Park

42 **J 60 Music Bar**
43 **308 Strone Road**
44 **Ruskin Arms**
45 **Itchycoo Park**
46 **9 Daines Close**

East London

The District Line underground train takes me to the mythical East End and the traditional lower class areas of the eastern parts of London. The East End was where the American author Jack London went in 1902, disguised as a tramp, to depict the terrible circumstances the very poorest population in England were living under. His findings were published in the book The People Of The Abyss. This was also the area in London that was hit the hardest by the German bombings during the Second World War, when more than 15,000 people died and 94,000 houses were destroyed in the East End. The aim was to bring the English people down on their knees, but the effect was rather the opposite. A poor and tough area to grow up in, but also an area with a lot of solidarity, where people would support each other when needed.

The Small Faces is one of the few groups of the Sixties who came from these parts of London, but the guitar virtuoso Peter Green also grew up here. It was quite unusual for working class kids from the East End to challenge the norms and conquer the heart of the city, which was located in the smarter West End. But during the Sixties

SMALL FACES

NEW to the charts

FOUR boys from London's East End make their chart début this week with " Watcha Gonna Do About It " which enters the NME Chart at No. 27.

The group was formed by Ronnie " Plonk " Lane, who plays bass guitar. When Plonk left school he started working in a fairground and took up playing guitar in his spare time, becoming quite efficient.

The SMALL FACES (l to r) STEVE MARRIOT, RONNIE LANE, JIMMY WINSTON and KENNY JONES.

He decided that the only way to get on was to form a group but he had difficulty finding a drummer. Plonk's brother suggested Kenny Jones, who at that time was playing in a pub. Kenny joined Plonk and formed a friendship which has lasted through several groups up until the present Small Faces.

Jimmy Winston, who plays guitar and organ, started playing guitar while he was still at school. When he was 16 he met a film producer who helped him get small parts in TV and film advertisements. He appeared in the film " Two Left Feet."

Lead guitarist Steve Marriot has also had acting experience. When he was 12 his father took him along to the auditions which were being held for Lionel Bart's " Oliver." Steve passed the audition and stayed with the show for a year and a half.

After " Oliver," Steve went to the Italia Conti Drama School and while there appeared in films and TV, including a part in a " Dixon Of Dock Green " episode   N.D.

*New Musical Express
September 3, 1965 ▲*

this suddenly became possible, and it didn't just apply to musicians. Other famous names from the East End were the successful photographers David Bailey, Brian Duffy and Terence Donovan, the actor Terence Stamp, the playwright Harold Pinter and the creator of the new hairstyle for Sixties women, Vidal Sassoon. But the tough conditions in the East End also created the notorious Kray Twins, who were the major gangster leaders in London during the Sixties.

The sign advertising Hammond organs is the only clue that this was once a music store. ▶

East Ham, Manor Park

After thirty minutes I exit the old underground station in East Ham and I'm struck by the contrasts of what I see in

176

front of me. East Ham still looks very much like an old English working class area, but there are plenty of people from countries such as Pakistan and Bangladesh. This means that the traditional pubs you usually see in every street corner are not there, and instead there are rows of vegetable grocers and small shops with signs in Urdu, Bengali or other languages. But although the area is old and worn it seems to be treated with respect, and there are no signs of graffiti or litter anywhere

I walk along the main street, High Street North, towards Manor Park, and after a while I reach my first destination.

J 60 Music Bar

445 High Street North in Manor Park was once the location of the music store *J 60 Music Bar*. Here, a meeting once took place between two young men, which was to be very important for the formation of The Small Faces. J 60 sold musical instruments and Steve Marriott was working here on Saturdays, starting January 2, 1965. The shop was popular among young musicians, since the staff was knowledgeable and there was a good chance they might meet likeminded musicians.

Shortly after Steve began working at J60, Ronnie Lane entered the shop together with his father. Ronnie had decided

J 60 Music Bar
East Ham/
Manor Park
445 High Street
North
Tube:
East Ham

Ronnie "Plonk" Lane
with his bass guitar
Harmony H22, in the
spring of 1966. Ronnie
Lane came from
Plaistow in east
London. His role in
The Small Faces and
then The Faces was of
great importance for
the success of both
groups. He also got the
chance to show what
an incredible song
writer he was when he
formed his own band,
Slim Chance, in 1973 ▶

to switch from guitar to bass, since it was hard to find bass players in East London; this would give him more gig opportunities. Ronnie and Steve immediately recognised each other from a year earlier, when Ronnie's old band The Outcasts performed together with Steve's group The Moments. Ronnie Lane was looking for a Harmony bass guitar and Steve Marriott took one down from the wall, making the remark that it was an excellent choice. Ronnie liked the bass guitar, but the price – £45 – made him hesitate. Steve decided to sell it to him for half the price. When this was discovered, he was fired.

Ronnie stayed behind in the shop until it closed and then went back with Steve to his home in Daines Close to listen to his collection of Stax and Motown records. It wasn't just the music that brought them together; both were mods and loved to party at the same places, for example the Scene Club and the Flamingo Club in the West End. Ronnie invited Steve to a jam session with his new band, The Pioneers, at a pub in Ilford, and he showed up one night with his harmonica. The newfound friends began partying and the gig ended in chaos: where Steve Marriott – using the pseudonym Jerry Lee Marriott – smashed the piano to pieces and band leader Ronnie Lane was banned from the premises. But Steve, Ronnie and the drummer of The Pioneers, Kenney Jones, had found each other, and just a few months later they formed The Small Faces.

At J60 Steve Marriott had also got to know Jimmy Langwith, whose parents ran the pub Ruskin Arms on the other side of the street, and Jimmy would sometimes play the guitar there. Steve and Ronnie visited the pub one night and offered Jimmy a place in the band, but then as

an organ player since Steve was playing the guitar. Jimmy Langwith accepted the offer and also changed his last name to Winston.

Steve Marriott ◀

What remains of the J60 Music Bar today is a big neon sign from the Sixties, advertising Hammond organs, which is on the gable facing Sherrard Road. The electric cable to the sign was cut off a long time ago and beneath the sign there is a shop repairing and selling second-hand sewing-machines. As I'm standing there the shop owner comes out and asks me what I'm looking at, and when I point to the sign he immediately offers to sell it to me. I tell him that I'd love to buy it, but that it's too large to bring back to Sweden. When I tell him about the sign and who met in the shop his face brightens. He is very familiar with The Small Faces and takes a look at the sign, this time with new eyes. I probably raised the price of the sign by telling him this story.

Strone Road

I turn back to walk along High Street North to Strone Road, where I visit number 308, where Steve Marriott was born in January 1947. He grew up on the ground floor of this two-storey building, together with his sister who was five years younger. Their father found it hard to get a job and opened a small booth outside Ruskin Arms. There he sold fish, mainly eel, which was Steve's main food as a child.

308 Strone Road
Manor Park/East
Ham
Tube:
East Ham

Steve's home, like all the other homes in the area, was poor, but he was surrounded by music. His father played the piano and sometimes performed in bars, at weddings and at parties; Steve would often tag along. His parents noticed his interest in music and when he was about seven years old he was given a ukulele, which he quickly learned to play. Soon he would walk around playing at bus stops in the area, making money for the household. Sometimes the entire family would perform at parties, with Steve on ukulele, his dad on a small bass, his mother on washboard and his little sister using the palms of her hands. When he was 12 he formed his first band together with his class mates and wrote his first song, inspired by Buddy Holly.

Without a doubt, Steve Marriott was a very talented young boy. This didn't just apply to music, but also to acting. When he was thirteen his parents sent him to an audition for the Lionel Bart musical Oliver!, which was based on Charles Dickens' Oliver Twist and was playing at the New London Theatre. The reason the audition was held was that the school-age child-actors had to take a break from the production after three months. The rules stipulated that those who auditioned were only allowed to perform one song, but when Steve Marriott has finished his first song he immediately started one more song, before anyone had the time to stop him (the song in question was Buddy Holly's 'Oh, Boy!'). Despite this violation of the rules he got the part as Oliver, and not only that part but they also wanted him to do several parts and perform different songs, depending on which character he played. He performed in the musical for one year, with a ten-day break every three months. He was paid £8 per week, which doesn't sound like very much, but it was a very high salary in those days. A cast album was also recorded at the legendary EMI studio in Abbey Road; it was released in 1960. Steve Marriott performed three songs, although those songs really belonged to the Artful Dodger character.

Ruskin Arms

From Strone Road, you just have to cross the street to get to *Ruskin Arms*, where The Small Faces would rehearse and play at the start of their career. Ruskin Arms is situated in a large, red Victorian brick building. From the old signs on the outside one may surmise that the pub has a long tradition of presenting live music, but also that boxing matches used to be arranged here.

The Small Faces began rehearsing on the upper floor of Ruskin Arms during the spring of 1965 and after just a few weeks they were playing in front of an audience on the pub's stage. They were quickly discovered by the owners of a new club in Leicester Square, the Cavern Club. When they were about to make their debut at the Cavern, they needed a name for the band and Steve's girlfriend came up with the name The Small Faces. The significance of "small" was pretty obvious, since they were all very

Ruskin Arms
East Ham/Manor
Park
386 High Street
North
Tube: East Ham

BLUEOPERA CLUB
ALEXIS KORNER'S
RHYTHM & BLUES
Ruskin Arms High St. North E.15.

Just like many other pubs
Ruskin Arms started a
blues club, which opened
in early 1964. ▲

short, Jimmy Winston excepted. They were all mods and "face" was an expression that meant that you were among the coolest of the mods. Thus, The Small Faces were formed, but in the autumn Jimmy Winston was replaced by organist Ian McLagan.

Ruskin Arms is a spacious pub, where people are sitting in groups and talking, playing billiards or darts. A door at the far end leads into the concert hall, with room for around threehundred spectators. Today, the black painted room shows traces of heavy metal and this was also where Iron Maiden began their career. But today Ruskin Arms is highly multicultural and the entertainment varies between rock and various ethnical performances with dance and music. After finishing my beer I walk out and take bus 147 to a park that has been immortalised in song.

New Musical Express
June 8, 1968 ▼

184

Itchycoo Park

Over bridge of sighs
To rest my eyes in shades of green
Under dreamin' skies
To Itchycoo Park, that's where I've been

(Itchycoo Park, lyrics: Marriott/Lane)

Itchycoo Park
Little Ilford/
Manor Park
Tube: East Ham
Bus: 147 from High
Street North

Many who have heard 'Itchycoo Park' by The Small Faces and then made vain attempts at finding it on a map, will probably believe that the name is a complete invention. But it's actually not an invention by songwriter Steve Marriott. Close to Little Ilford Park there is an empty site at the end of Millais Avenue, where Steve Marriott sometimes used to hang out with his friends. They called it 'Itchycoo Park' because of all the stinging nettles that used to grow there, and I'm curious to find out what it looks like.

After just a few minutes I step off the bus on Church Road and walk down to Millais Avenue. It turns out to be just a short street, right at the edge of a small housing area with low-rise buildings. I feel like I'm at the edge of nothing and the people I meet seem a little surprised to see me there, as if they're wondering what I'm doing there. A man walks up to me and asks where I'm headed and when I point at the empty site he looks even more surprised. I don't bother to explain, since it would probably confuse him even more to learn that of all places in London, a song was named after this one; most other places are much more beautiful and have more to offer.

Because Itchycoo Park certainly isn't a very nice and idyllic place, and for a while I wonder why Steve Marriott and his friends would hang out here. Not even the neighbourhood drunks or junkies seem to appreciate the place, despite its remote qualities. In the song about Itchycoo

Park the backing choir sings, "what did you do there?" and that's what I'm asking myself right now. But Steve Marriott thought this place was exciting and stimulated his fantasy: one day it was a jungle, the next day the Wild West or an unknown, faraway country.

The site measures about 55 x 30 yards and is surrounded by a low wooden fence which is all mouldy, and at the far end of its long side there is a hill leading up to the heavy traffic of North Circular Road. It seems some use the place as a dump, while someone has made a brave attempt at creating a small plantation. However, I can't see that anything grows there, except for something unidentifiable that I wouldn't want to put on my sandwich. Here and there, there are barrels of rusty sheet-metal or plastic, and a number of small ramshackle sheds that look

'Itchycoo Park' was released in early August 1967 and reached number three on the UK singles chart. It was the first time that phasing was used on a recording. This method was later used by artists such as The Beatles and Jimi Hendrix. ▼

like they're about to fall apart any minute. I have no idea what the sheds contain, but they look like the ones you see on film, which often contain something horrible. I don't bother to find out. Itchycoo Park may possibly be a place for boyish adventures, but it's not a place I would recommend for a romantic walk in the moonlight.

Daines Close

9 Daines Close
Manor Park
Tube:
East Ham, bus 147
from tubestation

My curiosity satisfied, I walk towards 9 *Daines Close* nearby, where Steve Marriott lived with his parents from the age of fourteen. I walk through Little Ilford Park, pass by the wide Romford Road and then reach a three-storey building where the family moved in 1961, when the building was new. It must have felt like a real luxury for the family to suddenly have a bathroom in the apartment. The house is very simple, built of brown bricks and with built-in balconies, many of which have laundry hanging on them. This was where Steve Marriott and Ronnie Lane would sit and talk and listen to music, trying to find the right songs for the band at the start of their career. But today the house is silent and I don't see a single human being.

Since Steve Marriott hated the ordinary school and his parents recognised his considerable talent, they arranged for him to try out for the prestigious theatre school Italia Conti Drama School. As the only pupil from the East End, he got into the school at age 14. His parents were unable to finance his education, but the school let him go there for free since they were certain they would be able to quickly find parts for him, so that he could pay the fee himself. And that's what happened: soon enough he was given parts in radio, theatre, film and television. He brought his guitar along to all his appearances, so that he

An ad for the Steve Marriott's Moments gig at the Noreik club on October 31, 1964. ▲

The Small Faces' song writers Steve Marriott and Ronnie Lane in early 1966. The two buddies, who at one time had been inseparable, would go their separate ways a few years later. Steve Marriott formed Humble Pie and Ronnie Lane was one of the founders of The Faces in early 1969. ▶

could play it whenever there was a break.

He had parts in films such as Heaven's Up, featuring Peter Sellers in the lead role, and Live It Up, where he had a more prominent part as the drummer in a band. Among the musicians in the film were Gene Vincent and a certain Ritchie Blackmore, the future guitarist of Deep Purple. The sequel was entitled Be My Guest, in which Jerry Lee Lewis replaced Gene Vincent. Steve Marriott would spend many of the fees from his various performances on cool clothes, which he often bought at Cecil Gee's in Shaftesbury Avenue or in Carnaby Street. By the time The Small Faces achieved their breakthrough a few years later, shopping for clothes was already a habit.

But after a while Steve Marriott tired of acting and his family and relatives were all highly disappointed when he quit at the age of sixteen and declared that he was going to devote himself to music instead. He wrote the song 'Imaginary Love', which he tried to sell on Denmark Street, without any success. However, the song finally reached the ears of Decca, and they immediately offered him a recording contract. His first single was 'Give Her My Regards', with his self-written song on the B-side. After that he put together a number of different bands, among them The Moments, before he met Ronnie Lane and found the right constellation in The Small Faces.

I leave Daines Close and walk back to Ruskin Arms, the same way that Steve Marriott and Ronnie Lane often walked 40 years ago. I can't help feeling a little sad when I consider the fact that both of them are gone today: Steve died in a fire at his home in April 1991 and Ronnie was diagnosed with multiple sclerosis, which he fought bravely until his death in 1997.

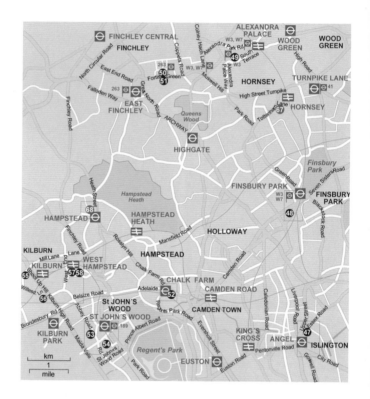

47 Camden Head

48 Astoria Finsbury Park

49 Alexandra Palace

50 6 Denmark Terrace
   Fortis Green

51 Clissold Arms

52 Roundhouse

53 Abbey Road Studios

54 7 Cavendish Avenue

55 33 Mapesbury Road

56 State Cinema

57 Klooks Kleek

58 Decca Studios

67 Konk Studio

68 10a Holly Hill

190

North and Northwest London

Islington

It is a Sunday afternoon as I board the underground train to the northern parts of London, to walk in the footsteps of The Kinks and also visit a couple of famous concert venues. I get off at Angel Station, located in what is now a prestigious middle class area: Islington. As I leave the station, I walk north on Upper Islington Street for a couple of hundred yards until I reach Camden Walk, which is a narrow passage filled with small antique shops, boutiques, galleries, cafés and bars. For those with plenty of time on their hands there are many interesting items to see in the shop windows. I stop for a minute at the Rockarchive photo gallery, where they have wonderful, well-made black and white portraits of a number of famous artists and bands from the Sixties.

Camden Head

After a short walk I reach 2 *Camden Walk*, where a painted sign announces that this is the location of the pub Camden Head, established as early as 1899. Outside there are plenty of guests, but many seem to skip the food and just enjoy a beer in the sunshine.

Camden Head
Islington
Camden Walk 2
Tube: Angel Station

In a small room above the pub, The Kinks began rehearsing in the autumn of 1963; previously, they usually rehearsed in their home area of Muswell Hill. When they began rehearsing here the band was called The Bo Weevils and consisted of Ray and Dave Davies on guitars, Ray's old class-mate Pete Quaife on bass and Mickey Willett on drums. On September 26, 1963, they managed to entice The Beatles' manager, Brian Epstein, to come down here. He felt that Ray Davies might possibly be interesting as a solo artist, but he had no interest in the rest of the band. A month or so later, they changed their name to The Ravens and performed at Camden Head several times during the autumn.

On January 24, 1964, Mick Avory came to the pub to audition as a drummer, after having advertised for a job in Melody Maker. By that time, the band had a recording contract, but desperately needed a new drummer when Mickey Willett left the band. They tried to get Viv Prince (later in The Pretty Things) to join the band, but he had a bad hangover and never turned up for the audition. Mick Avory was just as desperate as they were; he had turned Brian Jones down when he was forming The Rolling Stones 1 ½ years earlier and felt that this may be his last chance at boarding the rock'n'roll train.

Dave Davies felt uncertain when Mick Avory showed up. With his short hair and wearing his nicest Sunday suit, his look was in direct contrast to the others in the band, who had long hair and were wearing leather jackets. But they liked the same kind of music and the band knew that Avory had played in an early version of The Rolling Stones, so he was invited to join them and he began learning the group's repertoire. Apart from a few self-written songs, the repertoire mainly consisted of standards by Chuck Berry, Bo Diddley, Buddy Holly and Little Richard.

The band rehearsed intensely at Camden Head for a

week before they performed in public at the pub on January 31, 1964, calling themselves The Ravens. The following day they made their debut as The Kinks and after a few more days of rehearsals at Camden Head it was time to make their television debut in Ready Steady Go!, where they mimed to their recently-released first single, 'Long Tall Sally'. The song was not a hit, however, and it would take another half year before they achieved their big breakthrough with 'You Really Got Me'.

Camden Head is spacious and pleasant with beautiful cut glass window decorations in the Art Nouveau style. No-one in the staff is aware that The Kinks have rehearsed and played at this pub; they are very surprised when I tell them. A narrow staircase leads up to the old rehearsal and concert room and I'm allowed to walk upstairs to have a look. It turns out that the local stand-up comedy association is having a meeting in the room, but they don't mind my visit.

The room holds about thirty people standing and the small stage, where The Kinks rehearsed and played more than forty years ago, is still there in one of the corners. Behind the stage there are windows where you can watch the traffic running by on Essex Road, and at one of the walls there is a fireplace, but otherwise there isn't much to see. I walk outside and sit down to have a beer while I'm planning my next route. After thinking for a while I decide to take the tube back to Kings Cross and change to the Piccadilly Line, going north to Finsbury Park.

48

Astoria Finsbury Park
Finsbury park
232 Seven Sisters Road
Tube: Finsbury Park

Finsbury Park

Just outside the tube station is the *Astoria Finsbury Park* on 232 Seven Sisters Road. The "Finsbury Park" addition is used so as not to confuse it with the Astoria that's located in Charing Cross Road in central London. The building

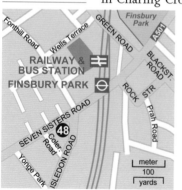

looks very dull, but when I go in I'm startled by how beautiful it is on the inside. Astoria Finsbury Park was one of the major rock venues in London, with room for 3,000 people, and this was where the really big artists and bands used to perform: both domestic stars and international visitors.

The first of these were The Beatles, when manager Brian Epstein arranged

The Beatles' Christmas Show for sixteen days, featuring two performances almost every day from December 24, 1963. 100,000 tickets were sold in just a few weeks. Apart from performing a number of songs The Beatles also took part in a few comedy numbers, which must have been a great challenge considering all the hysterically screaming little girls. In the show, a number of other artists from Brian Epstein's stable of acts performed, among them Cilla Black and Billy J. Kramer And The Dakotas.

Between two shows on December 18, Paul McCartney and John Lennon took the opportunity to visit The Rolling Stones, who were performing at the nearby, much

New Musical Express
January 3, 1964 ▼

January 3, 1964   NEW MUSICAL EXPRESS   3

Beatles have four spots in their Christmas show

WITH sketches, scenery and production, Brian Epstein succeeds in injecting show business into his " Beatles' Christmas Show" at the Finsbury Park Astoria in London. The whole thing adds up to the kind of entertainment that audiences are rarely treated to on rock 'n' roll shows.

By CHRIS HUTCHINS

The Beatles are seen on four occasions through the show which is good value in itself. But with the added talents of Rolf Harris and other 1963-born stars from Epstein's stable it makes for a bumper presentation.

The show has a clever opening with all the artists emerging from a helicopter to take their bow. But without Rolf Harris to keep the pace moving I doubt whether this introduction would have bridged the gap before the Beatles eventually made their initial appearance.

The Barron Knights did a surprisingly good warming-up job with numbers like " Big Girls Don't Cry" and " You Don't Have To Be A Baby To Cry" given the comedy treatment they deserve.

The subsequent sketch featuring the Beatles in doctor uniforms (giving us the first-ever glimpse of John Lennon wearing glasses on stage) was as weak as it was brief, but that hardly mattered as it gave the fans a second glimpse of the fab foursome.

The item that followed was probably the most successful as far as production was concerned. Backed by the Barron Knights, Tommy Quickly sang a well-chosen selection against an effective set. " Winter Wonderland " complete, with Christmas tree and snowman illuminated behind a gauze curtain was the highlight.

Tommy was followed by the Four-

most who suffered during the performance that I watched from ailing amps, but-their selection well spiced with wit kept the entertainment to a high standard and won the group an enthusiastic reception from the capacity (of course !) house.

The Beatles provided a further non-musical interlude by way of their " Sir Jasper" sketch, which was brilliant in both its conception and their performance of it.

Fortunately someone had had the foresight to present the words they spoke on a screen behind them for their couldn't possibly have been heard. At the display of the words " it is snowing," Ringo danced on stage wearing a grin we rarely see him with, scattering make-believe snow.

As the villain of the plot John Lennon in cloak and top hat secured " Mrs." George Harrison adorned in shawl and " her baby" to the railway line. But hero (of course) Paul McCartney saved George from the path of an on-coming train.

We were both with the twanging guitars as the Dakotas launched into " Cruel Sea" to herald the magnificent entrance on a four foot high moving rostrum of Billy J. Kramer. Understandably, somebody had forgotten to put a microphone on the rostrum, and Billy J. had to step down to make himself heard with " Beautiful Dreamer."

I have never seen him work so enthusiastically, in addition to his three big hits he also sang " Pride "

and an excellent version of " Scarlet Ribbons." He closed the first half to much deserved acclaim.

After Duke D'Mond and his Barron Knights had got things going again, red-haired Cilla Black took the stage for some lively numbers which she concluded with " Love Of The Loved." For a comparative newcomer, I like the way Cilla moves on stage and belts out her songs.

I can't think of any entertainer in the pop business who could have filled the pre-Beatles spot as well as Rolf Harris did. He opened with " Tie Me Kangaroo Down Sport," but gave his lyrics concerning each of the Beatles, and couldn't have failed with lines like " I'll scream and call 'Il I fall, Paul'' !

Then there was " San Aries," " English Country Garden " and—as the Beatles themselves were setting up their guitars behind the curtain—his latest record, " I've Lost My Mummy."

The Beatles closed the show in spectacular style. Overhead spotlights picked them out one by one on the darkened stage before they swung into the number which features George vocally, " Roll Over Beethoven."

They tempered things down with " All My Loving " and " This Boy" before Ringo went solo with the number John and Paul wrote for the Rolling Stones, " I Wanna Be Your Man."

Then there was " She Loves You " before Paul was singled out for " Till There Was You." The Beatles' current chart rider, " I Want To Hold Your Hand," preceded the final two rousing numbers which John came out with and " Twist And Shout."

Of course this enormous theatre was frequently drowned by screams — but there was laughter and applause, too. It's true to say that there was never a dull moment in this thoroughly enjoyable show.

...ast of " The Beatles Christmas Show," with the BEATLES in the front row; then (middle row, ..KE D'MOND, TOMMY QUICKLY, BILLY J. KRAMER, ROLF HARRIS, CILLA BLACK ..URMOST. Back row : the rest of the Foremost, DAKOTAS and the BARRON KNIGHTS.

E PRESLEY'S FILM SONGS TO BLAME ?

(continued from previous page)

..ard for Elvis Presley to ...following his disc decline " Now that his sales are ..we can't do himself any ...

NUMBER OF WEEKS AT No. 1 POSITION

Beatles .... 18 weeks

No. 20 on the strength of " Can't Get Used To Losing You " .... Bobby Vee and Tommy Roe (28th and 27th) show their consistency by retaining very similar positions to last year, but ...

simpler club Noreik, a former cinema that was converted to a show venue by throwing out the seats. But in order to avoid a riot the Beatle members never showed their faces in the actual venue, instead the two groups sat talking in the dressing room before the Stones entered the stage. Nine months later The Rolling Stones were so big that they could fill the Finsbury Park Astoria twice the same day, on September 5, 1964.

In August 1965 The Byrds came to England, fiercely promoted as America's answer to The Beatles, and played the Astoria on August 14. The inappropriate promotion led to unfair and inaccurate comparisons, which resulted in bad reviews in many papers. Donovan also performed at this concert and he felt that The Byrds' gig was great and publicly defended the band.

March 3, 1967 was the starting date for a package tour consisting of The Small Faces, Roy Orbison, The Jeff Beck Group and the brothers Paul & Barry Ryan. It was the very first concert played by The Jeff Beck Group and it was a very important gig for the band, which consisted of Jeff Beck on guitar, Ron Wood on bass, Rod Stewart on vocals and Ray Cook on drums. But the group's show was a disaster since the audience was shouting for either Roy Orbison or The Small Faces throughout the entire concert. As if that wasn't enough, the electricity died in the middle of the gig. The whole thing ended with Jeff Beck running off stage, firing Cook and declaring that the group would leave the tour. Rod Stewart was also angry and accused The Small Faces for shutting off the electricity, although they had already left the venue.

A package tour consisting of the curious line-up of The

Jimi Hendrix Experience, Engelbert Humperdinck, Cat Stevens and The Walker Brothers, began their tour here on March 31, 1967. Jimi Hendrix participated because his manager Chas Chandler felt it was important that Jimi made as many public appearances as possible, in order to boost sales of his 'Purple Haze' single. Chandler also knew that The Walker Brothers were about to split up, and so it was unlikely their hearts would really be in the tour. But Jimi Hendrix had his mind set on doing something out of the ordinary, since this was the group's first nationwide tour, and those who attended the second show at the Astoria this night would experience something they had never seen before.

After Jimi Hendrix had spent fortyfive minutes playing the guitar like he always did – with his teeth, behind his

The smooth-voiced baryton singer Scott Engel of The Walker Brothers hated his role as a teen idol in the group where none of the members were brothers, nor named Walker. Add to this internal personal differences, and the group had to split in 1967. ▼

neck, between his legs and lying down on the floor – the group had finally arrived at their very last song, 'Fire'. In the middle of the song, Jimi put his guitar down on the floor, doused it in lighter fluid and set fire to it. Neither the audience nor his fellow band members knew what was happening, when the guitar was suddenly on fire. Accompanied by a roar from the burning guitar, Jimi Hendrix left the stage, waving at the startled audience. The representatives of the press were just as upset and the event made the front page of most newspapers. Although Jimi Hendrix is often associated with setting fire to his guitar, this only happened three times during his career. The Astoria concert was the first time, the second time was at the Monterey festival during 'Wild Thing', and the last time was at a concert in Miami.

The name of the Astoria Finsbury Park was changed to the *Rainbow* in 1971, when The Who played the first three nights. Two years later Eric Clapton – backed by names such as Pete Townshend, Ron Wood and Steve Winwood – made his big comeback here, after a few years as a heroin addict. Today, a world-wide religious organisation occupies the premises, and they won't allow any pictures to be taken, nor are walking tours permitted, so I leave and take the W3 bus which leaves from the bus garage behind the underground station.

Muswell Hill

If you're travelling north to Alexandra Palace, I recommend that you take the bus since you may enjoy a nice trip up the high hill, through a charming small town area and leafy greenery. If you prefer going directly to Muswell Hill you may take the W7 bus, which will bring you the same way up the hill but which doesn't make the turn into Alexandra Park. While you're travelling up the hill you may also entertain your fellow passengers by singing a verse from 'London Song', written by the area's famous poet, Ray Davies:

> "But if you're ever up on Highgate Hill on a clear day
> you can see right down to Leicester Square
> Crystal Palace, Clapham Common, right down to Streatham Hill
> North and South, I feel that I'm a Londoner still".

(London Song, lyrics: Ray Davies)

If you haven't been thrown off the bus after singing, you will arrive at Alexandra Park after a while, at which time the bus will turn towards a gigantic building.

Alexandra Palace

Alexandra Palace is beautifully located and provides a spectacular view of the city in clear weather and then functions as the landmark of northern London. It's a

49

Alexandra Palace
Alexandra Pal. Way
Wood Green
Tube: Wood Green
Station
Bus W3

Brian Jones of The Rolling Stones at the Alexandra Palace, June 26, 1964, shortly after the group returned from their first US tour. The very same day the Stones released their single 'It's All Over Now', which would top the charts within a week. ▲

popular place to visit; for instance, there are many possibilities for recreation and pleasure. The gothic building consists of several large halls, out of which the largest one has room for more than 7,000 people. In here, exhibitions, events and concerts are arranged. Ally Pally, which is what Londoners call the building, was built in 1873 as a "The People's Palace". It was burned to the ground almost immediately, but was quickly built up again in 1875.

In 1980 the palace was on fire again and most of the halls were destroyed, but in 1988 parts of the palace were opened again. According to rock myths, Keith Moon was the one who set fire to the place, during one of The Who's concerts. It's difficult to see how this could have happened, since Keith Moon died in 1978.

Immediately after The Rolling Stones' return from their first US tour in 1964, a welcome-home party and a nightly gig was arranged on June 26 at Ally Pally. Apart from the Stones, John Lee Hooker, John Mayall's Bluesbreakers, Alexis Korner and Downliners Sect also played during the evening and night.

One of those present at the concert was a certain John "Hoppy" Hopkins, who would found the underground paper International Times (IT) and the UFO club a couple of years later. It was during this night that he got the idea of renting Ally Pally at some point. He realised this idea on April 29, 1967, when he arranged The 14-Hour Technicolor Dream, a big psychedelic happening which was attended by around 10,000 people. The purpose of the event was to raise money for the International Times, which was under threat of prosecution after a narcotics raid by the police at the paper's offices.

The event began at 8 pm and lasted until 10 am the following day, for those who managed to stay awake. As the title of the event suggests, there were light shows flowing constantly across the premises, while at the same time short underground films were projected on white sheets on the walls; it was all inspired by the new drug culture, centred around LSD. There were two stages at opposite ends of the cathedral-like hall and also a small one in the middle, where there were poetry, dancers, acrobatics and other small-scale performances. More than forty bands and artists were supposed to appear at the event, but the organisers forgot to book some of them and some artists forgot themselves that they were supposed to perform. And of those who did play, many have no recollection of doing so. But among those who probably made appearances are: Pink Floyd, The Crazy World of Arthur Brown, The Soft Machine, The Move, The Pretty Things and The Creation. Pink Floyd appeared at 3 am, directly from a gig in Holland.

The large audience were moving back and forth between the stages in a state of confusion, since they didn't know which bands would be playing were or when. Also, different bands were often playing at the same time on the two stages so that there was a cacophony of sound in the middle of the hall. The confusion wasn't helped by the rumour that The Beatles and The Who would be performing at some point during the night. The rumour was probably triggered by the presence of Who guitarist Pete Townshend and by John Lennon's arrival there in his Rolls Royce, after having seen a news story about the event on television. The organisers were pleased afterwards – having counted their revenue – and decided to arrange yet another event during the month of July.

On July 29, the *Love-In Festival* was held, featuring Eric Burdon And The New Animals onstage, plus more or less the same bands as during the earlier concert. According to eyewitnesses, the event was marked by quarrels, scuffles and fights, and the love message was literally kicked to the ground.

It was during Pink Floyd's performance that night that the drug abuse and burgeoning psychosis of band leader Syd Barrett became apparent for the first time to many of those present. At first, he failed to appear onstage and some members of the impatient audience started to whistle. When the band found him in the dressing room, he was sitting there completely transfixed and they all had

THE LOVE-IN FESTIVAL

THIS SATURDAY ALL NIGHT LOVING!
ALEXANDRA PALACE 9 P.M. TILL 9 A.M.

ERIC BURDON
THE ANIMALS
PINK FLOYD
BRIAN AUGER
CRAZY WORLD OF JULIE DRISCOLL AND THE TRINITY
ARTHUR BROWN
TOMORROW
BLOSSOM TOES
SOCIAL INTERVENTION
DREAM
FLOWER MACHINE
SAM GOPAL
LOVE IN FESTIVAL
ALEXANDRA PALACE SATURDAY JULY 29 9PM TIL 9 LONDON N22

TICKETS £1-0-0

available at:— LOVING BOX OFFICE until midnight; PHOTO CENTRE, 2 Shaftesbury Avenue; KEITH PROWSE, 19 New Bond Street; ABBEY BOX OFFICE, 27 Victoria Street; BETTER BOOKS, 94 Charing Cross Rd; INDICA BOOKS, 102 Southampton Row; HAMPSTEAD RECORD CENTRE, 72 Heath Street; TAKE 6, 66 Wardour Street; ASHTON & MITCHELL, ALFRED HAYS, 100 St. Martin's Lane JOHN TRAPP, 20 Crouch End Hill; One STOCK RECORDS, 40 South Molton Street; H. J. ADAMS, 5 Grosvenor Street and ALEXANDRA PALACE on night.

The Love-In concert on July 29, 1967, was anything but loving. Many guests, managers, journalists and even artists were attacked and beaten, both by prowling gangs and by over-zealous guards. ◀

to pull him to his feet and drag him out onstage. There, they hung his white Stratocaster on him and finally began playing, to the great cheers of the audience. But Syd Bar-

rett was just standing completely still, without moving so much as a finger. He stood there for a couple of songs, lost in his own world, before the group stopped the performance and led him off the stage.

Ironically, this disaster occurred on the very same day that the group's first major hit, 'See Emily Play', reached its peak position on the sales charts, and just a week before they were about to release their first album, *The Piper At The Gates Of Dawn*. The following week it was reported that Syd Barrett had suffered a nervous breakdown and that Pink Floyd would take a month-long break. But Syd Barrett would never be the same again. Five months later, in early January 1968, David Gilmour was asked if he wanted to join the group, and just a couple of weeks later Syd Barrett played his last gig as a member of Pink Floyd.

There is another sad memory associated with Alexandra Palace. The Small Faces played here on New Year's Eve 1968, together with blues veteran Alexis Korner, and there was a long line of expectant youths outside Ally Pally. Alexis Korner was warming up the audience and spirits were high when The Small Faces entered the stage. The band had enjoyed great success during the year with singles such as 'Lazy Sunday' and the album *Ogden's Nut Gone Flake*. The band started to play their hits quite energetically, but the show was plagued by technological problems. A screeching feedback from the amplifiers meant that they had to stop the show all the time, and lead singer Steve Marriott grew all the more irritated and frustrated from not being able to hear the band when he was singing.

When the time came to play the last song he asked Alexis Korner to join them onstage to see if matters improved. But the situation just grew worse. A deafening distortion occurred and in the middle of the song Marriott had enough. He threw his guitar on the floor so hard that it went to pieces and finished by kicking the microphone stand. Then he ran off the stage in front of his band mates and the audience, both of whom were shocked. The Small Faces finished the concert with Ronnie Lane and Alexis Korner on vocals. After the concert, Steve Marriott declared that he would leave the band and form a new group, Humble Pie, together with, among others, Peter Frampton. All Small Faces gigs were cancelled immediately, except for a tour of Germany to which the group were contractually bound. One of the very best bands of the Sixties had split up.

It's a grey day, so I can't see very much of the London that Ray Davies is singing about and I choose to go back to the main road to walk the last bit up the hill, towards central Muswell Hill. This is where The Kinks have their roots and I am slightly surprised that the district gives such a cosy and inviting impression. I knew that The Kinks' leading duo, the brothers Ray and Dave Davies, grew up in an old working class suburb, and I had imagined a considerably more shabby area. But now I understand why the brothers chose to remain in the area, long after they had achieved their breakthrough as musicians.

Denmark Terrace/Fortis Green

50

6 Denmark Terrace
Muswell Hill
Tube: East Finchley,
Bus 263
Tube: Finsbury
Park, Bus W7

I walk along Queens Avenue for a couple of hundred yards until I reach Fortis Green, which I follow until I reach a small, unassuming two-storey house, squeezed-in among a row of houses; for some reason its address is 6 Denmark Terrace. In this house, which is situated next door to a small workshop, Ray was born in 1944 and then Dave in 1947, the sons of a butcher. The mother grew up

Ray Davies, maybe the best individual song writer of the 60s. A sharp observer of the times and a depicter of the people and the everyday life in the suburbs. The picture was taken in early September 1965, when The Kinks had just released the single 'See My Friends', a song that Paul McCartney wishes he had written. ▶

in the slum areas of King's Cross, together with twenty (!) brothers and sisters, and learned to look after herself in the streets at an early age. The Davies brothers had six older sisters: there was a twentythree-year age difference between Dave and the oldest sister. Several of the sisters were married and had children of their own, which meant that the house was very crowded (the width of the house seems to be no more than four or five yards). It's easy to see how this affected the brothers' need of integrity and individuality, but also their feeling of solidarity.

Both brothers grew up with music, which was equally important for the entire family. In the living room there was a piano, which all the sisters played, and their father gladly played the banjo. On his 13th birthday, Ray's sister Rene gave him his first guitar and she taught him his first chords. She tragically died from a heart condition later the same night, when she was dancing at London's Lyceum. All the sisters loved to dance, which inspired Ray to write 'Come Dancing' and 'Don't Forget To Dance' many years later.

The two brothers didn't have much in common, but when Dave got his first guitar at the age of twelve their interest in music brought them closer together. In the living room they started doing their first recordings after a while – mainly instrumental songs – on a small mono tape recorder. Ray wrote 'You Really Got Me' here in March 1964 and the song's groundbreaking guitar sound was created through little brother David's experiments on a small amplifier that was in the room. When Ray Davies wrote the song, the intention was that he would give it to Georgie Fame and the Blue

Little brother Dave Davies, the creator of the classic riff in 'You Really Got Me', in 1965. With time, Dave also became a proficient song writer.

Flames, who were very popular at the Flamingo Club, where Ray also played sometimes before The Kinks were formed. But the brothers realised that the song would fit The Kinks perfectly, and upon release in August it became an enormous hit as well as the breakthrough song for the band.

At the family piano Dave Davies wrote his first solo single, 'Death Of A Clown', released in 1967, which is a melancholy autobiographical depiction of Dave's view of his own situation at the time. For several years he had been partying around as a rock star at the hip clubs in London, but now he was starting to regard himself as a clown, although he was only twenty years old.

If you're curious to know where Ray Davies wrote his 1970 mega-hit 'Lola', you may want to proceed to 87 Fortis Green, where Ray Davies lived at the time with his wife, Rasa. Personally, I'm getting hungry and thirsty and so I cross the street to the Clissold Arms pub, which is a must for all Kinks fans.

Clissold Arms

When they were around thirteen and sixteen years old, the brothers made their debut at *Clissold Arms*. As a regular, the father knew the owner and despite their age, they were allowed to play in the room at the back of the pub. They mostly played instrumentals at the time, most of which were written by Ray himself. While I have a beer I talk to a woman in the staff, who was here and saw them on these very first nights. She says they weren't especially good at the time. But they were still very young and would learn with time.

After a while, Ray's schoolmate Pete Quaife joined the band as a bass player and he suggested that his friend John Start became the drummer. The band now called themselves The Ray Davies Quartet and had expanded their repertoire to include songs by acts such as The Everly Brothers, Buddy Holly and Little Richard. They continued appearing at Clissold Arms, but then as a trio since there was no room for Start's drums.

Ray didn't enjoy singing and suggested that the band should get a singer. A certain Rod Stewart, known locally as the Elvis of Muswell Hill, made an audition and then began rehearsing with the band. But pretty soon it was clear that Stewart's musical tastes and personality were too different, so he and the band decided to go their separate ways.

With time, Ray Davies became the major depicter of London and its people; his songs are filled with stories about the city's madness and sinfulness, its joys, riches and pleasures. But the major social upheavals of the time and the simple everyday life in the unassuming suburbs were also

Clissold Arms
Fortis Green
Tube: East Finchley,
Bus 263
Tube: Finsbury Park,
Bus W7

given plenty of room in his songs. He has written so many songs about the different environments of London that you can take a bus from the centre of the city and sing a song about almost every area until you reach Muswell Hill.

Despite all their success and visits abroad, the Davies brothers never completely let go of Muswell Hill and Clissold Arms. When Dave Davies turned 50 in 1997, his older brother Ray held a birthday party for him at Clissold Arms. Most of the remaining Davies family participated, together with then-members of The Kinks and old friends. Filled with childhood memories, Dave then wrote the song 'Fortis Green':

> Mum would shout and scream when dad would come home drunk
> When she asked him where he'd been, he'd say "Up the Clissold Arms"
> Chattin' up some hussy, but he didn't mean no harm
> [...]
> Fortis Green, memories of days when I was young
> It can only be a memory. A time that now has gone
> Memories of Fortis Green, when I was just a lad
> Collecting bottle tops, threepenny bits, fishing with my Dad

(Fortis Green, lyrics: Dave Davies)

I drink my beer while I walk around having a look at the pub, which treasures the memory of the area's pride. The walls of the pub's inner room are filled with memories of The Kinks and the brothers Davies: here hangs one of Dave Davies' first guitars, a signed copy of the group's first single, 'Long Tall Sally', photographs and other memorabilia of the band.

It feels hard to leave Clissold Arms, so before I leave I sit down at a table outside and order a pie and another beer.

After resting for a while I take the bus westward from Fortis Green, towards East Finchley underground station, where I get off to take the Northern Line to Camden and the Chalk Farm underground station.

Camden

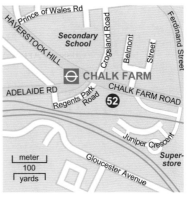

Roundhouse

99 Chalk Farm Road is the location of the *Roundhouse*, a large, round building, which opened as a steam engine repair building in the middle of the 19th Century, but which was taken over by Gilbey's Distillery, who used it as a storage facility.

Roundhouse
Camden town
99 Chalk Farm Road
Tube:
Chalk Farm Station

In the mid-Sixties, music entered the old premises, as part of the psychedelic wave that swept London, beginning in the autumn of 1966. The first rock concert was held on October 15, 1966, when the underground paper the International Times (IT) celebrated its birth and

213

Pink Floyd at the start of their career, before they had released their first record. But they were already established on the alternative underground scene and known for their psychedelic light shows. Left–right: Roger Waters, Rick Wright, Nick Mason and Syd Barrett in his usual perm. ▲

arranged a "happening" that lasted all night. Fairly unknown bands such as Pink Floyd and The Soft Machine provided the music and Pink Floyd displayed a psychedelic light show that made quite an impression on those who were there.

Although the premises were cold, dirty and damp, with hardly any lights and only two toilets, the event was a success, with more than 2,000 people in the audience. The insufficient lighting provided opportunities for those who were tired of waiting to get into the toilets, but also for those who wanted to explore the message of love a bit more thoroughly. Among the visitors were Paul McCartney, his girlfriend Jane Asher, Marianne Faithfull and a completely bored Mick Jagger.

214

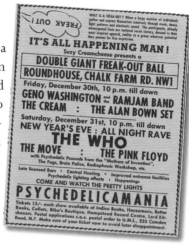

During the final two days of 1966, a major concert was held, featuring Cream and Geno Washington on the first day, and on New Year's Eve, Pink Floyd, The Who and The Move were playing. The year before, The Who had been the unrivalled favourites of London's mod movement, but a great number of mods had now got into the new, alternative "psychedelic" culture and the new bands that were formed in its wake. The premises were damp and cold, and so were the audience. Most of them had probably preferred celebrating New Year's Eve somewhere else, if it hadn't been for the bands.

Those who had the stamina could spend the entire New Year's holiday at the Roundhouse in 1966. The line-up of artists was impressive, but the audience complained that the premises were ice-cold. ▲

The bands were competing to make the biggest impression on the audience. The Who threw smoke bombs and guitarist Pete Townshend kicked down a couple of gigantic loudspeakers with his guitar, but the group suffered a couple of power failures during the concert, which caused them to stop completely and just look at each other. The Move made the biggest impression on the startled audience by using iron pipes to destroy first a representation of Hitler and then a car, as an ending to their concert.

On August 18, 1967, the psychedelic club the UFO moved to the Roundhouse and on the opening night The Crazy World Of Arthur Brown and The Incredible String Band performed. But the high rent and rising booking fees forced the club to close down as early as October. The low entrance fee was probably a part of the problem: in November 1967 you could go to the Roundhouse and watch a show featuring Jimi Hendrix, Pink Floyd, The

After a little over a year of psychedelic Happenings, many bands had tired of the experimental music. In early 1968 the straight-forward rock music was on its way back. (New Musical Express February 17 1968) ▲

Move, Amen Corner and The Nice for a sum corresponding to around £4 in today's money value.

In the summer of 1968, the Middle Earth club moved to the Roundhouse, and its first big event was a double show on September 6 and 7 featuring the American bands Jefferson Airplane and The Doors. The Doors' singer Jim Morrison took the opportunity to visit Carnaby Street during the daytime and in the evening he made his first performance dressed in a black leather outfit. The show was filmed and is available on VHS and DVD for those who are curious.

A couple of months later, Led Zeppelin (formerly The New Yardbirds) made their debut show in London at the Roundhouse under this name – the same day that singer Robert Plant was married – and in the ensuing months, bands like The Who, The Jeff Beck Group, Fairport Convention and The Pretty Things played there.

In the summer of 1969, the *Implosion club* opened. It was held there on Sundays and had a major importance for the music scene in London for a long time. The club had a big disco and for a small entrance fee one could usually watch five bands each club night. Among the many bands and artists who played at the club are names such as Frank Zappa, The Who, Deep Purple, Thin Lizzy, Tyrannosaurus Rex, Mott The Hoople, David Bowie and Elton John, all of whom were paid the same concert fee, irrespective of their status. The Roundhouse continued being a concert venue throughout the Seventies and Eighties, and this was the place where The Rolling Stones held their farewell concert, in March 1971, before they moved to France temporarily because of tax reasons.

I enter the building, which these days is mostly used for various exhibitions, but it's so dark that I can't really make out anything, except that the premises still look like old engine sheds with transverse iron girders under the high, dome-shaped ceiling. Camden Market is located nearby and I take the opportunity to walk around the shops and buy a few records before I decide to take the boat, choosing a more relaxing mode of transportation after a stressful day. Thus, I walk to Regent's Canal at Camden Locks, where I enter a canal boat and travel towards Little Venice in Paddington, where I take the tube home from Warwick Avenue. It is a beautiful and pleasant journey, where the boat slowly passes the London Zoo and travels along Regent's Park, through a tunnel and under bridges, before plenty of colourful houseboats appear along the canal quays as we approach the charming Little Venice. A nice end to a long day.

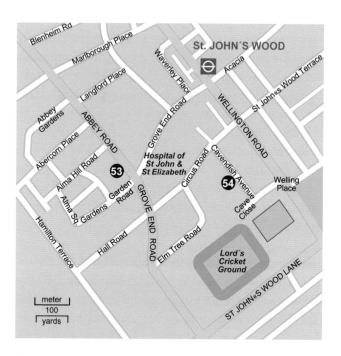

🛑53 **Abbey Road Studios**
🛑54 **7 Cavendish Avenue**

St. John's Wood

Abbey Road

A not entirely unfamiliar recording studio is located in St. John's Wood and I choose bus 189 from Oxford Street to take me there. After 15–20 minutes I get off at the crossing of Abbey Road/Grove End Road, where the familiar crossing from The Beatles' Abbey Road album is located, nearby the EMI building. The famous photograph was taken August 8, 1969, during a short coffee break, when The Beatles were recording the album.

The detached house on 3 *Abbey Road* was bought in 1929 by the company that was to become EMI, and in two years the 16 room house was converted into three studios of various sizes. The opening ceremony on November 12, 1931, was quite grand, as Sir Edward Elgar performed 'Land Of Hope And Glory' together with the London Symphony Orchestra. However, the studio was only truly immortalised in September 1969, when The Beatles released their final studio album, named after the

Abbey Road Studios
St. John's Wood
3 Abbey Road
Tube:
St. John's Wood
Bus: 189

The song 'All You Need Is Love' was recorded during a unique live broadcast across five continents in the programme Our World. (New Musical Express July 1, 1967) ▶

street where the studio is located. It was also the group's biggest-selling album.

By that time, innumerable famous recordings had already taken place at EMI's studios in Abbey Road. The first of these to take place in the Sixties was The Shadows' session for their 1960 number one hit 'Apache'. Helen Shapiro was only 15 years old when she recorded 'Walkin' Back To Happiness' in 1961. The Beatles finally entered the studio in 1962 and recorded their first single, 'Love Me Do', in studio 2. Over the following seven years they recorded 90 per cent of their records at Abbey Road; with few exceptions they used studio 2 for those sessions. By 1964, the group had released six singles, out of which four reached number one in England.

Perhaps the most famous recording was made on June 25, 1967, when BBC broadcast the programme Our World live across five continents with around 350 million people watching. In studio 1 The Beatles performed 'All You Need Is Love', written especially for the broadcast by John Lennon. The band invited all their friends to take part in the recording – which was organised as a party – and among the participants were Brian Jones, Mick Jagger, Keith Richards, Marianne Faithfull, Eric Clapton and Keith Moon. The single was released two weeks later and was a hit all over the world. On January 3, 1970, The Beatles made their last recording at Abbey Road; the song was 'I Me Mine'. In the following years, Pink Floyd took over their position as the "house band" at Abbey Road.

The Beatles were EMI's major triumph of the Sixties, but the company also made mistakes. On September 21, 1964, The Who – using the name The High Numbers – made a nervous audition in studio 2, but were turned

NEW MUSICAL EXPRESS ✳   On sale Friday, week ending July 1, 1967

...de EMI studios, JOHN LENNON, RINGO STARR and PAUL McCARTNEY ...for George Harrison, who was held up in traffic. Paul reads the BBC-TV handout ...them and the " Our World " TV show. His button says: " The Love Of My Life."

Expensive sandwich-men! The BEATLES wear boards which, when lined up (and the fifth board is seen) give the English, French, German and Spanish for the title of their next single, " Love Is All You Need." On George's board it seems that a little Russian has crept in!

Pictures by Napier Russell, Barry Peake and Alec Byrne ● Words by Andy Gray

EATLES USE THREE SATELLITES TO PLUG NEXT SINGLE!

...history was made on Sunday, when a new ...cord was plugged to the whole world at the ...me ! The honour rightly went to the Beatles, ...ng their " Love Is All You Need," an up-beat, ...sounding, simple-lyriced song which, John ...sound and pictures went out from the EMI ...where the Beatles make all their discs, via BBC- ...ross the world, on Early Bird space booster over ...antic, and spanned the wide Pacific via Lana ...d ATS/B satellites. The audience was estimated ...00,000!

...eatles were seen in action, John and Paul together ...chairs, with earphones on and miles in front of ...eorge farther back and Ringo at the back. They ...en playing and then the camera went to George ...in the control booth. He suggested the extra ...s come in and thirteen of them took their places ...the Beatles and facing them. While they filed in, ...road manager Mal Evans took sandwiches round ...boys and some sang " She Loves Me, Yeah Yeah ...off-key, ...with the violins at the start and brass at the end,

...the Beatles went through their new number, which has a chorus reminiscent of their songs of four years ago. It should be a big hit as it is simple and easy to sing. John spoke the message over a background of " Love, love, love " sung by Paul and George.

Press weren't invited to the actual transmission (only a few Beatles' friends, like Mick Jagger, Gary Leeds, Keith Richard, Marianne Faithfull, Jane Asher, Patti Boyd, Graham Nash and Keith Moon were present), but the day before the doors were thrown open for a free-for-all pictures session, at which I managed to have a quick word with—

PAUL: Someone's just asked if I'm leaving the group. And there seems to be another rumour I'm moving. Both very wrong. I've just finished my house and like it a lot. No, I haven't bought a kilt yet.

GEORGE: We will do a TV show before we do a film. Nothing new to tell you about the film project. No script yet.

RINGO: My garden is looking great now. Got some of my building men to help the gardening contractor and everything's okay.

JOHN: This song will be our next single. This TV show will give it a nice send off.

Indeed, with some 6,500 TV workers and 1,000,000 miles of telephone wire working for the disc, it couldn't be bad!

...general scene in the EMI studio, where some hundred photographers let flash at the BEATLES. When this picture was taken John was missing, but he soon appeared alongside the other three.

Our photographers think this picture is a triumph—all four BEATLES are looking at the camera, have all their eyes open, and three of them are smiling (George, why couldn't you have smiled, eh ?).

down by EMI. The Who knew that The Beatles had recorded their first album here, which certainly contributed to their anxiety.

People from all over the world still make the "pilgrimage" to Abbey Road to walk on the famous crossing and perhaps write their tribute to The Beatles – or some other famous band that has used the studio – on the wall outside the studio. The wall is washed clean very week, but before each cleaning it is photographed, section by section, and the pictures are then preserved for posterity. Unfortunately, there aren't any guided tours of Abbey Road since there are always recording sessions going on. And believe me, it's no use trying to talk yourself in! Today, there is a webcam at Abbey Road, pointed at the crossing. If you're curious to know who's crossing the street right now, you may visit this web page: http://www.abbeyroad.co.uk/virtual_visit/webcam/

Cavendish Avenue

7 Cavendish Avenue
St. John's Wood
Tube: St. John's Wood
Bus: 189

I turn back to Grove End Road and walk into Circus Road, which I follow a couple of hundred yards until I reach 7 *Cavendish Avenue*. There, only a few minutes' walk from Abbey Road, Paul McCartney found a sheltered 19th Century house, which he bought on April 13, 1965 for the sum of £40,000. However, he didn't move in until the end of March 1966, since he wanted to do some renovations first. Among the first things he did when he had moved into the house was to buy a sheepdog called Martha, who then inspired him to write the song 'Martha My Dear'.

During the years at the Asher family's house in Wimpole Street, Paul never had the opportunity to throw any private parties or indulge in any excesses, so after he had moved in he arranged a succession of dinners and parties. The parties were held in the big, bright living room with a fireplace at the back of the house, which had French windows facing the terrace. On the walls, there were paintings by the surrealist Magritte, whom Paul admired. In the living room there was also a colour monitor together with a large prototype of a video tape recorder, which he and the other members of The Beatles had been given by the BBC so that they could try them out. At this time, they were pretty much alone in owning video tape recorders in London.

In the garden, Paul had a large glass dome built, which he used for meditation. Later, a huge round bed was placed there, a gift from Alice Cooper and Groucho Marx (!). It was given to Paul after Cooper had visited him and said that this was the perfect place for the bed, which he himself had received from Groucho.

On the upper floor there was a music room with a large collection of instruments and tape recorders, and this was where many of The Beatles' most famous songs were written. Paul had a psychedelic rainbow painted on the piano in the room, and here, facing the street, he wrote songs such as 'Hey Jude' and 'Penny Lane'. Together with John Lennon he also wrote some of the songs for the *Sgt. Pepper's Lonely Hearts Club Band* album, among them 'Getting Better', 'She's Leaving Home' and 'A Day In The Life'.

Paul McCartney 1967 ▶ Someone who often called on Paul was Mick Jagger: he and Marianne Faithfull were frequent guests when they were living in Harley House, which is located nearby. Mick Jagger and Paul were the ones who decided when the Stones and The Beatles would release their singles, in order to avoid clashes in the release schedules. During the idyllic years of 1966–67 Paul would still open his door to visiting fans who wanted to ask him about The Beatles' records. And if they had travelled a long way, it happened that he invited them in for tea and a chat. I have heard that Paul still owns the house, but that he's hardly ever there; the street is quiet and still today, and there is no longer any music emanating from the house.

I walk back to Grove End Road, which I follow up to the St. John's Wood underground station. This is the location of the Abbey Road Café, which also functions as the studio's retailer, and those who are interested can buy Beatles souvenirs, T-shirts and other memorabilia there. I skip the souvenirs and instead I take the tube up to northwest London, where one of the places I will visit is connected to The Rolling Stones.

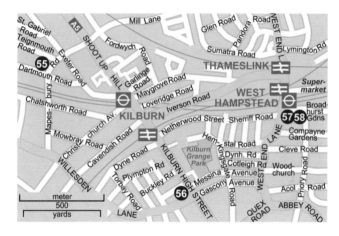

55 Mapesbury Road
56 State Cinema
57 Klooks Kleek
58 Decca Studios

Kilburn

Mapesbury Road

I get off at Kilburn Station and walk along Exeter Road for a few hundred yards until I reach 33 *Mapesbury Road*. At the corner there is a red two-storey brick house with a low brick wall in front of it. Mick Jagger and Keith Richards moved here in September 1963 and soon afterwards their manager Andrew Loog Oldham moved here as well. They moved into two rooms on the ground floor, to the left when you view it from the street.

The move to Mapesbury Road marked the start of the alliance between the Jagger-Richards-Oldham troika, which meant that the band's founder, Brian Jones, was left out in the cold. This was an intentional strategy on the part of Oldham, who realised that the independent Brian Jones was harder to manoeuvre into the more commercial path he was aiming for. He was also of the opinion that the focus should be on Mick Jagger's role as singer,

33 Mapesbury Road
Kilburn
Tube: Kilburn Station

MARIANNE GETS ROLLING WITH A STONES SONG

ALTHOUGH you wouldn't realise it at first, Marianne Faithfull's first disc was composed by two of the Rolling Stones, Mick Jagger and Keith Richard, along with their co-manager, Andrew Loog Oldham.

Marianne's debut is soft, melodic, folky and called "As Tears Go By." Whereas the Rolling Stones like to specialise in musical tear-ups.

But it suits Marianne. She likes and sings folk music with Americans Joan Baez and Bob Dylan as her favourites.

Disc producer Andrew Oldham discovered her at a party. Her boy friend—a mate of Peter and Gordon—took her there and, says Marianne: "This fellow came up and said, ' Hey, would you like to make a record.'"

The fellow was Andrew Oldham. He escorted Marianne to the recording studio where she recorded "As Tears Go By "—with all the lights turned off. Says she : "I was embarrassed to be the centre of attention."

Marianne is 17 and attends (like Dusty Springfield and Kathy Kirby before her) a convent school. This is in Reading where she lives and where she got a little singing experience in coffee bars for "about ten shillings a night."

At present Marianne is studying for her "A" level GCE examinations. If she passes, she would like to go on to a university — her father is a lecturer at London University.

But, of course, the success of "As Tears Go By " may change all that. Especially as she has just taken her first screen test as well . . .

Marianne's mother is Ava Sacher-Masoch, Baroness Erisso.

IAN DOVE.

MARIANNE FAITHFULL

From the NME ..

5 YEARS AGO
TOP TEN 1959—Week ending Aug. 2
Last This
Week

1	1	LIVING DOLL
		Cliff Richard (Columbia)
3	2	DREAM LOVER
		Bobby Darin (London)
4	3	LIPSTICK ON YOUR COLLA
		Connie Francis (MGM
2	4	BATTLE OF NEW ORLEAN
		Lonnie Donegan (Py

One of the first songs that the Jagger/Richards team wrote was 'As Tears Go By'. Marianne Faithfull, Mick's future girlfriend, made a breakthrough with the song in the autumn of 1964. Initially, they hated their own sweet ballads, which didn't stop them from recording the song a little over a year later. (New Musical Express August 21, 1964) ▲

but he had to accept that much of the attention continued to be directed at the charismatic Brian Jones. However, no-one can deny that Oldham's convictions laid the foundation for the group's eventual commercial success.

Even though the new apartment on Mapesbury Road was slightly better than the old one on Edith Grove (see Chelsea section), the difference from before wasn't too big. Apart from a bed in both rooms, there was no other furniture except for a closet, and the clothes that couldn't fit in there were spread around on the floors and the beds. A small record-player was on the floor next to Keith Richards' bed, so that he didn't have to get out of bed when he wanted to change records.

Mapesbury Road was where Mick Jagger and Keith Richards took their first few steps as songwriters. As their manager, Oldham realised that The Rolling Stones had to write their own songs if they were to become really big, and therefore he demanded one day that Mick and Keith must write a song before he would allow them to leave the house. The first songs the couple wrote they felt were terrible pop ballads, which they didn't want the band to play but instead gave to other artists.

The first song they wrote was 'It Should Be You', which never became a hit for anyone. However, the American singer Gene Pitney was successful with 'That Girl Belongs To Yesterday' (after he had reworked it), and Marianne Faithfull achieved her 1964 breakthrough with 'As Tears Go By'. Although Mick and Keith really tried to write a blues song for the group, the result was always yet another pop ballad, and the duo's first contribution to The Stones was 'Tell Me'. While Mick Jagger often spent his time at his girlfriend Chrissie Shrimpton's place, Keith devoted himself to his guitar and record-player, and in early 1964 he played The Four Seasons' 'Rag Doll' over and over again for several days in a row. Together with Oldham he finally wrote a pastiche on the song, 'All I Want Is My Baby', which was given to Bobby Jameson, another of Oldham's artists.

The Rolling Stones' breakthrough songs 'Not Fade Away' and 'Little Red Rooster' were recorded during the time that Keith Richards and Mick Jagger lived in Mapesbury Road, and their fame quickly grew. Soon it became common knowledge where Mick and Keith were living and outside the house the fans were gathering, scissors in hand, prepared to snatch a souvenir of whatever kind.

Friday, May 8, 1964

NEW MUS

RICHARD GREEN
continues the new
NME series . . .

STANDING on a platform at a railway station during the morning rush-hour, one day, a young r-and-b fan met a chap he had first come into contact with years before. They had drifted apart, but when they met again, they started talking about Chuck Berry and John Lee Hooker.

Nobody else on the station took any notice of the long-haired youngsters who were arranging to meet and listen to some LPs in a few days' time.

Really, they were like any two r-and-b fans. Except that they were Keith Richard and Mick Jagger.

"I had known Mick since I was at primary school, but I didn't see him for ages," said Keith. "We lost touch with one another, then when I met him again I was waiting for the train to go to work and he was off to the London School of Economics.

"I had a Chuck Berry record with me and Mick asked what it was. I told him 'Back In The USA' and we started talking about Berry and people like that. I had only a few records at the time, but Mick had a fantastic collection so we decided to get together and listen to them."

That was that. Within a few months, Mick and Keith were appearing together and the Rolling Stones were born.

If Keith hadn't met Mick that morning, he would have caught his train and travelled to an advertising office.

Keith peered through the window of his co-manager's office overlooking Regent's Park and told me : "I went to Dartford Technical School but our policies didn't agree so they asked me to leave. Then I studied for three years at Sidcup Art School.

Big deal!

"At the time, I was going into advertising. I finished my course and I was all ready to go into the big wide world of advertising full-time, but I never made it because the Rolling Stones overlapped."

When Keith and Mick teamed up they spent quite a time going round jazz clubs with all sorts of odd people. Then they heard of an r-and-b club that was opening in Ealing.

"We thought : ' Oh, big deal, this is it ' so we went along to have a

KEITH RICHARD
met Mick again on platform

look," Keith recalled. "Charlie was playing the drums there with Alexis Korner and Brian used to go there quite often."

It didn't take long for Keith, Mick, Charlie and Brian to get together and form a little clique. They spent hours talking and playing r-and-b. They had found something in common and they wanted to make the most of it.

Someone suggested forming a group. No need to tell you the name it was given.

"We began in 1962, but we didn't have a drummer. We had one that wasn't much good and when he left we were stuck. Charlie didn't begin with us, he stayed with Alexis, but by that time he had left that band, so he joined up with us and Dick Taylor, who played with us, left."

Georgio Gomelsky got the Stones to play at Richmond Station Hotel on Sunday nights where he ran the Craw Daddy Club. Suddenly, everything went mad and the Press

descended upon the place to get on the new craze. The Beatles were often among the audience.

"It got so bad that we le Keith went on. "We were play regularly four nights a week then and we had met And Loog Oldham and Eric Easton v became our managers and the is history."

While most people, especially th who have made the Rolling Sto LP what it is, happily accept the that the group are purely r-an Keith does not necessarily agree v that view.

Giggle

He says : "R-and-b's a bit o giggle. It's hard to say what r-an is. So many people say Ch Berry is r-and-b, then he says h rock and roll, so where do you from there ? Bo Diddley calls music Bo Diddley, so that's settled. Still, I don't mind what call it at the moment and for next ten years I'm happy. Whe it will last, I don't know."

Obviously, the Stones will last l enough for Keith to go on add to his collection of guitars. Ma they'll go on long enough for him buy the house he wants on Thames.   RICHARD GREE

SEARCHERS OKAY
CHAOTIC CONCER

DESPITE the presence of Searchers, Brian Epstein's "Pops Alive" concert at the Pri of Wales on Sunday was not the s cess one would have expected. Wat ing the first house was rather witnessing a rather chaotic d rehearsal.

You got the feeling it was going be "one of those nights" after c pere Alan Freeman gave a g build-up to the first act . . . and t had to refer to a piece of paper to the name of it !

The Searchers were great. T closed an exciting act with "Wh I Say" and went off to a tremend reception from an audience sounded capacity—even if it was Praise, too, for the dynamic Sou Incorporated, who replaced T o Meehan's disbanded Combo, and Bennett and the Rebel Rousers.

CHRIS HUTCHI

The red brick wall was covered with written declarations of love and many even tried to get into the apartment. They finally had to find somewhere else to live in the autumn of 1964.

Before I leave Kilburn I decide to visit an old concert venue and therefore I walk back towards the station and pass under the railway bridge, where Kilburn High Road begins. After a while I see a tall white building on my right side, with a tower that looks like a small skyscraper.

Gaumont State Cinema

197–199 Kilburn High Road is the location of the Gaumont State Cinema, also known as the State Theatre. The white building is seen from afar and today it gives a somewhat strange impression as it protrudes from the brown, run-down surroundings, as if it was left there while the city planners journeyed on to newer, more interesting areas.

Although today the building is a gigantic bingo hall, where some of the original neon decoration is hanging in shreds, one can still sense its former glory. Part of the magnificent interior decoration in Italian Renaissance style is still there, together with the biggest Wurlitzer Organ in Great Britain: a fantastic creation with 1,200 pipes that was formerly used during film screenings, and which is still used on special occasions a couple of times every year.

State Cinema was built in 1938 as

New Musical Express
May 8, 1964 ◀

56

State Cinema
Kilburn on Tube:
197-199 Kilburn High
Road
Tube: Kilburn Station

a miniature version of New York's Empire State Building and was one of Europe's biggest cinemas at the time. Seating 4,000 people and with standing room for just as many, it was also suitable as a concert venue for bigger events. There was also a dance hall adjacent to the cinema, which could room 1,200 people; in the Fifties world-famous jazz acts would perform there and later on there were also rock concerts.

The first rock act to perform here was Bill Haley And The Comets, in February 1957, while Buddy Holly, who was enormously influential in England, did two concerts on March 2, 1958, almost a year before he tragically died in a plane crash. The Beatles played in the dance hall twice, the first time on April 9, 1963, together with Gerry & The Pacemakers, and on October 23, 1964, they performed two concerts, right in the middle of the recording period for the Beatles For Sale album.

On November 19, 1963, The Rolling Stones played to a sold-out house and the police had to calm down the many disappointed fans who failed to get in. After the concert many in the audience stormed the stage, but everybody managed to escape except Charlie Watts who ended up on the floor with a bunch of girls on top of him. He was finally rescued by the guards, but his newly purchased pink shirt was ripped to shreds.

State Cinema remained as a live venue for rock music during the Seventies. For example, Jethro Tull started their UK tour here on February 27, 1971, and Keith Richards and Ron Wood performed at the State Cinema on July 13 and 14, 1974, when Ron Wood was launching his first solo album, I've Got My Own Album To Do. The Who's Keith

Moon did one of his last live performances at the State Cinema, on December 15, 1977, when an extremely drunk Pete Townshend really made a fool of himself by shouting insults at the audience during the unsuccessful concert.

In the Eighties, the State Cinema was under threat of being torn down, but the building was saved for posterity thanks to new investors who renovated the building and converted it into a bingo hall. You can tell from the magnificent building that it was once built with grand visions, and it's a little sad that it hasn't been afforded a more dignified old age.

West Hampstead

Klooks Kleek

Heavy clouds are gathering and I rush back to the underground to get off at the next stop, which is West Hampstead. When I arrive it's starting to rain and I walk into the Rat & Parrot pub, which is close to the station, at 100 West

Klooks Kleek
West Hampstead
100 West End Lane
Tube:
West Hampstead

Klooks Kleek started
their R&B nights on
April 13, 1964. The first
act was one of the
main attractions at the
time, Georgie Fame. ▶

MEET GEORGIE FAME !
at the opening of KLOOKS KLEEK'S
Regular MONDAY R 'n' B SESSIONS
MONDAY, APRIL 13th, 3/6

End Lane. In the Sixties the pub was called The Railway
Hotel and the club *Klooks Kleek* was located above it.

Klooks Kleek was started by Dick Jordan, who had the
ambition to present a wide spectrum of jazz and R&B.
But in November 1964 he was forced to give up the jazz,
since the blues had taken over the audience's interest completely. Klooks Kleek quickly became a popular venue for
recording live albums, the reasons being that the mood

DECCA

JOHN
MAYALL
PLAYS
JOHN
MAYALL

RECORDED LIVE AT KLOOKS KLEEK !

John Mayall
recorded his first
album at Klooks
Kleek in December
1964. In the
Sixties, his group,
Bluesbreakers, was
mostly known as a
nursery for future
world-famous gui-
tarists such as Eric
Clapton, Peter Green
and Mick Taylor. ▶

was warm and enthusiastic and that Decca Records was located next door. Cables would simply be drawn out of the window of Klooks Kleek and then into Decca, where the songs were recorded.

The first band to record a live album here was The Graham Bond Organisation. *Live At Klooks Kleek* was recorded in October 1964, featuring Jack Bruce on bass and Ginger Baker on drums; later, both would be members of Cream. On December 7, 1964, John Mayall's Bluesbreakers recorded the live album *John Mayall Plays John Mayall*. At the time, the band consisted of John Mayall, mainly playing the organ, Hughie Flint on drums, John McVie on bass and Roger Dean on guitar. Roger Dean was more of a country music guitarist and was replaced by Eric Clapton six months later.

John Mayall's Bluesbreakers went on to perform several times at the club, for example during the summer of 1965, featuring Clapton on guitar. On February 1, 1968, Jimi Hendrix went onstage to jam with the band. On March 17, 1966, a temporary constellation using the name The Peter B's performed there: Rod Stewart, Peter Green on guitar, Mick Fleetwood on drums and Peter Barden on keyboards. Shortly afterwards, the band formed the nucleus of Shotgun Express.

A couple of months later the blues legend Zoot Money and his Big Roll Band recorded the live album *Zoot!* at the club. One of the members in the band was guitarist Andy Summers, who much later became a member of The Police. The club was packed that night and hundreds of people were turned away. Brian Auger, leader of the group The Trinity, introduced the band and in the audience, offering moral support, were Georgie Fame and Chas Chan-

Zoot Money and his
Big Roll Band offered
a big show when they
recorded the live album
Zoot! on May 31, 1966 ▶

dler, The Animals' bass player. The band had an enormous
repertoire to choose from, but elected to record their
nine most popular club songs. The biggest cheer erupted
during the closing song, 'Barefootin', when Zoot suddenly stopped singing and ran around tearing the shoes
off the band members, and then tore the shows off the
audience members in front of the stage.

Cream made their London debut here in August 1966
and in November they tried to make a live recording. The
recording was a failure, however, since the volume was
much too high for the microphones, and the record was
never released to the general public. Ten Years After had
better luck with their recording of the *Undead* album in

the spring of 1968. Among the songs they performed was the original version of 'I'm Going Home', which gave them their international breakthrough at the Woodstock Festival the following year.

Other bands who played at Klooks Kleek were Steampacket (featuring Long John Baldry, Rod Stewart and Julie Driscoll), Led Zeppelin, Yes, Jethro Tull and Uriah Heep. On August 26, 1969, Deep Purple did an acclaimed performance at the club. However, audience interest in club gigs was diminishing and the owner, Dick Jordan, closed down Klooks Kleek in January 1970. Later in the Seventies, the Moonlight Club opened here; it was a centre for punk and new wave music.

Even though the premises are closed today, fortunately the spacious pub on the ground floor is still there. I feel as if I can still hear the music in the walls: the atmosphere inspires you to have more beers than is probably good for you. Since the rain is pouring down outside I choose to remain for a while, sitting at one of the large windows facing the street, watching people rush by. Many of them have umbrellas, but for some the downpour was not part of the plan and they try to shield themselves with whatever they have handy: a jacket, a hood or just a newspaper. A gentleman in a suit, white shirt and tie seems to have realised the hopelessness of the situation and resignedly walks along with his clothes pasted to his body like a wet suit, carrying his newspaper under his arm.

Ten Years After recorded their *Undead* album at Klooks Kleek in May 1968. Many regard this as one of the best live albums made in the Sixties. ▼

But the rain usually comes in showers in London and after a while I head out on the streets again. I walk around the corner and look up at the windows above the pub, where the cables were drawn out of Klooks Kleek, and I feel a little melancholy that they are completely closed these days. The cables ran into the building next door, where Decca Records once had their offices.

Decca Studios

Decca Studios
West Hampstead
165 Broadhurst
Gardens
Tube:
West Hampstead

This was where The Beatles went to make an audition on January 1, 1962, although they were eventually given the thumbs down by Dick Rowe of Decca. To be quite honest, the songs The Beatles played didn't reveal the group's true potential, nor their originality: they played quaint numbers such as 'Besame Mucho', 'The Sheik Of Araby' and a carbon-copy arrangement of Chuck Berry's 'Memphis, Tennessee'.

The following year, Dick Rowe got his own back when he signed The Rolling Stones to the label, thanks to a tip-off from George Harrison. But the pressure on him was

The top floor of this building, behind the locked-up windows, was once the location of Klooks Kleek. From here the recording cables were drawn to the next door Decca house, with the characteristic blue windows. ▶

so hard at the time that he was forced to enter a unique agreement: the Stones were allowed to use whichever studio and producer they wanted, without Decca having any say about it. Also, the band were given a higher royalty than The Beatles were given by EMI.

After the mistake with The Beatles, it was said that Decca signed everybody and everything, and if their doorman had started whistling he would have been given a record contract in a flash. But that wasn't true, and Dick Rowe was to make more mistakes. In the autumn of 1963 he turned down a group called The Ravens; the following year they would become world-famous as The Kinks. But the most embarrassing blunder occurred a few years later. In November 1966, Rowe was courted by the manager Michael Jeffrey, who had a couple of completed recordings by a new artist that he wanted to launch, but he was turned down on the spot. The artist was Jimi Hendrix and the songs were 'Hey Joe' and 'Stone Free'!

The Decca house looks like it did way back when, with its characteristic blue window-frames, but today the building belongs to the National Opera, and it's probably safe to assume that no young rock groups dreaming of a recording contract will show up here.

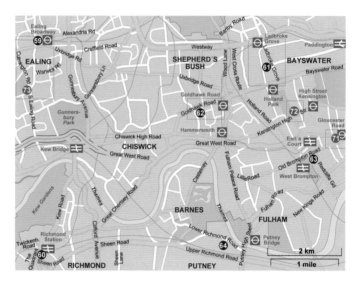

59 Ealing Club

60 Crawdaddy Club

61 Lansdowne Crescent

62 Goldhawk Club

63 Troubadour

64 Half Moon

71 1 Courtfield Road

72 Sticky Fingers

73 35 Sunnyside Road

West and Southwest London

Ealing

The London variation of American rhythm & blues that turned into a British amalgamation of rhythm & blues and rock, didn't start in one of the clubs in the West End or Soho. Those clubs were exclusively jazz clubs and some of them, such as the Flamingo Club, might possibly allow some jazz-influenced blues on the premises. This new wave actually began outside central London, in the suburb of Ealing, west of London. Therefore, I take the tube towards Ealing Broadway, and after less than half an hour I arrive and exit the station. One may also take the train from Paddington Station, which is a little quicker.

Ealing Club
Ealing
42a Broadway
Tube:
Ealing Broadway
Train from
Paddington Station

Ealing Club

It's raining outside, so I rush across the street towards Broadway 42a, where there's a white house with a sign that says Azur Nightclub on the wall. On the short side, there are some steep steps leading down to a narrow passage between the houses, where I find the entrance to what was once the G Club, better known as

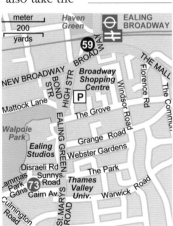

In order to reach Ealing Club you had to walk down the steps to the right. ▲

the Ealing Club. It is wet and only a few rays of light find their way down to the narrow walkway, which seems unchanged since the club opened on March 17, 1962. Blues pioneers Alexis Korner and Cyril Davies were the ones who started the Ealing Club, the reason being that it was so hard to get gig opportunities at the conservative London jazz clubs. The club was open on Saturday nights and the house band was Alexis' own band, Alexis Korner's Blues Incorporated, featuring harmonica player Cyril Davies, Jack Bruce (later in Manfred Mann and Cream) on bass, Charlie Watts on drums and Long John Baldry on vocals. But it was a very loose line-up, which was constantly changing and largely functioned as a nursery for new blues musicians and blues band. Ealing Club and Alexis Korner inspired the formation of a number of other bands.

MASSIVE SWING TO R&B

MM special

The R&B grip on the London music scene is highlighted on this special map showing the strongholds where the clubs are thickest and busiest

RICHMON

TWICKENHAM

KINGST

Two years after the opening of Ealing Club many of its visitors had started their own R&B bands. The success for the British variation on rhythm & blues, which also contained a large portion of rock, forced most of the jazz clubs to change their direction if they wanted to survive. (Melody Maker, April 18, 1964) ◀

THERE has been a lot of talk about Greater London's swing to the left. But it's been swinging to rhythm-and-blues for some time. R&B is, in fact, the London sound. And it's spreading, although there is, as yet, little to be heard north of Newcastle or west of Bristol.

"everything is exploding," declares Bill Carey, manager of the Band and General Agency, recently formed by Ted Morton of Jazzshows.

And Bill quotes figures to prove it. He claims that within a 40-mile radius of Central London some 300,000 people pay to hear R&B every week.

According to Bill there are some 300 groups in the country aiming to play R&B—140 of them in the Greater London area.

'In beat, the audience screams at the group... in R&B the group screams at the audience'

BILL CAREY

R&B is quite distinct from the beat scene," says Bill. "I reckon that each week groups are pulling in around £750,000 worth of business—and will pass the million mark soon. It may be a all-time entertainment industry but it certainly has a big future.

"I would say R&B is a southern scene—not forgetting that the Animals played for years in Newcastle and there are plenty of groups outside London.

Fight

"It's curious thing about it is that the males outnumber the females in the audiences. You see great swing lines in front of the stages.

"And the London audience is definitely increasing. Any club presenting R&B that doesn't pull in 500

by BOB DAWBARN

people can consider it is doing poor business. At 100 Oxford Street, R&B is pulling in between double and treble the number of customers who come for trad.

"Every agent seems to be after every band at the moment. I believe far too many agents are signing every group they can get hold of, just to have them on the books. It may do the agents good, but I'm sure it will be bad for the groups in the long run.

"Up-and-coming groups? In the next four months, as far as the South is concerned, I think it will be a hard fight between the

Animals, the Pretty Things and the Yardbirds.

"And two groups I'd love to have on my books are The Tridents and a Northampton outfit called The Apex."

The name certainly get further and further out, with titles like The Who, Them, the Bluebottles and the Pretty Things.

Release

"Using the leader's name is going out," says Carey. "Many of them pick names from tunes they like. The Pretty Things are named after the Bo Diddley tune, for example, and the Ground Hogs were called after a John Lee Hooker number.

"R&B even has its own National Anthem, 'I've got my mojo working',

just as 'The Saints' used to be compulsory for the trads."

Hamish Grimes, manager of the Yardbirds, asserts, "They the working seven nights a week at very high prices. They are booked almost solid for the next three months—and that is without a record."

Their first release is due out next month.

"R&B is beginning to go down extremely well in the Midlands and North," asserts Grimes, "But I think there are two distinct kinds of followings.

"One set follows the Georgie Fame type of music which is essentially a London thing. Other groups, like the Downliners Sect, Jimmy Powell and the Five Dimensions, and the Yardbirds, appeal more on the fringe scene with beat."

Perhaps the biggest bookers of R&B are the Malcolm Nixon Agency.

Future

Their John Martin told me: "Apart from London the big centres are Newcastle, Manchester, Birmingham, Stoke, Sheffield and Norwich. The South Coast uses between 20 and 25 of the groups every week.

"We recently signed our tenth band and they are all earning good money. But you have to be terribly careful to make sure that what you have is good. It's no good flogging a second-rate group to somebody just because he needs one in a hurry.

"My tips for the future? Long John Baldry's groups, of course. They not only took over where Cyril Davies

stopped but had pushed further ahead. Alex Harvey is getting really big, his first LP sold 1,000 copies in the first week.

"I think Jimmy Powell and the Five Dimensions could be the first with a really big record hit among the lesser-known groups. And then the Animals and Georgie Fame have ever-increasing support.

"In terms of pure R&B I feel the Ball, Barber and Bilk of the music will be Harvey, Baldry and Fame. The rest lean more towards the pop side."

Crowds

John Gee, manager of the Marquee, admits the club books R&B because "these groups bring in the money."

"In the last three days," he told me, "I've had ten groups ringing me—and I'd never even heard of any of them. It's getting that ridiculous.

"Jazz, however, is holding its own at the Marquee. Saturday, admittedly a good night for anything, we have modern jazz and attendance compares favourably with R&B nights. The same goes for Sundays when Stan Getz has pulled in fantastic crowds over the past month.

"I must admit that our one bad night is Wednesdays when we present mainstream or trad.

"My tips for R&B stardom? The Yardbirds have got what the kids seem to want. Another excellent group is the Cheynes, who dropped at the club while Manfred Mann was on tour."

WHO will be the new big-timers in the ever-growing R&B scene. MM asked people intimately connected with the business for their tips. John Martin of the Malcolm Nixon Agency—Georgie Fame, Long John

Baldry, Alex Harvey, Jimmy Powell's Five Dimensions and the Animals. Bill Carey, of the Band and General Agency — the Pretty Things (pictured above), the Animals and the Yardbirds.

243

On the first Saturday, 100 people came to the club, which had room for 200 persons, but after just four weeks the club had 800 members. Ealing Club was always packed with people and many would pay the entrance fee just to get in and hear the last number. Those who went there certainly didn't end up in an elegant and swanky club. The premises were rough, dirty and very damp, and above the stage there was a mouldy piece of cloth so that there wouldn't be too much condensation water dripping down on the musicians.

Alexis Korner encouraged everybody who wanted and had the guts to go up onstage and perform with the band. On April 7, 1962, Brian Jones – using the pseudonym Elmo Lewis – and Paul Pond made a guest appearance together with the house band, and were a big hit. They performed 'Dust My Broom', with Brian Jones on slide guitar and Paul Pond on vocals, and especially Brian Jones attracted a lot of attention with his guitar playing. Alexis Korner recruited Paul Pond for Blues Incorporated after the performance, but Brian Jones turned him down since he had decided to form a band of his own. Paul Pond would later be known as Paul Jones, the lead singer with Manfred Mann.

This night was of great significance in rock history, since Mick Jagger and Keith Richards were in the audience together with Dick Taylor. Just like everybody else, they were very impressed by the performance and went up to speak with Brian Jones afterwards. Through Brian they got in touch with Ian Stewart, but it would be a few more months before they would all be onstage together.

A couple of weeks later, Mick Jagger and Keith Richards performed at the club. Mick Jagger was offered a position as one of the singers in Blues Incorporated, but

Harmonica player Cyril Davies and Alexis Korner at the Ealing Club in the spring of 1962. They started the club because no club in central London would allow electric blues music. Behind the drums is a young man named Charlie Watts, and this was where Brian Jones recruited the future members of The Rolling Stones. Many other club visitors would become famous musicians, among them Eric Clapton, Jeff Beck, Eric Burdon, Pete Townshend, Paul Jones and Art Wood. ▶

Keith Richards' rocky Chuck Berry style was a little too much for Alexis Korner. Every time Keith made a guest appearance, Alexis Korner managed to break one of the strings of his guitar, so as to avoid having to take part in the performance.

Eric Burdon got wind of the club and hitch-hiked down from Newcastle for some well-received guest appearances. Filled with inspiration, he hitch-hiked back and persuaded his friends in the Alan Price Combo to become a real blues band, and a couple of years later they

achieved their breakthrough as The Animals. According to Eric Burdon he was there one night and had been promised the opportunity to appear as guest vocalist, but when he jumped up on the stage, another young guy appeared at the same time. Alexis Korner diplomatically suggested that they should sing together. They accepted and began discussing which songs to sing. Korner introduced them to each other: "This is Eric Burdon and this is Mick Jagger." But you shouldn't be to certain that it actually happened this way; Eric Burdon seems to be very fond of spreading tall stories.

In the middle of April, Alexis Korner's Blues Incorporated began getting gigs at the Marquee Club in Oxford Street and then also at the Flamingo Club in Soho. Many of the blues fans went along to the West End and Alexis Korner abandoned the Ealing Club, which got new owners.

In the summer of 1962 The Rolling Stones were formed, but they could hardly get any gigs except at the Ealing Club. Their first performance there happened on July 28. That night the line-up was Brian Jones, Mick Jagger, Keith Richards, Ian Stewart on piano, Dick Taylor on bass and Tony Chapman on drums. During the autumn they played a handful of gigs per month at the club, but things didn't really start happening for them until Bill Wyman joined them in December and then Charlie Watts in mid-January 1963.

One of the group's most avid supporters was Eric Clapton, who would also get up and sing a song every now and then, usually 'Roll Over Beethoven', but he still didn't dare perform with his guitar. Although the place was often packed on Saturdays, the Stones hardly got paid after their gigs, since the new club-owners maintained that the audience hadn't paid any entrance. The Stones were very angry and when they began getting gigs at other places, they decided to stop playing the Ealing Club. Their last gig there was on March 2, 1963. Later that year, an early version of John Mayall's Bluesbreakers made one of their first public appearances at the Ealing Club, and The Who also played a few gigs here at the beginning of their career, in the early spring of 1965.

Unfortunately, neither the old club, Azur Night Club, nor the present one, The Red Room, has protected the memory of this historical site. There is absolutely nothing to remind you that the British blues wave began here, and the lack of a sense of history feels very sad. The middle class suburb of Ealing Broadway is fairly run-down, but pretty charming and there are plenty of students here. This is also the location of Ealing Art School, which was attended by names such as Pete Townshend, Art Wood (of The Artwoods) and his more famous younger brother, Ron Wood. Later on, Freddie Mercury of Queen also studied there.

Before I leave the place I cross the street and enter the pub The North Star. The pub has a rich selection of small dishes and most of the tables are occupied by young people who are eating and talking. I make do with a beer and after a short while I go to the bus station, taking the number 65 bus to Richmond and another club surrounded by legends. If you're going directly from London you may go by underground to Richmond or take the train from Victoria Station.

Richmond

Crawdaddy Club
Richmond
1 Kew Road
Tube:
Richmond Station
Train from
Victoria Station

Crawdaddy Club

After a 40-minute bus ride through the suburbs, I reach the station in Richmond. But it's hard to find the Station Hotel, which was once the location of the *Crawdaddy Club*. I'm walking up and down Kew Road, before I finally decide that the building with the name Railway Hotel 1888 engraved in the façade is the right address. I go into the nice and spacious pub on the ground floor, order a beer and walk around snapping pictures. After a while I start talking to the helpful staff and find out that the address I have is not the right one.

I'm confused as I go out to talk to a policeman outside the station. He directs me to the address I'm looking for, which is right across the street. I walk into a big, ultra-modern hamburger restaurant and this is the right address: 1 Kew Road. And yet everything is so damned wrong! There is not even a sign left of the legendary club and the old pub environment has been completely erased.

Even the green sign on the wall, which for many years told the proud story of the Crawdaddy, has been taken down.

No-one could imagine that this used to be the Station Hotel, where different jazz clubs had been located since the early 1950s, before Russian immigrant Giorgio Gomelsky started a rhythm & blues club on Sundays at the end of 1962. The house band, Dave Hunt's Confederates – originally a trad jazz band – enlisted future Kinks founder Ray Davies and transformed itself into a blues band, Dave Hunt's R&B Band. The result was a repertoire that shifted between trad jazz and jazz-inflected blues, which made Ray Davies leave the band after just a month.

In the beginning of 1963, Gomelsky was growing tired of the house band, which chose not to show up every now and then, and began looking for a new band. Brian Jones knew Gomelsky from before, since The Rolling Stones had played a couple of times at Gomelsky's former club, the Piccadilly Club, and asked him that the band would be given a chance. The group got their chance and the Crawdaddy Club is the club where The Rolling Stones achieved their definitive breakthrough.

But it didn't start out well. They were offered £1 for each band member and a percentage of the entrance, but when they were about to make their debut on February 24, a terrible snow storm broke out. According to Gomelsky, there were only three people in the audience at the Station Hotel, which was still the name of the venue. There were twice as many people onstage as there were in the audience, but the Stones put on a show as if it were 100 people in the audience. For every week, the audience grew in number, and after a month or so they numbered a hundred, which in turn grew into several hundred.

The Rolling Stones managed to attract most of the young blues lovers in London, largely because the few others who played the blues were much older and still had a strong connection to jazz. The Stones represented the new, raw, electrified sound which you could dance to, and they were also just as young as their audience and had a challenging and fairly aggressive stage show, which attracted young people of both sexes. During this time, Brian Jones was the uncontested leader of the band – not only musically but in terms of style – and he was the one who constantly pushed the band forward.

I enter the walkway between the houses to reach the back of the house where the entrance to the club was: today it is the back door of the hamburger restaurant. I try to imagine what it must have looked like at the time, with a long line of people patiently waiting for five hours before the door opened, many of whom were disappointed when they had to turn back home because the place was full.

In front of the stage there were young and enthusiastic boys, who would soon become famous musicians in bands of their own: Don Craine (Downliners Sect), Phil May and Dick Taylor (The Pretty Things), Pete Townshend (The Who), Rod Stewart, Ian McLagan (later of The Small Faces) and of course Eric Clapton. In the audience there was also often a bunch of guys who, together with Eric Clapton, would replace The Rolling Stones at the club six months later: Keith Relf, Chris Dreja, Paul Samwell-Smith and Jim McCarthy. They became famous as The Yardbirds.

A local reporter got wind of the Stones' gigs and when he arrived at the packed club even the tables were full of dancing youths. Afterwards the reporter wanted to know the name of the club, which actually didn't have a name. But since the Stones used to end their show with Buddy Holly's 'Doin' The Crawdaddy', the name Crawdaddy was mentioned, and the club went down in history under this name. The article about the club and The Rolling Stones was published in the local paper in early April 1963. Peter Jones of the Record Mirror got wind of the rumour and assigned the reporter Norman Jopling to write an article about the Stones and the Crawdaddy Club, which became the first article about the group in the national press.

On April 14, The Beatles visited the club after a television recording in London. They had heard the rumour about The Rolling Stones' ventures at the club and were curious to see them with their own eyes. Dressed in long, black leather coats they entered the club and placed themselves discreetly in the background, but they were immediately noticed by the audience as well as the Stones onstage. There was a murmur in the room, but nobody went up to them, so they were allowed to listen in peace. They were impressed by what they saw and after the gig they went back to Brian, Keith and Mick's apartment in Edith Grove.

Now that they had been discovered by The Beatles as well, it was just a matter of time before some manager would sign The Rolling Stones. At the end of April, nineteen-year-old Andrew Loog Oldham entered the Crawdaddy. Astonished by what he saw, Oldham – still a minor – quickly found a partner, the veteran Eric Easton. The following week, the couple signed a three-year contract with the group. In the beginning of May, Dick Rowe at the Decca record label received a tip-off from George

THE ROLLING STONES

AS the trad. scene gradually subsides, promoters of all kinds of teen-beat entertainments heave a long sigh of relief that they have found something to take its place. It's Rhythm and Blues, of course—the number of R & B clubs that have suddenly sprung up is nothing short of fantastic.

One of the best-known — and one of the most successful to date—is at the Station Hotel, Kew Road, in Richmond, just on the outskirts of London. There, on Sunday evenings, the hip kids throw themselves about to the new "jungle music" like they never did in the more stinted days of trad.

And the combo they writhe and twist to is called the **Rollin' Stones**. Maybe you've never heard of them —if you live very far away from London the odds are you haven't. But by gad you will! The **Rollin' Stones** are probably destined to be the biggest group in the R & B scene if it continues to flourish. And by the looks of the Station Hotel, Richmond, flourish is merely an understatement considering that three months ago only fifty people turned up to see the group. Now club promoter bearded **Giorgio Gomelsky** has to close the doors at an early hour—over four hundred R & B fans crowd the hall.

GENUINE

And the fans who do come quickly lose all their inhibitions and proceed to contort themselves to the truly exciting music of the boys —who put heart and soul into their performances.

The fact is that, unlike all the other R & B groups worthy of the name, the Rollin' Stones have a definite visual appeal. They aren't the Jazzmen who were doing trad. eighteen months back and who have converted their act to keep up with the times. They are genuine R & B fanatics themselves, and they sing and play in a way that one would have expected more from a coloured U.S. R & B team than a bunch of wild, exciting white boys who have the fans screaming—and listening—to them.

Lineup of the group is Mick Jagger, lead vocal and harmonica and student at the London School of Economics. The fierce backing is supplied by Brian Jones, guitar and harmonica, and also spokesman and leader of the group. He's an architect, while Keith Richards, guitar, is an art student. The other three members of the group are Bill Wyman, bass guitar, Ian Stuart, piano and maraccas, and drummer Charles Watts.

Record-wise, everything is in the air, but a disc will be forthcoming. It will probably be the group's own adaptation of the **Chuck Berry** number, **"Come On"** (featured on Chuck's new Pye L.P.). The number goes down extremely well in the club's session on Sundays — other Chuck Berry numbers that are in the group's repertoire are **"Down the Road Apiece"** and **"Bye, Bye, Johnny"**—which is one of the highlights of the act.

DISC/FILM

Even though the boys haven't dead-certain plans for a disc, they do have dead-certain plans for a film. For club promoter Giorgio is best known as a film producer, and he has made several imaginative films dealing with the music scene. But for the Rollin' Stones film, there are some truly great shots of the team in action, singing and performing **"Pretty Thing"**, the Bo Diddley number. The film itself lasts for twenty minutes, and will be distributed with a main feature film.

The group are actually mad about Bo Diddley, although pianist Ian is the odd man out. Diddley numbers they perform are "Crawdad", "Nursery Rhyme", "Road Runner", "Moaner" and, of course, "Bo Diddley".

They can also get the sound that Bo gets too — no mean achievement. The group themselves are all red-hot when it comes to U.S. beat discs. They know their numbers inside out and repertoire of about eighty most of them are the number every R & B fan in the knows and near enough lo

The boys are confident they make a disc, it should They are also confident abo own playing, although on at the end of the session mond they are dead-beat. because on Sunday afterno also play the R & B sessio Ken Colyer Club.

SUPERFICIAL

But despite the fact that & B has a superficial rese to rock 'n' roll, fans of parade music would not f familiar material performed Rollin' Stones. And the not use original material— American stuff. "After all say, "can you imagine a composed R & B number

ENUINE R & B !

OLLING STONES in
at the Station Hotel,
nd, Surrey. They are
g them in" with their
aterial. (NRM Picture
BILL WILLIAMS.)

make it."
oup that thinks a lot of the
stones are The Beatles.
y came down to London
week, they were knocked
he group's singing. They
ll the evening at the
Hotel, listening to the
ind away. And now they
e word around so much in
that bookings for the
ve been flooding in — in-
veral at the famed Cavern.
s can't be bad for the R
ip who have achieved the
sound better than any
oup over here. And the
t in all likelihood will soon
eading R & B performers
untry. . . .

MARTIN YALE AGENCY
30a St. Peter's Ave.,
Cleethorpes
Representing:—
**CARTER-LEWIS
KEITH KELLY
HOUSTON WELLS
and the MARKSMEN
THE SOUND OF
THE ECHOES
with PAUL KEENE
JAMIE LEE and the
ATLANTICS
RICKY WILSON and
the YOUNG ONES
ERIC LEE and the
4 ACES
The SHELL CARSON
COMBO**
and many other attractions
for stage and ballrooms.

The first article about The Rolling Stones in the national music press. The description of the scenes at the club made the owner of the Station Hotel stop the club. (Record Mirror May 11, 1963) ◄

New Musical Express
December 27, 1963 ▶

Harrison about the new group The Rolling Stones, who were reaping great rewards at the Crawdaddy Club. Earlier, Rowe had turned down The Beatles and now he was keen to restore his reputation. He didn't waste any time but went directly to the club, and the enthusiastic scenes at the Stones' gig raised his hope of getting his own back. The following day he signed the Stones to a recording contract with Decca.

The articles about the wild concerts at the Crawdaddy Club caught the attention of the brewery that owned the Station Hotel, and caused them to close down the club. After a couple of weeks Giorgio Gomelsky opened the club again, but now at the Richmond Athletic Ground. The Rolling Stones were soon too big for the club and on September 22, 1963, they played their last gig at the Crawdaddy Club.

Giorgio Gomelsky didn't succeed in becoming the manager for the Stones, but he quickly signed The Yardbirds. They replaced the Stones at the Crawdaddy Club, but they had a rough start since the audience were missing their old favourites. However, with time they built up their own circle of loyal admirers, as the band developed. Gomelsky also arranged for the band to be the backing band for blues giant Sonny Boy Williamson when he toured Great Britain, with one of the concerts taking place at the Crawdaddy on December 9, 1963. In early 1964 Gomelsky recorded a number of live songs with The Yardbirds at the club; the quality of the recordings turned out to be surprisingly high when they were released, thirtyfive years later.

IT'S RHYTHM-AND-BLUES THAT'S BOOMING NOW

Say The Rolling Stones

By RICHARD GREEN

RHYTHM 'n' blues is as popular in Britain today as trad was in its boom period, say the Rolling Stones, who are currently enjoying their second hit parade success.

The group, which began like so many others playing weekly in an out-of-town club and which shot to fame almost overnight, had much to say about r-and-b in this country when I spoke to them this week.

"In the trad boom a couple of years ago, only British bands made any real impression, but look what is happening to r-and-b today," said Mike Jagger. "British and American acts are getting into the charts, and everywhere you go groups are playing it.

"Even with the trad boom, none of the bands did all that well as far as the hit parade went."

Since the Rolling Stones have achieved national status—via songs by Chuck Berry and Lennon and McCartney—it has been said that they have deserted their r-and-b style and gone over to more commercial numbers.

"That's untrue," exclaimed Mike. "We play the same now as we have always done. So many people have suggested that we have changed our style that we are a bit tired of hearing it.

"When we played at the Craw Daddy and Eel Pie Island we did exactly the same type of stuff, and the scenes were really raving."

He went on to explain: "It is like this: if we play two numbers and one goes down a bomb and the other falls flat, we drop the unsuccessful one. Obviously we are not going to play a tune if audiences are not going to like it, but that is as far as it goes.

"All I can say, and this goes for the rest of the boys, is that we have not changed our style and do not intend to."

While the r-and-b influence has been around for a good many years, with artists like Chuck Berry, Jerry Lee Lewis and Ray Charles having big hits, it is only lately that the British public has gone for that music in a big way.

With the advent of so many groups trying to hitch a ride on the r-and-b bandwagon, an outfit that is going to stay on long after others have fallen off must have something different and extra about it.

The Rolling Stones can claim a collection of differences.

Ask anyone to name something about the Stones and it is a fair bet that the group's hair styles will be in the answer. Their shoulder-length hair, which dances wildly as they fling themselves about the stage in reckless abandon, is really unusual.

Then there is Mike's own individual shake routine, which he lapses into during a number. It has caught on in such a big way that teenagers all over the country are emulating it on the dance floors.

Above all this, is the sound which the Rolling Stones create. A sound so exciting and gripping that few other groups can come within shouting distance of it. When they really get worked up during a performance, an electric current seems to surge through the listener's body.

"We are going on tour with the Ronettes soon," said Brian Jones, "and after that there is talk of a Continental tour, and a television series."

Talking about the Continent, Brian added: "We don't want to play at the Star Club, though. This is because British groups are only booked there to fill in.

"The club features American names and any British outfits that have appeared there have not starred.

"I know the Beatles, the Searchers and Gerry and the Pacemakers have all played the Star Club, but that was a long time ago, before they became famous. It is all right for experience, but that is all."

If the Rolling Stones have the courage to admit that they do not want to play at a scene that is among the biggest attractions on the Continent, and at the same time strike a blow for the prestige of British groups, they deserve to succeed.

Rolling Stones successors are

AT a party last Saturday night, the Yardbirds talked about their record very much in the same style as a car salesman illustrating to a prospective customer the finer points of the latest model. They were giving an outward appearance of great confidence, though inwardly they were, I felt, slightly apprehensive about the outcome.

By Richard Green

So when I telephoned them on Monday to tell them that "I Wish You Would" had entered the NME Chart at No. 26, there was a moment of stunned silence, during which I thought I had been cut off.

Then one Yardbird said: "You're joking! I never thought it'd do it this quick." Five Yardbirds then

YARDBIRDS ARE IN!

flew off in the direction of the nearest tavern to celebrate.

Actually, the Yardbirds are five nice guys who have gained a fantastic reputation among r-and-b fans by taking up residency at Crawdaddy clubs in Richmond and later Croydon. They had the unenviable task of following the Rolling Stones

to the first club, but before long they had the crowds flocking back again.

Their large, bearded manager, Georgio Gomelsky, took a chance and sent the Yardbirds to Liverpool's Cavern to play. They were an immediate hit and the offers poured in.

Recently, they taped a Granada spectacular with Peter, Paul and Mary.

One of the group's main assets—apart from their excellent music, of course—is the way in which they manage to blend in with their audiences. In between numbers, or when a string breaks, they chat to the fans and often break off into impromptu numbers.

The Yardbirds comprise Eric Clapton (lead guitar), Keith Relph (harmonica and lead singer), Chris Dreja (rhythm guitar), Paul Samwell-Smith (bass guitar) and Jim McCarty (drums).

They play because they enjoy doing so and consider it a release from all the everyday pressures that young people experience.

While the Yardbirds are not really Mods, their audiences essentially are. But I wouldn't mind betting that within a very short space of time, the Rockers and the in-betweens will be raving about the group, too.

New to the Chart

The YARDBIRDS' lead singer has his arm in a sling in the pict above, but it is now okay again. He's KEITH RELPH, and the oth are (l to r, top) JIM McCARTY, PAUL SAMWELL-SMITH (l t bottom), CHRIS DREJA and ERIC CLAPTON.

The Yardbirds replaced The Rolling Stones at the Crawdaddy Club in September 1963. The following month, Eric Clapton became the solo guitarist in the group. At the start The Yardbirds were not a remarkable band, apart from grooming Eric Clapton as a guitarist. The group became more interesting when the innovative guitarist Jeff Beck replaced Clapton in March 1965. Beck's distinct and original guitar sound gave the band a large international following. (New Musical Express May 29, 1964)   ▲

Having established that there is not a single trace left of the Crawdaddy, I don't bother to sit down, but instead I cross the street and return to the Railway Hotel. There I have a sandwich together with both a whisky and a beer, in order to put the cultural homicide I've witnessed today out of my mind.

Notting Hill

It's cloudy and grey as I exit the Notting Hill Gate underground station, which is suitable weather for the melancholy visit I plan to start this day with. I walk westward along Holland Park Avenue until I reach Ladbroke Grove, where I walk a few hundred yards to a bow-shaped street named Lansdowne Crescent. The area consists of palatial three-storey buildings with adorned white façades, high pillars and arched balconies at the front. The small park in front of the houses has a locked gate, for which only the residents have the key – a signal that this area is not meant for just anybody.

Lansdowne Crescent

At 22 *Lansdowne Crescent*, large green plants and palm trees have been planted in large pots on the steps leading up to the front door. I have a vision of a young woman stepping out of the house, just before 10.30 am on Friday, September 18, 1970, to buy a pack of cigarettes. Her name is Monika Danneman and left behind in her bed in the apartment is a sickly Jimi Hendrix, perhaps already half-choked on his own vomit. According to Danneman herself, she found him covered in vomit when she returned. She then called her friend Alvenia Bridges, who was at Eric Burdon's place, to ask for advice. They told her to call an ambulance immediately, but for some reason it wasn't until 11.18 that she finally made the call. When the ambulance finally arrived at 11.27, Hendrix still showed small signs of life,

22 Lansdowne
Crescent
Notting Hill
Tube:
Holland Park
Station

but when they arrived at St. Mary Abbot Hospital there were no signs of life.

But according to Eric Burdon's statement the same day to Jimi's friend, the reporter Sharon Lawrence, Monika Danneman first called him several hours earlier and got the advice to call an ambulance. It wasn't until the second call, around 11.00, that Danneman was finally convinced that she should call an ambulance. Whatever really happened, it was made clear in the ensuing investigation that Jimi Hendrix had been lying unsupervised in his vomit much too long; his vomiting was mainly caused by the sleeping pills (Vesperax) he had taken. There were forty sleeping pills in the bottle and Hendrix had taken nine of those, which perhaps proves that he didn't have any intention of killing himself, as many speculated he may have.

Jimi Hendrix met Monika Danneman during a tour of Germany in early 1969 and according to Danneman, during the summer of 1970 he had asked her to find

somewhere to stay in London so that they could meet when he got back after his tour. In those days, 21 and 22 Lansdowne Crescent were combined into one hotel, the Samarkand Hotel, where she found a basement apartment that she began renting in early August 1970. During this period, Jimi Hendrix stayed at the Cumberland Hotel at Marble Arch when he was in London. On the night of September 17, he was at a private party. Monika Danneman picked him up in her car at 3 am, driving him home to her apartment. Upon arriving there, she later stated, she made a few tuna fish sandwiches for the two of them, before they finally went to bed.

That last night of his life at Lansdowne Crescent, he wrote a song that included this prophetic last verse:

> The story of life is quicker
> than the wink of an eye
> The story of love
> is hello and goodbye
> Until we meet again

(The Story of Life, lyrics: Jimi Hendrix)

When Monika Danneman published her memoirs, The Inner Life Of Jimi Hendrix, she ended up in a bitter courtroom fight with her rival, Kathy Etchingham – Jimi's previous girlfriend – in 1996. The outcome was that Monika lost; shortly afterwards she gassed herself to death in her car.

Shepherd's Bush

> People try to put us d-down (Talkin''bout my generation)
> Just because we g-get around (Talkin''bout my generation)
> Things they do look awful c-c-cold (Talkin''bout my generation)
> I hope I die before I get old (Talkin''bout my generation)

(My Generation, lyrics: Pete Townshend)

Like amphetamine-chewing mods, The Who stuttered out the song 'My Generation' in 1965, achieving their international breakthrough. Now my plan is to visit the area where they began their career. Therefore, I walk down to Holland Park Avenue to take the 148 bus west, towards Shepherd's Bush. If you're in a hurry, you may take the tube to Goldhawk Road Station and from there you take the bus to the lower part of Goldhawk Road.

The farther I go along Goldhawk Road, the more suburban the area becomes, although it's fairly close to central London. Even if it's giving off a quiet impression these days, this used to be a rough area in the Sixties, and the bands who came to play here got out as quickly as they could after the gigs. After a while I reach 205 Goldhawk Road, a stand-alone two-storey house that reminds me of an old people's home.

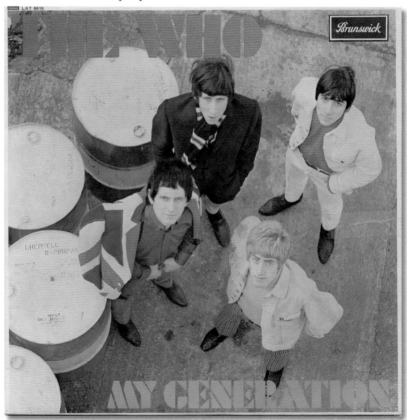

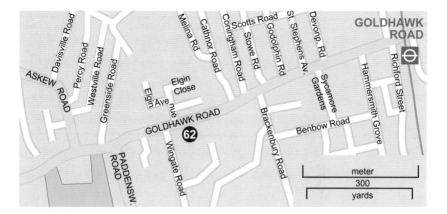

Goldhawk Club

In the Sixties, this was the location of *the Goldhawk Social Club*, which was a meeting-place for the growing mod movement in West London. There would often be fights between different groups in the garden outside the house. The Goldhawk Club, which was a members-only club, began arranging live concerts on Fridays and Saturdays in the autumn of 1963. Several artists performed here, such as The Yardbirds, The Kinks, The Animals and Georgie Fame.

But the Goldhawk Club is primarily famous because this was where The Who achieved their breakthrough. On November 22, 1963, they began performing here, using the name The Detours. They soon changed their name to The Who, and it was at the Goldhawk Club that they built up their reputation and conquered their first avid fans. Vocalist Roger Daltrey was born and grew up nearby, on *15 Percy Road*, which was important for the local patriots that made up the audience.

As I'm standing there, contemplating the house, an elderly man walks towards the front door and I walk up to

Goldhawk Club
Shepherd's Bush
205 Goldhawk Road
Tube: Goldhawk
Road Station

261

him. He tells me that these days the house belongs to the members-only club Shepherd's Bush Social Club, but he is kind enough to let me have a look inside. In the Sixties there was a giant guard standing at the massive oak front door, and you were allowed in only after showing your blue membership card, which I don't have to do now.

I enter the foyer, which in the Sixties functioned as the bar section. A staircase leads down to the room where the bands played and the audience were dancing. The stage is still there at the far end of the short side of the brown and drab room. In those days there were large sofas along the walls, but they have been replaced by small tables and chairs. Directly to the left when you get down, the small bar is still there with a few bar stools. But there were seldom or never any strong beers sold here, partly because the audience didn't have a lot of money, but also because many preferred to pop assorted pills that were washed down with a small beer or a coke. These drugs had been used by the Army as stimulants during the Second World

War, and when the war was over, there were plenty of pills left. Therefore, 100 pills didn't cost more than a large beer in 1963–1964, which partly explains all the pill-popping during the clubs up until the mid-Sixties.

On July 31, 1964, The Kinks played at the club with The Who as the supporting act, although they called themselves The High Numbers. The Kinks performed 'You Really Got Me', which was released as a single a few days later. The song inspired Pete Townshend of The Who to write a similar tune: 'I Can't Explain'. That night was the first time that The Who performed with Keith Moon behind the drums at the club. Many in the audience were sceptical and suspicious before the gig, since Moon was not from the area but from Wembley. But thanks to his personality and his artistry behind the drums, Keith Moon quickly became a favourite with the tough core audience at the Goldhawk Club.

In January 1965, The Who were to make their first appearance on television, playing their newly-released single, 'I Can't Explain', on Ready Steady Go!. The pro-

Smashing time costs WHO fortune!

ANYONE who has ever seen a demolition gang smashing down a building will know what it's like when the Who get up steam. Their music rolls and crashes and throbs like a berserk thunderstorm—and naturally, it doesn't do their instruments any good.

Vocalist Roger Daltrey slumped into a chair at the NME this week and told me: "This isn't a gimmick and I'm telling you no lies, but we have to get new guitars and drums every month or so. They just get smashed up. And it's costing us a fortune!"

Then he sat up and gave it to me straight: "It's so expensive, you could even say we Who are running at a loss at the moment."

There wasn't even the slightest trace of a smile. For Roger Daltrey, helping to produce the group's screaming, searing brand of music, is the most serious person in the world.

Jumps up

This is the kind of dedication that has sent the Who's "My Generation" absolutely C—C—CRASHING up the NME Chart this week. It stands at No. 3 in the current list, a jump of 13 places.

So many theories have been advanced about the disc and its stuttering gimmick that I asked Roger if one story credited to him—that the number is about someone who was "blocked" (or on drugs)—was true.

He denied he had ever said that. "The song just tells about a young kid who's tryin' to express himself, y'know?"

Then he grinned: "Apart from that, it was freezing in the studios when we recorded it. That's why I stutter on the lyrics!"

As usual with the Who, "My Generation" was recorded and released in about two weeks flat. They have always done this and they intend to go on for as long as possible. Even

The WHO (l to r) JOHN BROWNE, ROGER DALTREY, PETER TOWNSHEND and KEITH MOON.

the song itself was written only a few days before the session.

There was also a lot of disagreement about "My Generation" and the treatment they should give it. "Near punch-ups," according to Roger.

He has never disguised the fact that quite often the members of the Who can't stand each other. He claims that this is all to the good.

"Don't believe whatever you've seen before," he says heatedly. "The Who will never split up. We have arguments all the time but this is what gives us that extra spark. The Who thrives on friction."

Like it or not Roger's regarded by many as an avant-garde Mod spokesman in the pop business. I asked him for his views on the current pop scene.

He feels that it is in "a bad state"

at the moment, but that discs like Ke Dodd's "Tears" are purely a momentary lapse !

At the same time, according t Roger, he doesn't want to stick hi neck out by making a prediction abou the next big pop trend. "We don' want to follow anybody else's trend," he told me. "We want to set it.

"The worst thing about startin something new, like we have, is tha everybody else jumps on the band wagon ! Then you get dozens o imitations."

He looked thoughtful. "In one wa I suppose it's a good thing, because i makes us change to something new And that's what we want to do—kee changing. We just feel we never wan to get in a rut or grow old."

ALAN SMITH

New Musical Express
November 12, 1965 ▲

gramme was broadcast live and in order to ensure that the audience were positive, The Who appropriated the tickets and gave them to their devoted fans at the Goldhawk Club. The fans' wild dancing and cheering in front of the television cameras gave a proper boost to the band's continued career. The Who played the Goldhawk Club for the last time on December 3, 1965, when they gave a farewell performance for their faithful audience. By that time the band had achieved their breakthrough and the small room was no longer sufficient. They hadn't played at the club for six months and for the first time in the club's history there was a long line up Goldhawk Road. On the previous occasion the band had been paid £50 for their gig, this night the fee was £300.

There was another band that found favour with the local patriots at the Goldhawk Club, and they were The Small Faces. They were a big hit there in the winter of 1965; it was particularly Steve Marriott's vocals and Ian McLagan's Hammond organ that made the critical audience disregard the fact that the group was not from the area. The present club seems to have a considerably older and quieter membership, and there are no signs of any fights as I walk to the underground train to go to West Brompton Station in Earl's Court.

Earl's Court

Troubadour
Earl's Court
265 Old Brompton
Road
Tube: West
Brompton Station

The Troubadour

The Troubadour on 265 Old Brompton Road is one of the few popular places from the Sixties that is around today and still has a lot to offer a visitor. The Troubadour attracts attention, and passers-by slow down or stop for a while at the café. In the shop window there are several shelves of coffee pots in various colours and models, and the beautifully carved front door has been decoratively painted with colourful Medieval motifs. You immediately feel like you want to enter the café, which these days is also a restaurant with an alcohol licence and a generous choice of good food. Nor are you disappointed when you enter the premises; it's as if an entire gang of creative interior decorators have been given free hands to contribute their talents.

The Troubadour opened as a café as early as 1954, as part of the great coffee revolution in London. The philosophy of presenting new contemporary music was impor-

tant even from the beginning. The music is just as important today, and concerts featuring a wide array of artists
are arranged several times each week. Up-and-coming
acts are also welcomed at least once a week.

I walk down the stairs to the refurbished basement
room, where a long row of famous artists have performed
or jammed over the years: Jimi Hendrix, Bob Dylan, Keith
Moon, Led Zeppelin, Joni Mitchell, Rod Stewart and Paul
Simon, just to mention a few. In recent years both the
basement room with the stage and the actual café have
been extended and renovated, but without compromis-
ing the charming atmosphere that has always characterised the place.

Charlie Watts used to be a frequent visitor and began
playing the drums in different bands at nights. This was
also where he met Alexis Korner in November 1961 and
got the offer of joining Alexis Korner's Blues Incorporated. In conjunction with his London visit in the winter of 1962–1963 Bob Dylan was a frequent visitor at
the folk music clubs, and his British colleagues taught
him several traditional songs, which he then transformed
into his own. At the Troubadour he heard 'Lord Franklin'
and 'Scarborough Fair' for the first time, thanks to Martin
Carthy. He then rewrote the songs and turned them into
'Bob Dylan's Dream' and 'Girl From The North Country',
respectively. Bob Davenport taught him 'Nottamun Town'
and 'Poor Miner's Lament', which became 'Masters Of
War' and 'Only A Hobo' in Dylan's versions, and from Nigel Denver he picked up 'The Patriot Game', which was
turned into 'With God On Our Side'.

Bob Dylan was really in London to take part in a BBC
television play, after the director Philip Saville had seen

Bob Dylan at the Singers Club, December 22, 1962, where he was not welcomed with open arms by the narrow-minded and conservative audience. He liked it better at the Troubadour, where he was a frequent guest while spending a month in London in late 1962 and early 1963. The contact with the British folk musicians inspired many of the tunes on his second album, *The Freewheelin' Bob Dylan.*
▶

him perform in New York's Greenwich Village and felt that Dylan would be a good actor. However, it proved impossible to direct Dylan during the taping and his part was taken over by a real actor, while Dylan got a small part where he played himself, more or less. Whether the outcome was successful or not is not possible to ascertain, since the BBC destroyed the tapes immediately after the broadcast.

January 14, 1963, is a memorable date, since Bob Dylan appeared at the club and made his first public performance of the newly-written 'Don't Think Twice, It's All Right', and also a drunken version of 'Blowin' In The Wind'. Some remember the gig mainly because he was so inebriated that he almost fell off the stage! Earlier that day, Dylan had taken part in a recording session in the basement of Dobells record shop, at 77 Charing Cross Road, together with his American friends Eric Von Schmidt, Ethan Signer and Richard Farina. For contractual reasons, Dylan used his alias Blind Boy Grunt in something that was more like a drunken gig, where Dylan arrived at the studio with a big bag of Guinness.

I sit down at one of the tables in the café and order an omelette and a glass of wine, while I watch all the decorations and details on the cosy premises. Some tables are occupied by temporary diners, while at others there are small parties or single visitors, all of whom look like they use the Troubadour as a home away from home, comfortably huddled up in the wooden sofas with their papers, magazines and books. After finishing my meal I'm in a considerably better mood and take the underground to Putney, where I get off at Putney Bridge Station.

Putney

Half Moon

Half Moon
Putney
93 Lower Richmond
Road
Tube: Putney
Bridge

From the station I walk via Putney Bridge over the Thames and then turn right on Lower Richmond Road, walking up to number 93. After a few minutes I see the well-known half-moon shaped sign of the *Half Moon pub* on my left side; the pub occupies the entire ground floor of the beautiful brick-red corner house.

Half Moon has had a live stage since August 1965, when Gerry Lockran and Cliff Aungier started the Folksville Club, but unfortunately it's hard to get information about which groups played here originally. What is completely certain is that artists such as Bert Jansch, Ralph McTell and Roy Harper played here many times. The latter received a tribute from Led Zeppelin in the song 'Hats Off To (Roy)

Harper' on their Led Zeppelin III album. Many years earlier, Jimmy Page appeared on one of Harper's albums and he greatly respected his song writing. American blues artists such as Champion Jack Dupree also appeared here.

Many bands and artists who became famous in the Sixties played at the Half Moon at one point or another; some of them still appear here. On the walls there are photographs and posters of the most famous artists and bands who have performed in the concert room behind the pub: The Rolling Stones (2000), The Who (1995), The Kinks, The Yardbirds, John Mayall's Bluesbreakers, The Pretty Things and The Small Faces. However, The Small Faces never actually played at the venue, although their front men, Steve Marriott and Ronnie Lane, have both performed here individually.

Stepping out of the Sixties for a moment, Kate Bush made her debut here and Elvis Costello played at the pub while he was still using his real name, Declan Patrick Mc-Manus. U2 performed here four times during their first UK tour, and Van Morrison and Nick Cave have also been on the stage.

I talk to the pub's sound engineer Doon Graham for a while. He has been working at the club since 1982 and his opinion is that the Half Moon is the best place to work in London, since great artists are appearing at the pub continually. He also tells me that he was working the night that Steve Marriott did one of his last concerts, in January 1991, before he tragically died in a fire at his home in April. At the end of the concert, Marriott's old friend, Peter Frampton, got up on stage, and together they played their old hit from their time together in Humble Pie, 'Natural Born Bugie'. According to Doon Graham it was an incredibly great concert, and a worthy conclusion to an amazing musical career.

For my part, I can find no more fitting conclusion to my London rock walks than having a beer at the Half Moon, surrounded by photographs of many of the artists in whose footsteps I have walked for a few weeks.

Appendix

In addition to the places I have covered extensively in the book, I want to mention a few other London addresses that may be of interest.

The Beatles

Apple Boutique. This was the location of The Beatles' famous boutique. The group invested £100,000 to design it and get it started. The four-storey house was painted in a psychedelic style. The boutique was opened on December 5, 1967, but was a financial disaster and had to close down only eight months later.

Map p. 122

Apple Boutique
94 Baker Street,
Marylebone
Tube: Baker Street
Station.

Palladium Theatre. On October 13, 1963, The Beatles performed on the television show Sunday Night At The London Palladium, with thousands of fans blocking the streets during their performance. The chaos that followed is regarded as the start of "Beatlemania".

Map p. 14

Palladium Theatre
Argyll Street,
Oxford Circus
Tube: Oxford
Circus Station.

At the same place and on the same programme, The Rolling Stones created a major scandal on January 17, 1967, when they refused to take part in the traditional waving to the viewers after the programme. The headlines were just as big and black as after The Beatles' performance, but now with a negative message.

The Kinks

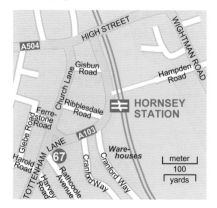

67

Konk Studio
84-86 Tottenham
Lane, Hornsey Vale
Tube: Turnpike
Lane Station, and
from there bus 41 to
Hornsey Station

Konk Studio. Ray Davies' recording studio, where The Kinks recorded many albums and which is still used by various bands. However, you should be aware that you will not be let in to have a look inside the studio.

The Rolling Stones

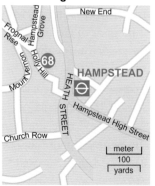

68

10a Holly Hill
Hampstead
Tube: Hampstead.

10a Holly Hill. In the autumn of 1964, Mick Jagger and Keith Richards moved to a house of their own at the top of a steep street in Hampstead. In December 1964, they wrote the group's first self-written single here: 'The Last Time'.

274

7 Elm Park Lane. Brian Jones moved to this cosy garden mews in the heart of Chelsea in early March 1965. Up until this time, Brian Jones had been satisfied playing the guitar, bottleneck and harmonica, but now he blossomed as a multi-instrumentalist who made significant contributions to the Stones' music: sitar, dulcimer, marimba, mellotron, harpsichord, saxophone, recorder, piano, organ and Arabian wind-instruments are just some of the instruments he played on future Rolling Stones records.

Among Brian's closest friends at this time were Pete Townshend and George Harrison. Outside the house a Rolls-Royce Silver Cloud was parked that autumn: it had been purchased by Brian from Harrison. In September 1965 Brian met Anita Pallenberg in Munich and a few months later she moved in with Brian.

Map p. 158

7 Elm Park Lane
Chelsea
Buses 11, 22 from Trafalgar Square.
Tube: South Kensington.

52 Marylebone Road. In the spring of 1966, Mick Jagger moved here together with Chrissie Shrimpton. Late that autumn, his new girlfriend Marianne Faithfull moved into the apartment and after the first night together here Mick Jagger wrote 'Let's Spend The Night Together' according to Faithfull. Marianne Faithfull didn't feel comfortable in the apartment since she felt it was too closely connected to Chrissie, and when the neighbours began complaining about all the fans that were gathering in front of the house, they moved to Chester Square in the spring of 1967.

Map p. 122

52 Marylebone Road
Harley House
Tube: Baker Street.

1 Courtfield Road. Today this house is an hotel, but this was once the location of Brian Jones' apartment. He lived there during 1966 and up until May 1967, most of the time together with Anita Pallenberg.

This was where Brian Jones wrote the music for the Volker Schlöndorff film Mort und Totschlag (A Degree Of Murder). The film featured Anita Pallenberg in one of the leading roles and was nominated for the Golden Palm at the 1967 Cannes Film Festival. For the recording sessions Brian recruited the services of Jimmy Page on guitar, Kenney Jones on drums and Nicky Hopkins on piano, while Brian himself played instruments such as sitar, organ, dulcimer, alto saxophone, banjo, harmonica and autoharp. To Brian's disappointment the film was never shown in English cinemas and few people were aware of what Schlöndorff felt was his brilliant work on the soundtrack, which consisted of self-written blues, country, soul and Eastern music.

When Anita Pallenberg left Brian Jones for Keith Richards in early 1967, his life collapsed. He entered into disastrously self-destructive behaviour, which turned him into a tormented wreck in just a few weeks. He had never received any support from the other members in the band he once formed, The Rolling Stones, not even now when he needed it more than ever.

However, there were others who were considerably

1 Courtfield Road
South Kensington
Tube: Gloucester Road.

Brian Jones plays the sitar in the hit song 'Paint It, Black' on the programme Ready Steady Go! in the summer of 1966. ◄

The founder of The Rolling Stones, Brian Jones, died just when his life started to look a little brighter and he was about to form a new band. (New Musical Express July 12, 1969) ▶

BRIAN JONES

By Editor
ANDY GRAY

THE coroner's verdict: "Misadventure." This is the final word on the tragic death of Brian Jones, 25, an original Rolling Stone who left the group only four weeks ago to concentrate on giving the world the music he loved — rhythm-and-blues — which he felt the Stones had deserted.

Brian was working on his new music until late on the evening of July 2, and decided after a dinner and a few drinks, to cool down with a midnight swim in the pool beside his Cotchford Farm mansion at Hartfield, Sussex.

His companions—interior decorator Frank Thorogood, and Swedish girl friend Anna Vohlin, 22—left him in the pool and a nurse, Janet Lawson, visiting Frank, found Brian at the bottom. He was rescued, given the kiss of life and massage, but pronounced dead by a doctor at about 3 am on July 3.

Brian Jones was the Stone who loved r-and-b the most ardently. That music was his life. As Jimmy Miller, the Stones' recording manager, said: "He was entirely a musician. He never quite adapted to the commercial and image aspects of the Stones.

"As a musician he should be remembered for the brilliant bottle-neck country guitar work on 'Beggar's Banquet,' for his interpretation of blues — played honestly as a white man. And he composed a brilliant score for the German film 'Mort Und Totschlag'."

Mick Jagger spoke for all the Stones when he said: "I am just so unhappy. I am so shocked and wordless and so sad. Something has gone. I have really lost something.

"We were like a pack, one family in a way. I just say my prayers for him. I hope he becomes blessed, I hope he is finding peace . . . and I really want him to."

The concert in Hyde Park last Saturday, with 250,000 fans attending, was the greatest tribute any pop star could ever have . . . and the Stones dedicated it to Brian Jones.

His father sums up what we all feel: "We had our violent disagreements, but we never stopped loving him."

25

TEN feet
ger pou
looked de
and sad, lea
down, sui
generally e
manner we
14 months
recognised
He also she
his wont and
earthly conta
made the
pressing my
could lever n

more empathetic and sympathetic, among them Jimi Hendrix, John Lennon and George Harrison. In interviews after Brian's death in 1969 George Harrison said that he liked Brian very much and that they had been close. He said that he felt great sympathy with his situation in the Stones, since it resembled his own position in The Beatles. He also stated that Brian Jones was very sensitive and that there wasn't enough love and understanding from the people around him. "I hope that people give him a better deal in death than they did in life," said Alexis Korner after Brian Jones' mysterious and insufficiently investigated death on July 3, 1969. Tragically, he was just getting back on his feet at the time.

Sticky Fingers is Bill Wyman's London restaurant and a very good museum if you're interested in the Stones. This is where you'll find items such as Brian Jones' white eye-

72

Sticky Fingers
Phillimore
Gardens 1a,
Kensington.
Tube: High Street
Kensington.
Buses 9, 10.

drop guitar, Bill Wyman's first bass guitars, the Stone's gold record awards and lots of cool photographs, newspaper clippings and posters.

The Who

Map p. 240

35 Sunnyside Road
Ealing Broadway
Tube: Ealing
Broadway.

35 Sunnyside Road. This apartment belonged to the American Tom Wright, whom Pete Townshend got to know at art school in Ealing in 1961. Wright was the owner of an enormous record collection of American artists, which led to Pete Townshend's discovery of blues musicians such as John Lee Hooker and Jimmy Reed. When

Tom Wright had to leave England in great haste, after he'd been arrested for possession of marijuana, Townshend and his friend, Richard Barnes, took over both the apartment and the record collection. This was the place where The Detours changed their name to The Who in 1964, at the suggestion of Richard Barnes.

Acknowledgments

I want to take this opportunity to extend my thanks to a number of people who have made this book possible. First of all I want to thank my children, Jennie and Martin, who have read through the manuscript and offered constructive suggestions for improvements.

A big thank you to Carl Magnus Palm, who not only translated this book into English but also contributed important suggestions and comments. Thanks also to Carl Magnus' friend, Ian Cole, who proof-read the English-language manuscript for us.

Another important person is my friend Benjamin Jónsson, who has provided encouragement as well as valuable opinions.

A special thanks to Jan "Rock Ola" Olofsson, who spent a couple of days showing me around and who shared many interesting stories from Sixties London.

Thanks also to everybody else who happily let themselves be interviewed and told me what they knew about various places.

I also want to thank the young Swedish photographer Klara Rådström, who accompanied me for a few days in London; and made the long days seem a little shorter and the sky a little bluer.

For their contributions of photographs, records, papers and magazines I would like to give a special thanks to Val Weedon, John Hellier, Jan Olofsson, Bertil Lundberg, Pontus von Tell, Rolf Hammarlund, Roger Holegård, Per Magnusson and Lennart Taflin.

Recommended books

I would like to call attention to the books that have been the most important to me and which I am happy to recommend to the interested reader.

Bacon, Tony: London Live. Balafon Books, London 1999.

Badman, Keith & Rawlings, Terry: Quite Naturally The Small Faces. Complete Music Publications Ltd 1997.

Black, Johnny: Eyewitness The Who. Carlton Books Limited 2001.

Booth, Stanley: The True Adventures Of The Rolling Stones. Abacus 1986.
In my opinion, the best on-the-spot account of The Rolling Stones.

Brunning, Bob: Blues, The British Connection. Blandford press 1986.

Davies, Dave: Kink, An Autobiography. Boxtree Limited 1996.

Fletcher, Tony: Dear Boy; The Life Of Keith Moon. Omnibus Press 1998.

Henderson, David: The Life Of Jimi Hendrix : 'Scuse Me While I Kiss The Sky. Omnibus Press 2002.

Hewitt, Paolo: The Small Faces – Young Mods Forgotten Story. Acid Jazz Books Ltd 1995.

Hewitt, Paolo & Hellier, John: All Too Beautiful. Helter Skelter Publishing 2004.
An excellent biography of Steve Marriott of The Small Faces, which has been very useful.

Hinman, Doug: The Kinks: All Day And All Of The Night. Backbeat 2004.

Lakey, Alan: The Pretty Things: Growing Old Disgracefully. Firefly publishing 2002.

Lawrence, Sharon: Jimi Hendrix: The Man, The Magic, The Truth. Harper Collins Publishers 2005.

I feel that this is the most interesting and accurate book about Jimi Hendrix as a human being.

Levy, Shawn: Ready, Steady Go!. Fourth Estate 2002.

Marsh, Dave: Before I Get Old: The Story Of The Who. Plexus Publishing Limited 1983.

The best book about The Who.

McLagan, Ian: All The Rage. Watson-Guptill Publications 2000.

The Small Faces' organist has written one of the best rock memoirs I have ever read.

McDermott, John with Eddie Kramer: Hendrix, Setting The Record Straight. Warner Books 1992.

Oldham, Andrew Loog: Stoned. Secker & Warburg 2000.

A book that deals not only with the early years of The Rolling Stones, but above all an interesting insider's view of the music scene in London during the early Sixties.

Phelge, James: Nankering With The Rolling Stones. A Cappella Books 1998.

Phelge lived together with Mick Jagger, Keith Richards and Brian Jones for almost all of 1963, and provides a very interesting, entertaining and detailed description of the early Rolling Stones.

Twelker, Uli & Schmitt, Roland: The Small Faces & Other Stories. Sanctuary Publishing 2002.

Rawling, Terry: British Beat 1960-69. Omnibus Press 2002.

Savage, Jon: The Kinks, The Official Biography. Faber and Faber 1984.

Shapiro, Harry: Alexis Korner, The Biography. Bloomsbury 1996.

Schaffner, Nicholas: Saucerful Of Secrets: The Pink Floyd Odyssey. Helter Skelter Publishing 2003.

Wyman, Bill with Ray Coleman: Stone Alone. Viking Penguin Books 1990.

Bill Wyman is a reliable eye-witness and diarist from the day he became a member of The Rolling Stones, in December 1962. Naturally a must for anyone who's interested in the Stones.

Index

Photo credits

Cyrus Andrews/Redferns: 168; Bo Arrhed/© Premium Rockshot:
39, 59, 69, 121, 149, 179, 197, 214, cover, inside rear jacket; Calle
Ballonka/© Premium Rockshot: inside rear jacket; Stephen Berkeley-
White: 82, 88, 99, 133, 219, 231; Torbjörn Calvero/© Premium
Rockshot: 173; Sven-Eric Delér/© Premium Rockshot: 30, 42, 155,
180, 207, 208, 280, cover, inside rear jacket; Evening Standard/
Getty Images: 32; Jeremy Fletcher/Redferns: 27; Kent Gustavsson:
6; Ulf H. Holmstedt/© Premium Rockshot: 106, cover, inside rear
jacket; John Hopkins/Redferns: 200; Roy Jones/Getty Images: 60;
Lars-Åke Madelid: 19, 24, 28, 33, 36, 46, 48, 52, 54, 58, 61, 63, 71,
75–76, 92, 96, 108, 113–114, 116, 123-125, 127, 130, 136, 138,
141, 144, 148, 153, 161, 163, 169, 170, 177, 183, 192, 210, 213,
222, 227, 238, 242 (two images), 248, 258, 262-263, 266, 270–
271, 273-275, 277; Bengt H. Malmqvist/© Premium Rockshot:
inside rear jacket; Mirrorpix: 17, 67; Petra Niemeier/Redferns: 128;
Michael J. Nordström/© Premium Rockshot: 95, cover, inside rear
jacket; Jan Olofsson: 31, 44, 142, 276; Pictorial Press: 74, 84, 137,
189; Privat: 18, 29, 89, 186; David Redfern/Redferns: 245; Rex
Features/IBL: 104, 139, 147, 167; Klara Rådström: 77, 195, 199,
206, 279; Lars Göran Rådström: 233; Brian Shuel/Redferns: 269;
Ewa Säfwenberg: 225; Andrew Whittuck/Redferns: 34

Every effort has been made to acknowledge correctly and contact the
source and/or copyright holder of each illustration, and Premium
Publishing apologies for any unintentional errors and omissions.

More books from Premium...

The Encyclopedia of Swedish Progressive Music 1967–1979
From Psychedelic Experiments to Political Propaganda –
with fully illustrated discography
& valuation guide
Bonus CD included
by Tobias Pettersson & Ulf Henningsson (Editor)
ISBN 978-91-89136-22-9

The Beatles
Film & TV Chronicle 1961–1970
by Jörg Pieper & Volker Path
ISBN 91-89136-05-5

The Look for Roxette
The Illustrated Worldwide
Discography & Price Guide
by Robert Thorselius
Bonus CD included
ISBN 91-971894-8-0

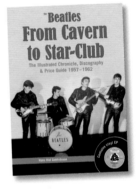

The Encyclopedia of Swedish Hard Rock & Heavy Metal Vol. II
by Janne Stark.
Bonus CD included
ISBN 91-89136-13-6

Benny's Road to ABBA
by Carl Magnus Palm
ISBN 91-89136-14-4

The Beatles
From Cavern to Star Club
by Hans Olof Gottfridsson
Bonus vinyl EP included
ISBN 91-971894-7-2

For Premium Publishing's complete catalogue, please visit our website:
www.premiumpublishing.com

Our international books can be ordered from our UK distributor:
Turnaround Publisher Services Ltd., Unit 3, Olympia Trading Estate, Coburg Road, Wood Green,
London. N22 6TZ, United Kingdom
Tel: +44 20 8829 3000   Fax: +44 20 8881 5088
www.turnaround-psl.com   info@turnaround-uk.com